Y0-BRY-080

HANDEL

HANDEL

BY

R. A. STREATFEILD

WITH TWELVE ILLUSTRATIONS

GREENWOOD PRESS, PUBLISHERS
WESTPORT, CONNECTICUT

Library of Congress Cataloging in Publication Data

Streatfeild, Richard Alexander, 1866-1919.
   Handel.

   (The New library of music)
   Reprint of the 1909 ed. published by Methuen,
London.
   Includes index.
   1. Händel, Georg Friedrich, 1685-1759.   2.   Com-
posers--Biography.   I.   Series.
ML410.H13S7 1978   780'.92'4 [B]   77-28261
ISBN 0-313-20248-6

First published in 1909

Reprinted in 1978 by Greenwood Press, Inc.
51 Riverside Avenue, Westport, CT. 06880

Printed in the United States of America

10 9 8 7 6 5 4 3 2 1

PREFACE

TO the inquiring student the ebb and flow of fashion in the world of music present phenomena of remarkable interest. The stone that the builders rejected becomes the head of the corner, and the idol of one age is trodden under foot; by the next. A mute antagonism reigns between one generation and another, and the sons delight in nothing so much as in consigning the cherished treasures of their fathers to the dust-heap. This is the rough-and-ready process by which immortality, or what, according to Mr. Arthur Balfour, passes for such in the world of music, is ultimately achieved, and even the greatest composers have to submit to it. For a musician to please his own age is no very severe test. At any given point in the history of music successful composers may be counted by the hundred. But their day is brief. Fashion turns her wheel, and the favourites of an hour sink into oblivion. Then comes the final test. Will the fallen god be lifted from the mire and restored to his old splendour? Will the dead musician be rediscovered by a later generation and live a second life in their new-born love and veneration? A second life it must be, for the first is dead for ever. A man's work can never mean to a later age what it meant to the men of his own time. But it is characteristic of great art that it carries a message to every generation in turn. We can all find in it something to suit our own idiosyncrasies. It may be something entirely different from what our forefathers found, but it is none the less valuable and none the less true on that account.

What the music of Handel meant to the men of his own time it is now difficult to say, but we know well enough what it meant to our fathers and grandfathers. To them Handel was the musician in ordinary to the Protestant religion. He had been taken over bag and baggage by the Church of England. Handel is himself partly responsible for the popular view of his genius. One of the most often quoted of his sayings relates to the production of *The Messiah*. Some one congratulated him upon having given the town a fine entertainment, whereupon he replied : "My lord, I wish not only to entertain them, but to make them better." This was a very natural and proper observation to make, but unfortunately to the average Englishman to "be good" means only to go to church or chapel on Sunday morning and to conform externally to whatever form of Christianity happens to suit the exigencies of his temperament; and thus Handel's *obiter dictum* was gradually twisted into meaning that he wrote with a definitely evangelistic purpose, and in consequence he was held up as an example of a composer who had consecrated his genius to the service of religion. So widely was this view disseminated that in time even his secular works were claimed by the Church. In the year 1862 we find Dean Ramsay—an amiable divine usually credited with a sense of humour—declaring in a lecture on Handel that "Lascia ch'io pianga" was "like all Handel's fine Italian airs, essentially of a sacred character."

This was the Handel that the present generation in its boyhood was expected to fall down and worship. No wonder that, like the enterprising youth in the nursery rhyme, we took him, metaphorically speaking, by the left leg and threw him downstairs, though in his case it was not because he wouldn't say his prayers, but because he would say them and nothing else.

But even in those days there were a few who recognised the real Handel beneath the black gown and white tie in which his ecclesiastical friends had disguised him. In 1863 Edward FitzGerald wrote: "Handel was a good old Pagan at heart, and, till he had to yield to the fashionable Piety of England, stuck to Opera and Cantatas, where he could revel and plunge and frolic without being tied down to Orthodoxy." Twenty years later Samuel Butler, the author of *Erewhon*, comparing Handel to Shakespeare, in the opening words of his *Alps and Sanctuaries* said: "It is as a poet, a sympathiser with and renderer of all estates and conditions whether of men or things, rather than as a mere musician, that Handel reigns supreme. . . . There has been no one to touch Handel as an observer of all that was observable, a lover of all that was lovable, a hater of all that was hateable, and, therefore, as a poet.

Shakespeare loved not wisely but too well. Handel loved as well as Shakespeare, but more wisely. He is as much above Shakespeare as Shakespeare is above all others, except Handel himself; he is no less lofty, impassioned, tender, and full alike of fire and love of play; he is no less universal in the range of his sympathies, no less a master of expression and illustration than Shakespeare, and at the same time he is of robuster, stronger fibre, more easy, less introspective."

In those days these were voices crying in the wilderness, yet a change was at hand. The year after Butler published his *Alps and Sanctuaries* appeared Rockstro's biography of Handel, in which the then traditional view of the composer was exaggerated to the verge of caricature. I am inclined to think that Rockstro's book dealt the death-blow to the Christian Handel. From that time forward a certain impatience of the national Handel-worship began to manifest itself, which, growing stronger year by year, has ended in practically dethroning Handel from the position that he occupied for so many years.

There is no doubt that at the present time, in England at any rate, Handel is unpopular with those who are the mouthpieces of cultivated musical opinion. Dr. Ernest Walker, for instance, in his *History of Music in England*, though much of his criticism of Handel is very much to the point and is obviously derived from a careful study of his works (which is more than can be said for a good deal of modern Handelian criticism), says that "no other composer can even attempt to rival

Handel in his power of intensely irritating those who
have the strongest and sanest admiration for his genius,"
and talks light-heartedly about consigning the old idol to
the rubbish-heap.   I am well aware that many thousands
of Englishmen habitually attend performances of *The
Messiah* as a religious exercise, just as many thousands
habitually go to church; but you cannot for that reason
call *The Messiah* popular as a work of art any more than
you can call the Book of Common Prayer popular as a
masterpiece of literature.   If Handel were really popular,
his other works would not be shelved so completely as
they are.   Thirty years ago *Samson, Solomon, Jephtha,
Judas,* and *Joshua* were frequently performed in London.
Now they are practically unknown.   No, the Handel of
our forefathers is dead; it remains for us to revive a new
Handel from the ashes of the old.   Handel the preacher
is laid for ever in the tomb, but Handel the artist, with
his all-embracing sympathy for human things and his
delight in the world around him, lives for evermore.

   In spite of the obvious trend of modern criticism, I
anticipate a return of popularity for Handel, or if not of
popularity, at least of more general appreciation; and,
paradoxical as it sounds, this will be accomplished by
the gradual acceptance of the theory of the poetic basis
of music.   For as the comprehension of the meaning of
music grows, so will less and less value be attached
to mere questions of form.   At present the advocates
of abstract music are sticklers for certain forms of
music, and they maintain, I understand, that the interest

of music lies in the manner in which these forms are used—they even talk of the "plot" of a symphonic movement, referring only to the development of the themes employed. When people have grasped the fact —and in time I have little doubt that they will grasp it —that it is what a man has to say that matters, and that the way he says it is comparatively unimportant, there is bound to be a reaction in favour of a man who had a great deal to say, even though the way in which he chose to say it now seems absolutely out of date. I know that this sounds as if it should apply chiefly to instrumental music, whereas Handel's most characteristic works are vocal. But though Handel set words to music, he often used the words merely as a peg to hang his ideas upon, or perhaps one should say as a spring-board from which to take dives into the infinite. I mean that in order to find his real meaning one often has to go behind the words to some remote idea lurking in the background, the existence of which a casual hearer might hardly suspect. I will give an instance of what I mean. Every one knows the famous air "Ombra mai fu" from the opera *Serse*, which is played by every violin student in the kingdom in a vulgarised modern version usually described as "Handel's celebrated Largo." This air is sung by the hero Xerxes, who is standing beneath the boughs of his favourite plane tree. The words mean: "Never was the shade of aught that grows more grateful." I had known the air from childhood, but I confess that I never realised what Handel meant

by it till I happened to stroll one Sunday evening last
summer into Lincoln's Inn Fields at the hour when one
of the excellent London County Council bands was
playing in the gardens. I paused to listen under the
shadow of a magnificent plane tree, broad and spreading
as Xerxes's own, and as the familiar melody with its
broad rich harmonies floated to my ears through the
dense foliage I knew that it was the hymn of the tree
that Handel was singing, not only of the plane tree
beloved by Xerxes, but of that other tree, emblem of
growth and strength and purity, that "bulk of spanless
girth, which lays on every side a thousand arms and
rushes to the sun."

It is the inner meaning of Handel's music, and its
power of searching the profoundest recesses of the soul,
that in the following pages I have endeavoured, so far as
I am able, to elucidate. Its merely technical qualities
have already been discussed enough and to spare. Books
on Handel written by musicians already abound, but
musicians as a rule take more interest in the means by
which an end is attained than in the end itself. They
tell us a great deal about the methods by which a
composer expresses himself, but very little about what
he actually has to express. I have tried, how feebly and
with what little success no one knows better than myself,
to find the man Handel in his music, to trace his
character, his view of life, his thoughts, feelings, and
aspirations, as they are set forth in his works. That
Handel, like other men, had his faults and weaknesses I

readily admit. Writing as he did *currente calamo*, he had
not always time to weigh the worth of his ideas. He
was content to employ certain conventional formulas
and certain well-worn cadences, which to modern ears
seem threadbare, and if a second-rate idea occurred to
him he did not always wait for a first-rate one. Yet
to me the mighty soul moving behind seems to give life
to the driest of bones, and I feel the tremendous personality of the man even in his most perfunctory strains.
Handel's warmest admirer could perhaps scarcely claim
for him that he was a greater musician than Bach or
Mozart or Beethoven. What he could claim, and I
think with justice, would be that of all who have written
music Handel was the greatest man.

It remains for me to conclude with a tribute of
gratitude to the authors from whose works I have derived
assistance. To Friedrich Chrysander, whose biography
of Handel stands alone as a monument of painstaking
erudition, my debt is greatest. It is a grievous misfortune
to the student of Handel that Chrysander's labours upon
his great edition of Handel's works prevented him from
carrying his biography beyond the year 1740. So far as
it goes it is invaluable, and the points upon which I have
ventured to differ from the learned historian are few in
number and of no great importance. I have also been
much helped by the biographies of Rockstro and
Schoelcher and the more recent monographs of Dr.
Hermann Kretzschmar and Dr. Fritz Volbach. With
regard to Handel's Italian journey in 1706–10 Signor

Ademollo's *G. F. Haendel in Italia* has been of the greatest assistance to me. To the other authorities that I have consulted due reference has been made in the body of the work, but I must mention with especial gratitude Mr. Randall Davies's *English Society in the Eighteenth Century*, which gives so admirable a picture of London life during the Handelian epoch.

My warmest thanks are due to the Earl of Shaftesbury for permitting me to make use of the MS. record of Handel's operatic career compiled by his ancestor the fourth Earl, which is now among the Shaftesbury papers in the Record Office; and to the Earl of Malmesbury for his kindness in allowing me to publish a reproduction of his portrait of Handel by Mercier, which was painted about the year 1748 and is undoubtedly the most lifelike and characteristic presentment of the composer that has come down to us. It is impossible for me to thank by name all the friends who have helped me in my work, but I must record my gratitude to Mr. Montgomery Carmichael, H.M. Consul at Leghorn, to Senhor Manoel de Carvalhao, and to Dr Guido Biagi, the Keeper of the Laurentian Library at Florence, for the kind assistance that they gave me in my attempt to unravel the history of the production of Handel's *Rodrigo*.

R. A. STREATFEILD

August 1909

CONTENTS

b

LIST OF ILLUSTRATIONS

xvii

HANDEL

CHAPTER I

HANDEL AT HALLE, 1685–1703

THE political and religious wars of the seventeenth century, so fertile and far-reaching in their issues, accomplished nothing more important for the future of European society than the elevation of the middle class to the rank of a power in the state. In England the Civil War stamped out the last traces of feudalism, in Germany the Thirty Years' War, though less sweeping in its apparent results, cleared the field quite as effectively. At the close of the struggle the burgher class awoke to the fact that it was practically its own master. The bogey of the Church was exorcised, the fangs of the aristocracy were drawn. A Frederick the Great and a Maria Theresa were still possible, but the command of the body politic had passed from the belly to the brain. The results of this social revolution, for so it practically was, were not immediately perceptible, but the habit of self-reliance and the acquired faculty of independent thought and judgment bore rich fruit in the ensuing generation. From the loins of the sturdy race that had won its way to liberty by blood and iron sprang the giants who were to build the shining citadel of German art. Only a line of heroes— mute, inglorious heroes, it may be, but heroes none the less—could father such a man as George Frederick Handel.

The Handel family originally belonged to Breslau, but early in the seventeenth century the coppersmith Valentine Handel migrated to Halle. His youngest son George, the composer's father, was born in 1622. George began life as a barber, but like many of his craft blossomed into a surgeon. His fortune was made by a lucky operation performed in 1660 upon Duke Augustus of Saxony, who in gratitude appointed him "Geheimer Kammerdiener und Leibchirurgus," which being interpreted is Groom of the Chamber and Private Surgeon. In 1665 he bought the house Am Schlamme, now famous as the birthplace of George Frederick. The latter, who was the second son of his father's second wife, Dorothea Taust, was born on the 23rd of February 1685, and was baptized on the following day.

Halle in 1685 was in some ways but a shadow of its past self. It had been for many years the favourite residence of Duke Augustus, who ruled over the archdiocese of Magdeburg in the name of his father, John George, the Elector of Saxony. His court at the Moritzburg, if not the most dazzling, was one of the most artistic in Germany. The Halle theatre had been famous not only for its history—for it was one of the earliest to cultivate the German Singspiel as opposed to the fashionable Italian opera of the day—but also for its *personnel*, since on its staff were to be found many of the most illustrious musicians of the time. Records survive, too, of court festivities of no common splendour, of ballets, tournaments, and spectacles, which prove that life at Halle was something very different from the trivial round of the ordinary German provincial town. But in 1680, after the death of Duke Augustus, all this gaiety came to an abrupt conclusion. In accordance with the terms of the Peace of Westphalia, Halle was handed over to the Electorate of Brandenburg, and the young Duke Johann Adolf of Saxe-Weissenfels, who succeeded his father, transferred his court to Weissenfels. The muses fled from the banks of the Saale, and Halle relapsed from courtly splendour into the dull monotony of burgherdom. Yet though the glory of Halle had departed, the quaint old town upon which Handel's eyes opened was not without its charm. The Moritzburg, not yet degraded into a Calvinistic church, still frowned down upon the city in stately splendour; the mysterious Rothe Thurm and the stone Roland still whispered the secrets of the Middle Ages to a later and more prosaic race; and from the towers of Our Lady's Church the sweet-voiced bells still chimed the evening hymn, that to the ears of the infant musician must have sounded like a message from another world.

The chief authority for the events of Handel's childhood is the memoir by the Rev. John Mainwaring, which was published in 1760, a year after Handel's death. Mainwaring did not himself know Handel, but he collected his anecdotes from those who did, particularly from John Christopher Smith, who had been Handel's secretary and was the son of one of his oldest friends, and, if due allowance is made for the legendary atmosphere that invariably gathers round the head of an illustrious man, there is no particular reason for doubting the general truth of his statements, though his details are often obviously pure romance and his chronology is not to be relied on. According to Mainwaring, therefore, the future composer "from his very childhood discovered such a strong propensity to Music, that his father, who always intended him

for the study of Civil Law, had reason to be alarmed."
His alarm took the practical shape of consigning to the
flames all the musical toys, drums, trumpets, and so forth,
with which the boy had filled his nursery. George
Frederick himself was packed off to school, although he
cannot very well have been more than five or six years
old. However, in spite of parental sternness, he was not
altogether severed from his beloved music. He contrived,
with the aid of an amiable relative, possibly his mother
or the aunt Anna who we learn from the baptismal
register was his godmother, to smuggle a clavichord—
doubtless one of the miniature sort which could be carried
under the arm—into a garret at the top of the house.
Thither in the stillness of the night the tiny boy would
creep and practise to his heart's content, while the rest
of the household was wrapt in slumber. No better instrument for these nocturnal concerts could have been devised
than the clavichord, with its sweet muffled tone, which is
barely audible a few yards from the instrument itself.
From early association the clavichord should have been
dear to Handel,—as dear as it undoubtedly was to Bach,—
yet he seems to have written nothing for it, at any rate
nothing has survived.

The next recorded event of Handel's childhood took
place, according to Mainwaring, when he was seven years
old. At Weissenfels, some forty miles from Halle,
occupying a subordinate position in the household of
Duke Johann Adolf, dwelt George Christian, a grandson
of old George Handel of Halle, sprung from his first
family, and a full ten years older than his little half-uncle
George Frederick. Thither, in spite of his seventy odd
years, George Handel proposed to go to visit his grandson,
and to pay his respects to the Duke. Boylike, his little

seven-year-old son wanted to go too, and, in the words of
Mainwaring, "finding all his solicitations ineffectual, he
had recourse to the only method which was left for the
accomplishment of his wish," that is to say, he ran after
the chaise as well as he was able, contrived to get picked
up when he was too far from Halle to be sent back alone,
made his peace with his father, and drove to Weissenfels
in triumph. At Weissenfels the stars in their courses
fought his battles for him. His astounding precocity won
the hearts of all the musicians in the Duke's orchestra,
and the Duke, who happened to hear the boy playing the
organ in the chapel one day after service, talked seriously
to his father about devoting him to the musical profession. Old Handel stood out as firmly as he could in
favour of a legal career, but the Duke was too much for
him. Doubtless the precedent of Schütz was quoted, who
had died at Weissenfels some twenty years before.
Schütz had begun life by studying law, but ere long had
yielded to the seductions of music, with such results as
even the obstinate old surgeon could scarce cavil at. In
the end he gave way, and promised that his boy should be
allowed to study music when he got home again. He
kept his word, and when they were safely back at Halle
he submitted George Frederick to the instructions of
Friedrich Wilhelm Zachow, the organist of the Liebfrauen-
kirche, while insisting that at the same time he should
continue his school work just as before.

Zachow was at that time about thirty years old, and a
fair average specimen of the cantor of the period. A few
of his works have survived to our day, and show talent
and sound musicianship if not genius. The man himself
we may judge to have been worthy and conscientious.
Handel was not a man who suffered fools gladly, yet he

retained his regard for Zachow to the end of his days.
He spoke of him invariably with affection and gratitude,
and he supported his widow in her old age. Zachow was
evidently a believer in hard work. It is said that he re-
quired his pupil to produce a church cantata every week.
Handel himself admitted, according to Burney, that he
worked "like a devil" in those days. This was said à
propos of a set of trios for two hautboys and bass, which
was discovered by Lord Polwarth in Germany many
years afterwards. He brought them to England and they
were shown to Handel, who recognised them at once as a
production of his boyhood. If they are the trios printed
by Chrysander in the Händel-Gesellschaft edition, they
are the best possible proof of Handel's astounding precocity. As a specimen of the work of a boy of ten years
old they stand alone in the history of music. Even
Mozart wrote nothing at that age that can be compared
with them for freshness of melody and maturity of
musicianship. Of Handel's other works written at this
time little has survived. An interesting record of his
studies with Zachow, in the shape of a volume of extracts
from the works of his contemporaries, dated 1698, was
known to exist so late as the year 1799, but all trace
of it has now disappeared. It would have been doubly
valuable if it had proved that even at that early age
Handel had already began the practice, which he carried
in his later years to such extreme lengths, of adapting the
work of his predecessors and contemporaries to his own
use. Three years of hard work with Zachow gave Handel
all the learning that his master could impart, as the latter
himself confessed, and the boy looked round him for more
worlds to conquer. Berlin was at that time the goal
of every German musician's ambition. The Elector of

Brandenburg, afterwards King Frederick I of Prussia, was a monarch of liberal tastes, and the Electress Sophia Charlotte ruled a court which would willingly have rivalled Versailles in its encouragement of art and artists. Thither Handel was taken by his father, probably in the year 1696.

The Berlin with which he made acquaintance was, it need hardly be said, very different from the spacious and handsome city of to-day. It contained but twenty thousand inhabitants, and in its outward appearance seemed not far removed from the country village from which it originally sprang. Trees grew in the narrower streets, and swine grouted among the refuse that collected under the lime trees of the now famous Unter den Linden. Many of the houses were thatched with straw, and wooden chimneys added to the ever-present danger of fire. The countrified aspect of the town was accentuated by the fences and palings which still surrounded the houses. The lighting of the streets was characteristically managed. Every three houses had to provide a lantern, which was hung at night over the door of each one in turn. Till the very end of the seventeenth century there was no pretence at anything like a watchman in Berlin. The inhabitants were a quiet, law-abiding race, and the Berlin street-life was very different from that of London. No Mohock orgies troubled the placid banks of the Spree, and when the Elector instituted his new police, the good Berliners indignantly declared that they were quite capable of looking after themselves. But though the city of Berlin lingered in its primitive state of civilisation, the court was nothing if not advanced and cultured. The Electress Sophia Charlotte consoled herself for a loveless marriage by surrounding herself with scholars and artists. Her husband was a typical German soldier-monarch. He rose at 4 a.m., just the time when his wife went to bed, and worshipped etiquette a good deal more fervently than he worshipped God; whereas Sophia Charlotte cared little for rules and regulations, and took a malicious pleasure in bestowing her patronage upon persons who were not *hoffähig.*

The great literary light of the Berlin court was Leibniz, whose friendship with Sophia earned her the title of the Philosophic Queen, though it may be doubted whether she was quite as competent to act the part of Egeria to the great philosopher as her courtly flatterers tried to make her believe. At any rate, we find her writing in a petulant mood to a friend: "Il traite tout si superficiellement avec moi. Il se défie de mon génie, car rarement il répond avec precision sur les matières que j'agite."

However, when Leibniz snubbed her, Sophia Charlotte could take refuge in music, for she was an accomplished performer on the harpsichord, and had collected a good library of music. She is said, too, to have dabbled in composition. In her younger days she had been a pupil of Steffani, who was Kapellmeister at the court of her father, the Elector of Hanover, and she remained his trusted friend all her life.

Her husband, though not himself troubled by artistic leanings, liked to think that he was at the head of a cultivated court, and encouraged her artistic tastes. She invited celebrated musicians to Berlin, and organised operatic performances among her household. On one occasion she incurred the wrath of the court preacher by summoning one of her performers to a rehearsal from the communion table itself. Possibly it was the same preacher who was refused admission to Sophia Charlotte's chamber when she lay on her death-bed some ten years later. "Laissez-moi mourir," whispered the poor lady to her attendants, "sans disputer."[1]

On what pretext the youthful Handel went to Berlin is not clear, but probably his fame had overstepped the limits of his native town, and a sedulous courtier may have desired to gratify his royal patrons by introducing a new infant prodigy to their musical circle. Handel's visit to Berlin was an unqualified triumph. The Elector and Electress were at his feet in a moment. The bonds of etiquette dissolved in his presence, and the courtiers vied with each other in singing the praises of the wonderful child whose performance upon harpsichord and organ put to shame the grey-haired professors of music.

The story of Handel's encounter with Bononcini and Ariosti at the court of Sophia Charlotte must be regretfully dismissed to the limbo of legend. Mainwaring relates with a profusion of detail how the gentle Ariosti welcomed the boy with rapture, applauded him with sincere delight, and held him on his knee for hours together while they talked of music and her inexhaustible treasures.[2]

Bononcini, on the other hand, we are told, stood

[1] Erman, J. P., *Mémoires pour servir à l'histoire de Sophie Charlotte, Reine de Prusse*, Berlin, 1801, 8º ; Hahn, W., *Friedrich, der erste König in Preussen*, Berlin, 1851, 8º.

[2] Ariosti is usually described by his contemporaries as an amiable and unambitious man. An epigram, however, by Paolo Rolli, published in his *Marziale in Albion* (1776), gives a less attractive view of his character. It may be roughly translated as follows :—

> " Here lies Attilio Ariosti—
> He'd borrow still, could he accost ye.
> Priest to the last, whate'er betide,
> At others' cost he lived—and died."

sullenly aloof, ignoring the boy when possible, and when
he was compelled to notice his existence, presenting him
with the most difficult test of musicianship that he could
devise — a cantata bristling with chromatic harmonies,
which the lad was to accompany at sight from the figured
bass. Handel fulfilled the task with complete success,
and Bononcini was forced to admit his young rival's
attainments, but he nursed his jealous envy in secret, and
when they met many years afterwards, memories of
Berlin added rancour to his hatred of the man who had
vanquished him in London.

All this, unfortunately, is pure romance. As Handel's
father died early in 1697, the Berlin visit cannot have
taken place later than 1696. Modern research has discovered that Ariosti did not reach Berlin until the spring
of 1697, and Bononcini not until 1702. It is just possible
that when Handel left Halle in 1703 he may have passed
through Berlin on his way to Hamburg. In that case
he would probably have met both Ariosti and Bononcini,
and possibly may have submitted to Bononcini's test. In
any case, the romantic picture of the youthful Handel
sitting upon Ariosti's knee must be abandoned, for it
would have needed a man of stouter build than the frail
little Italian *abate* to nurse an eighteen-year-old stripling
of Handel's sturdy build.[1]

The Elector gave the boy more than barren eulogy.
Wishing like a true Mæcenas to attach so brilliantly
gifted a genius to his own court, he offered to send him
at once to complete his education in Italy, and on his
return to give him a suitable position at Berlin. But

[1] Ebert, *Attilio Ariosti in Berlin*, Leipzig, 1905 ; " Briefe der Königin
Sophie Charlotte von Preussen." (*Publikationen aus den K. Preussischen
Staatsarchiven*, Bd. 79.)

CHAPTER II

HANDEL AT HAMBURG, 1703–1706

HAMBURG at the opening of the eighteenth century stood apart from the other great cities of Germany. Its isolated position had not only saved it from the terrors of the Thirty Years' War, but had induced many wealthy citizens from other towns to take refuge within its walls. Strengthened thus in substance and consideration, it had an advantage over its rivals when peace at last came, and during the latter half of the seventeenth century it easily established itself as the chief trading centre of Germany. Its commercial prosperity reacted upon its social life. The wealthy burghers could afford to send their sons on the grand tour, and to educate their daughters in the age's best accomplishments. Thus, while many German towns were still lingering in the mists of medievalism, Hamburg boasted an almost Italian degree of culture. In 1678 a theatre was opened, in which the German tongue was for the first time employed for operatic purposes. At first the operas given were sacred, but though the range of subject was strictly limited, no bounds were placed upon the splendour of decorations and accessories. Contemporary writers vie with each other in describing the sumptuous scenery and dresses. Even the French critic Regnard was compelled grudgingly

to acknowledge that "les opéras n'y sont pas mal repre-
sentés ; j'y ai trouvé celui d' ' Alceste ' très beau."

As time went on, sacred operas gave way to secular,
and the last sacred opera was performed in 1692. But
before that date, opera, even in cultivated Hamburg, had
to live down a good deal of prejudice and opposition.
The pietistic pastors of the period undertook a new
crusade against this latest snare of Satan. They
fulminated against opera from their pulpits, they denounced it in the streets. So successful was their
campaign that in 1684 they induced the civic council to
order the closure of the theatre. But the triumph of
blindness and bigotry was shortlived. In the following
year the theatre was reopened, and ere long reached the
zenith of its success under the auspices of Reinhard
Keiser, who rose upon the Hamburg horizon in 1694.

When Handel reached Hamburg in 1703 the decline
had already begun. German opera was yielding its pride
of place before the advance of the stranger. Not merely
were operas given in Italian and French, but even
German works were interspersed with Italian airs. The
taste of the city, too, was not what it had been. Opera
wavered between idle pomp and gross buffoonery, and
Keiser, who had undertaken the management of the
theatre in 1703, was dissipating his brilliant talents in
riotous living and debauchery. Still, there was much for
a boy of Handel's age to learn in Hamburg, and he
plunged into the enchanted world of music with the
eagerness of a neophyte.

Soon after his arrival at Hamburg, Handel fell in with
Johann Mattheson, one of the cleverest men of his time,
who, though only four years older than Handel, was
already a personage of considerable influence in Hamburg

musical circles. Mattheson was everything by turns, and nothing long. He sang at the opera, played in the orchestra, was an organist, poet, and composer, and, in fact, was ready to turn his hand to anything. He is now famous chiefly for his writings on music, of which one of the most entertaining is his *Grundlage einer Ehren-Pforte*, a biographical dictionary of musicians of priceless value to students of the period, though it is always necessary in reading it to make allowance for Mattheson's inordinate vanity and his jealousy of rival composers. Of the youthful Handel he writes: "Handel came to Hamburg in the summer of 1703, rich only in ability and goodwill. I was almost the first with whom he made acquaintance. I took him round to all the choirs and organs here, and introduced him to operas and concerts, particularly to a certain house where everything was given up to music. At first he played second violin in the opera orchestra, and behaved as if he could not count five, being naturally inclined to a dry humour. (I know well enough that he will laugh heartily when he reads this, though as a rule he laughs but little. Especially if he remembers the pigeon-fancier, who travelled with us by the post to Lubeck, or the pastrycook's son who blew the bellows for us when we played in the Maria Magdalena Church here. That was the 30th July, and on the 15th we had been for a water-party, and hundreds of similar incidents come back to me as I write). But once when the harpsichord player failed to appear he allowed himself to be persuaded to take his place, and showed himself a man—a thing no one had before suspected, save I alone. At that time he composed very long, long airs, and really interminable cantatas, which had neither the right kind of skill nor of taste, though complete in harmony, but the lofty schooling of opera soon trimmed him into other fashions. He was strong at the organ, stronger than Kuhnau in fugue and counterpoint, especially *ex tempore*,[1] but he knew very little about melody till he came to the Hamburg operas. At that time he came nearly every day and took his meals at my father's house, and he gave me many hints about counterpoint. I helped him, too, in the dramatic style, so one hand washed the other.

" On the 17th of August in the same year we journeyed to Lubeck, and in the carriage made many double fugues *da mente non da penna*. I had been invited by Magnus von Wedderkopp, the president of the council, to compete for the post of successor to the renowned organist Dietrich Buxtehude, and I took Handel with me. We played on almost all the organs and harpsichords in the place, and made an agreement, which I have mentioned in another place, that he should only play the organ and I only the harpsichord. However, it turned out that there was some marriage condition proposed in connection with the appointment, for which we neither of us felt the smallest inclination, so we said good-bye to the place, after having enjoyed ourselves extremely, and received many gratifying tributes of respect."

In another book Mattheson makes a further reference to Handel's early days at Hamburg : " There is a world-renowned man, who when he first came to Hamburg only knew how to make regular set fugues, and imitations were as new to him as a foreign tongue, and as difficult. No one

---

[1] In his *Critica Musica* (i. 326) Mattheson makes special reference to Handel's talent for improvisation : " And among the younger men I have not found one who has such readiness as Herr Capellmeister Handel, not only in composition but also in extemporisation, as I have hundreds of times heard with my own ears in the greatest amazement and admiration."

knows better than I how he used to bring me his first
opera scene by scene, and every evening would take my
opinion about it—and the trouble it cost him to conceal
the pedant! Let no one be surprised at this. I learned
from him just as he learned from me. *Docendo enim
discimus.*" [1]

The friendship between Handel and Mattheson lasted
for some time after their Lubeck adventure, and Mattheson
in his *Ehren-Pforte* quotes an affectionate letter written
to him by Handel in 1704. But later in the year matters
became somewhat strained between the two friends,
though their quarrel did not break forth into open
wrath until the 5th of December, at a performance of
Mattheson's opera *Cleopatra*, in which Handel played the
harpsichord and Mattheson himself sang the principal
part. But we will let Mattheson tell his own story: " I
as composer directed the performance and also sang the
part of Antony, who has to die a good half-hour before
the end of the opera. Hitherto" (*i.e.* at the previous
performances, *Cleopatra* having been produced on Oct. 20)
" I had been accustomed after finishing my part to go into
the orchestra and accompany the remaining scenes, and
this is a thing which incontestably the composer can do
better than any one else. However, on this occasion
Handel refused to give up his place. On this account we
were incited by some who were present to engage in a
duel in the open market-place, after the performance was
over, before a crowd of spectators—a piece of folly which
might have turned out disastrously for both of us, had not
my blade splintered by God's grace upon a broad metal
button on Handel's coat. No harm came of the encounter,
and we were soon reconciled again by the kind influences

[1] *Critica Musica*, i. 243.

of a worthy councillor and the manager of the theatre. Whereupon I entertained Handel at dinner on that very day, the 30th of December, after which we went together to the rehearsal of his opera *Almira*, and were better friends than ever."

What the rights and wrongs of the quarrel actually were it is now of course impossible to say, but there is no particular reason to suppose, as all Handel's previous biographers have taken for granted, that the fault rested entirely with Mattheson.

Mainwaring actually falsifies chronology so as to make Handel out to be a lad of fourteen at the time of the duel, and speaks of that historic event as an "assassination more than a rencounter," while Rockstro cannot speak too bitterly about Mattheson's effrontery, treachery, and so forth, whereas the saintly Handel is "too good a Christian to bear malice," and altogether behaves in a manner that would at once qualify him for admission into the angelic choir. As a matter of fact, Handel was the last person in the world to play the part of an injured and long-suffering innocent, and in this quarrel, as in all others in which he was engaged, he probably gave as good as he got. The misunderstanding between the two friends seems to have originated in Mattheson's appointment, in October 1704, to the post of tutor to the son of Sir Cyril Wyche, the English envoy at Hamburg. Handel had previously been engaged to give the boy music lessons, but his duties not unnaturally ceased on Mattheson's appointment. Handel considered himself ill-used, and probably suspected Mattheson of underhand dealings. His suspicions may or may not have been well-founded, but there is no evidence to prove that Mattheson behaved badly. As to the trouble about the accompaniments to

Cleopatra, Handel was evidently in the wrong, since he seems to have made no difficulty about giving up his place at the harpsichord to Mattheson before the fatal 5th of December. As Mattheson had accompanied the closing scenes of the opera for more than six weeks on end, he certainly had every reason to feel aggrieved at Handel's sudden determination to stand upon his rights as cembalist. However, the matter is of little enough importance, especially as it ended in the friendly and comfortable manner above recorded.

Meanwhile Handel's talents were winning wider and wider recognition. We have seen that by the autumn of 1704 he was seated in the conductor's chair at the harpsichord, in succession to Keiser, whose loose life was fast losing him popularity and employment in the city which a few years ago had been at his feet, and on the previous Good Friday he had produced his setting of the *Passion* according to St. John. This little work, though trifling compared to Handel's subsequent achievements, is specially interesting to us not only as being the earliest authentic composition of the composer that has survived to our day, but as the subject of one of the first and by no means the least elaborate essays in criticism that musical history can show. On the subject of Handel's *Passion* music, Mattheson is discreetly silent in his sketch of the composer's life published in his *Ehren-Pforte* (1740), yet in his *Critica Musica* (1722) he printed a most venomous criticism of the work, treating it in the utmost detail and riddling it with every shot in his locker. What prompted this attack we cannot now say with certainty, unless it may have been Handel's repeated refusals to contribute a sketch of his career to Mattheson's *Ehren-Pforte.* A letter politely declining Mattheson's offer written in 1719 is extant, which may well be the *fons et origo mali.* However that may be, Mattheson's criticism remains a ridiculous outburst of splenetic malice. No one would claim that Handel's early *Passion* is a masterpiece, or anything like one. With many faults of immaturity and inexperience, it has passages of remarkable freshness and beauty, and on the whole is rich in promise. Mattheson's onslaught upon the work, twenty years after its production, injured Handel's reputation as a composer far less effectually than it blackened Mattheson's character as a friend.

But if the John *Passion* did little to spread Handel's fame, his next work, the opera *Almira*, lifted him at once to the front rank of living composers. The libretto was originally designed for Keiser, but the latter, between his duties as manager and the excesses of his private life, found little time for composing. However, he wanted a new opera for the winter season, so he passed the libretto on to Handel, little dreaming that in the youthful cembalist he was to find a rival who would seriously threaten his own supremacy.[1] *Almira*, which was produced on the 8th of January 1705, with Mattheson in the principal tenor part, was one of those strange mixtures of German and Italian which were popular in Hamburg at the time. Many of the Hamburg operas, including *Almira*, were translated from the Italian, and it was usual to leave a certain number of solo numbers in the original for the sake of the singers who wanted to show off their voices to the best advantage, and fancied that they could do so more effectually in the liquid accents of the south. The audience, on the other hand, unlike opera-goers of to-day,

[1] F. A. Voigt, " Reinhard Keiser." (*Vierteljahrsschrift für Musikwissenschaft,* Jahrg. vi.)

wanted to be able to follow the plot, so for their benefit the recitatives and the songs of the comic characters were translated into the vernacular. The result must have been somewhat surprising, but we must not be too hard upon Hamburg taste, for the same polyglot system was employed in London as well about that time. *Almira* was a triumphant success, and ran uninterruptedly until the 25th of February, when it was replaced by Handel's second opera *Nero*, a work of which the music has unfortunately perished. Its freshness and originality charmed the ears that were weary of Keiser's waning talent, and its faults of inexperience were forgiven in the dazzling splendour of a sumptuous mounting.

Almira made Handel many friends, and one enemy. Keiser alone looked on gloomily at his young comrade's success, and listened unwillingly to his praises. To such lengths did his jealousy carry him that he determined to challenge Handel's supremacy by setting the libretto of *Almira* himself. He did so, and produced his version in the following autumn with so little success, that very soon afterwards he shook the dust of Hamburg from his feet, and retired to the seclusion of his native village, a defeated and disappointed man.

Meanwhile, the success of *Almira* turned Handel's thoughts to wider fields and ampler skies. Some years previously he had made the acquaintance of a man who was destined to exercise an important influence upon his career. This was Prince Giovanni Gastone dei Medici, the second son of Cosmo III, the Grand Duke of Tuscany, a man of most unsavoury reputation, whose thousand vices have so long been notorious that his one virtue —that of having turned Handel's thoughts to Italy— should in common kindness be given its proper place in history. Gian Gastone, as he was always called, who was born in 1671, was a man of truly Tuscan refinement, culture, and sensibility, though his morals were deplorable. He was hardly more than a boy when his father, anxious for the Medici succession, hurried him into a loveless marriage with a princess of Saxe-Lauenburg, a woman homely of feature, excessively stout, coarse in nature and violent in temper, who cared for nothing but hunting, and loved animals more than men. Exiled from his beloved Florence to a castle in the wilds of Bohemia, linked to a virago whom he detested, Gian Gastone sank almost involuntarily into debauchery and turpitude. At times he would escape from the loathsome embraces of his gaoleress, and seek consolation in such dissipation as the neighbouring German cities could offer. It was no doubt but a poor substitute for the luxurious enchantment of Italy, but it was something to hear music and to meet men who could talk to him of other things than shooting birds or chasing stags. On one of these excursions fate led his steps to Hamburg. In the winter of 1703–4 he stayed there for several months, lost a great deal of money at play, and made friends with Handel. Gian Gastone was something of a musician himself. In his younger days he had played the flute, and like a true Florentine he adored opera. It is easy to imagine with what eloquence he discoursed upon his lost fatherland, upon the art of Italy, and the magic of her wondrous sky. Handel listened with greedy ears, and within him rose longings for that enchanted land of the south, whose very name was music, where genius blossomed as it could never blossom in the mists of the northern ocean. Mainwaring's account of Handel's relations with Gian Gastone, which has been followed by subsequent biographers, is obviously sown with inaccuracies. He represents their acquaintance as dating from the production of *Almira*, which is out of the question, since by the autumn of 1704 Gian Gastone was back in Bohemia trying his utmost to persuade his wife to accompany him to Florence.[1] We may be pretty certain also that the Prince never offered to pay Handel's expenses on a trip to Italy.

Gian Gastone wanted all the money he could lay hands upon for himself, and never was a man in a worse position for playing Mæcenas to a promising young musician. He was always in debt, and his correspondence with his father is one long cry for money. As a matter of fact, while he was actually at Hamburg, his sister, the Electress Palatine, was moving heaven and earth on his behalf to raise money to pay his gaming debts, and before he could leave Prague for Italy in 1705 he had to raise a hundred thousand florins in order to satisfy his creditors. But if Gian Gastone was not in a position to play the princely patron, he could promise Handel a warm and kindly reception at his father's court whenever he was able to make the journey south. With this object in view, Handel settled down to a course of steady work, in order to make the money necessary for the journey to Italy which he felt was necessary for his artistic development. After the production of *Nero* he seems to have had little to do with the theatre. Probably he found that he made more money by giving private lessons, and the atmosphere of envy, malice, and all uncharitableness which seems to have brooded permanently over the Hamburg theatre was no doubt distasteful to a man of his honest and straightforward character. Some time in 1706 he

---

[1] Robiony, *Gli Ultimi dei Medici*.

wrote a third opera, *Florindo und Daphne*, which, however, was not produced until 1708,[1] when it was given in two sections on account of its extreme length. But by that time Handel was far away.

The date of his departure from Hamburg is not known. Most likely it took place in the summer or early autumn of 1706, for Prince Gian Gastone was at that time staying in Florence, and it is reasonable to suppose that Handel would wish to be introduced to the Grand Ducal court under his friend's auspices. According to Mattheson, he travelled in company with another friend named von Binitz, who paid all his expenses. In all probability we shall not be far wrong if we picture Handel leaving Hamburg in July, paying a flying visit to his mother at Halle on his way south, entering Italy by the well-trodden Brenner route, and reaching Florence in September or October 1706.

[1] Mattheson, *Der Musikalische Patriot*.

CHAPTER III

HANDEL IN ITALY, 1706–1710

TUSCANY was groaning beneath the brainless and bigoted sway of the Grand Duke Cosmo III when Handel first set foot in Florence. The glorious traditions of Florentine art and science were a thing of the past, and the country was sunk in priest-ridden sloth, squalor, and poverty. Of all the arts, music alone received any encouragement at the court, and this was due not to the Grand Duke, but to his eldest son Ferdinand, the *Gran Principe*, as he was always called, who was an excellent musician, and an enlightened and intelligent patron of the art. Ferdinand kept up the best traditions of the Medici family in this respect. All forms of music received his patronage, but to opera he was especially devoted. In his beautiful villa at Pratolino, high up in the lovely valley of the Mugnone, some dozen miles from Florence, he had built a magnificent theatre, where every year operatic performances were given under his auspices, that were the talk of all Italy. To Ferdinand music was a second religion. It was the guiding principle that regulated his life. Early in the autumn it was his custom to repair to Pratolino, where his *villeggiatura* was spent in the society of the choicest singers and musicians that Italy could produce. The opening of the Carnival drew him to

Florence, where masquerades, festivals, and operatic performances alternated in a bewildering whirl of gaiety. From Florence he went to Pisa for hunting, and in the sultry days of summer he sought the sea-breezes of Leghorn, a city for which he had a special predilection, and whose theatre under his patronage became famous for the excellence of its operatic performances.[1] Ferdinand was on the friendliest terms with Alessandro Scarlatti and other noted musicians of the day, indeed Scarlatti's letters to him which are preserved in the *Archivio Mediceo* show that his musical culture was something far above that of the average dilettante princeling. We find Scarlatti thanking him for suggestions, and consulting him as to the composition of his operas in a manner very different frcm that in which the humble composer usually adopts in addressing his princely patron. To Ferdinand Handel was introduced by his friend Gian Gastone, who was in Florence from June 1705 to November 1706, and had doubtless given his brother a glowing description of the new musical genius whom he had discovered in far-away Hamburg, long before Handel had appeared upon the scene.

Handel probably reached Florence in the autumn of 1706, and was no doubt speedily summoned to Pratolino, where Ferdinand was by that time established with his court. For three or four years Alessandro Scarlatti had been Ferdinand's favourite musician, and had had the honour of supplying Pratolino with its annual novelty, but in 1706 a coldness seems to have arisen between the composer and his Mæcenas, and he was succeeded in the latter's good graces by Perti. It is possible that during

[1] Anonymous MS. biography of Ferdinand in the possession of Mr. Herbert Horne.

the interregnum Handel may have enjoyed a brief period of court favour. Ferdinand used to complain of the "melancholy" character of Scarlatti's operas, and possibly he turned to Handel in the hope of hearing something more vivacious.

Handel's first opera, _Rodrigo_, was certainly written during his stay at Florence, and probably in response to a commission from Ferdinand, but no record of its production has survived. It is not mentioned by Allacci, whose _Drammaturgia_ (Venice, 1755) is a tolerably complete record of the Italian opera of the period, though he duly records the performance of a certain _Roderico_, which was given in the presence of Ferdinand in 1692 by the Accademia degli Innominati. Very possibly it was the libretto of this opera which, according to the fashion of the time, was re-set by Handel. Had _Rodrigo_ been given at Pratolino, some mention of it would almost infallibly have occurred in the Medicean archives. But Puliti, whose valuable _Cenni storici della vita di Ferdinando dei Medici_ gives an exhaustive catalogue of the musical works performed at Pratolino, knows nothing of the details of its production, though he corrects Mainwaring's statement with regard to the present which Handel received in return for his opera. According to him it was Prince Ferdinand, and not the Grand Duke, who gave Handel a hundred sequins together with a service, not of silver, as Mainwaring states, but of porcelain.

I had imagined that _Rodrigo_ might have been performed at Leghorn, during one of Ferdinand's summer visits to the sea, but Mr. Montgomery Carmichael, who has investigated the matter with the utmost kindness and assiduity, assures me that this is not the case. Probably _Rodrigo_ was produced in Florence itself. At that time the Teatro della Pergola was not used for opera, but the Teatro di Via del Cocomero (now the Teatro Niccolini) was open, and this may have been the scene of *Rodrigo's* production. It is more likely, however, that it was privately performed in the Pitti Palace, as was the case with an opera called *Enea in Italia*, which was given there in 1698 in honour of the birthday of the Grand Duchess Vittoria.

It is, of course, possible that the production of *Rodrigo* took place not on the occasion of Handel's first visit to Florence, but when he was there for the second time in the autumn of the same year on his way to Venice. Of this second visit we know but little, and in all probability it was a short one. Handel was in Florence for the third time on his way to Venice in the autumn of 1709 before leaving Italy altogether, but it is almost impossible that *Rodrigo* can have been performed then, owing to Ferdinand's bad health. On the whole, the probility is that *Rodrigo* was written in the autumn of 1706, and produced during the Carnival season of 1707.

Rodrigo has proved a stumbling-block to Handel's biographers in many ways, not least in the romantically sentimental legend of Vittoria Tesi the singer, which has twined itself around the story of the opera's production, and which it is now my mournful duty to disprove. Let us trace the legend to its source. Mainwaring writes : " Vittoria, who was much admired both as an actress and a singer, bore a principal part in this opera. She was a fine woman, and had for some time been much in the good graces of His Serene Highness." The reverend gentleman then suggests that " Handel's youth and comeliness, joined with his fame and abilities in music, had made impressions on her heart." It will be observed that Mainwaring

speaks of the lady merely as Vittoria. It was left for
Chrysander to jump to the conclusion that the famous
Vittoria Tesi was the singer in question, and under his
fostering care the legend grew to ample proportions, so
that the passion of la Tesi for Handel, her pursuit of him
to Venice, and the triumphs that she there won in his
Agrippina, are now part of the stock-in-trade of every
hack musical historian. Neither Chrysander nor his
copyists seem to have remembered the fact that Vittoria
Tesi was a contralto, whereas the heroines in *Rodrigo*
and *Agrippina* are both sopranos. But biographers are
notorious sentimentalists, and in the supposed necessity of
fitting out their hero with an appropriate love story such
trifles as this are easily ignored. As a matter of fact,
Vittoria Tesi at the date of the production of *Rodrigo* was
precisely seven years old. Her baptismal register exists
in Florence, and has been recently printed by Signor
Ademollo,[1] to whom is due all the credit of exploding
Chrysander's absurd legend. Vittoria Tesi was born in
1700, and did not make her début until 1716, when she
sang at Parma with the celebrated Cuzzoni in a pastoral
entitled *Dafne*. The heroine of *Rodrigo* was a very
different person—to wit, Vittoria Torquini, familiarly
called *la Bombace* or *Bambigia*, a brilliant singer who had
adorned Ferdinand's court since 1699, and had taken a
promiment part in the operatic performances at Pratolino.
As for *la Bombace's* penchant for Handel, I am not inclined
to treat it very seriously. She was a clever woman, and
contrived to remain in the good graces of the Prince
almost up to the day of her death. The story of her
ousting a long-established favourite is told with much
gusto in Luca Ombrosi's sketch of Ferdinand's career,

---

[1] *Nuova Antologia*, 16th July 1889.

and evidently she knew far too well which side her bread
was buttered to venture into a damaging liaison with a
travelling musician. She did not sing in *Agrippina*, the
cast of which is perfectly well known, and the story of
her following Handel to Venice is obviously pure
romance.

Soon after the production of *Rodrigo*, Handel started
for Rome, intending doubtless to spend Holy Week
and Easter there, in order to hear the world-famous
music associated with the services of the Church. With
regard to Handel's arrival at Rome we are on comparatively safe ground. We know by the signed and
dated autograph of a setting of the *Dixit Dominus* that
he was there on 4th April 1707, and the autograph of
a *Laudate Pueri* further assures us that he was still
there on 8th July. The general impression of his
biographers seems to be that he then returned to
Florence, driven from Rome by the unhealthy climate of
the summer and autumn months. But this theory is
founded upon a delusion. In those days there existed
no prejudice against the Roman summer, and the smart
society of Rome braved the terrors of the dog-days with
the utmost equanimity—indeed August seems to have been
a favourite month for social festivities.[1]   Moreover, con-
clusive proof of Handel's presence in Rome during the
summer months is furnished by an interesting letter now preserved in the Medici archives, written in Rome on the 24th
of September 1707.[2]   It is addressed by a certain Annibale
Merlini to Ferdinand dei Medici, giving a description of a
juvenile prodigy who was at that time the great musical
sensation of the Eternal City.   " He is a lad of twelve

---

[1] Ademollo, *I teatri di Roma*, pp. 107, 165, etc.
[2] *Archivio Mediceo*, Filza 5897.

years," writes Merlini, " a Roman by birth, who, though of
so tender an age, plays the *arciliuto* with such science and
freedom that if compositions he has never even seen are
put before him he rivals the most experienced and celebrated professors, and wins great admiration and well-
deserved applause. He appears at the concerts and
leading academies of Rome, as, for instance, at that of His
Eminence Cardinal Ottoboni, and at that which continues
daily for all the year at the Casa Colonna, and in the
Collegio Clementino, and at these as in other public
academies he plays *a solo* and in company with all kinds
of *virtuosi*. And all this can be testified by the famous
Saxon, who has heard him in the Casa Ottoboni, and in
the Casa Colonna has played with him, and plays there
continually."

In Rome, indeed, there was much to detain Handel.
The composor of *Rodrigo* was a person of consideration,
and Handel doubtless brought letters of introduction from
his friends at Florence to the leaders of cultivated society in
Rome. Of these Cardinal Ottoboni, the nephew of Pope
Alexander VIII, and the friend and correspondent of
Ferdinand dei Medici, was the most famous and brilliant.
Ottoboni was at that time a man of forty, handsome in
feature, aristocratic in manner, profoundly versed in all
the culture of the age and a devoted lover of music. He
was enormously rich, his revenues from the various bene-
fices that he held amounting to 80,000 scudi a year,
exclusive of his private fortune. His charity was inexhaustible. He founded a free dispensary for the poor,
entertained pilgrims at his own table, and inaugurated
various benevolent institutions. But his pet hobby was
his " Accademia poetico - musicale," to which Merlini
refers. The aim of the Academy, which was founded

3

in 1701, was the revival of the ancient glories of Italian sacred music. Ottoboni gathered around him all the poets and musicians of Rome. He held frequent concerts, instituted competitions and gave magnificent prizes. He was something of a poet himself, and wrote some capital opera and oratorio libretti for Scarlatti. In his young days, too, he had tried his hand at musical composition, though the failure of his opera *Colombo* in 1692 seems to have checked his ambition in that direction.

Blainville, who had been secretary to the States-General at the Court of Spain, was in Rome in the spring of 1707, and has left an account of a concert at Cardinal Ottoboni's, at which in all probability Handel himself was present: " His Eminence," he writes, " keeps in his pay the best musicians and performers in Rome, and amongst others the famous Archangelo Corelli and young Paolucci, who is reckoned the finest voice in Europe, so that every Wednesday he has an excellent concert in his palace, and we assisted there this very day (14th May 1707). We were there served with iced and other delicate liquors, and this is likewise the custom when the Cardinals or Roman princes visit each other. But the greatest inconveniency in all these concerts and visits is that one is pestered with swarms of trifling little *Abbés,* who come thither on purpose to fill their bellies with these liquors, and to carry off the crystal bottles with the napkins into the bargain." [1]

Handel was, as we have seen, a welcome visitor at Ottoboni's splendid palace, hard by the Church of St. Lorenzo in Damaso, but, being a foreigner, he does not seem to have been actually admitted to membership of the Academy. Under Ottoboni's roof he rubbed shoulders with some of the most famous of living musicians, among

[1] Blainville, *Travels*, vol. ii. chap. xl.

them Caldara, Corelli, and Alessandro Scarlatti.
Here also he met Cardinal Benedetto Panfili, who wrote
for him the libretto of *Il Trionfo del Tempo*, and the
Marquis di Ruspoli, one of Scarlatti's chief patrons, in
whose house Handel was staying when he wrote his
oratorio *La Resurrezione* in April 1708. Ruspoli was
one of the leading lights of the famous Academy of the
Arcadians, which had been founded in 1690 "to further
the cultivation of the sciences and to awake throughout
Italy the taste for humane letters, and in particular for
poetry in the vulgar tongue." Everybody in Rome who
had any pretensions to culture was an Arcadian. Prelates
and painters, musicians and poets met on equal terms
in the delicious gardens of the Roman nobility, where
the academical meetings took place. The fiction of
Arcadia was kept up even in nomenclature. Every
Arcadian was known by a pastoral name. Corelli was
Arcimelo, Alessandro Scarlatti Terpandro, and Pasquini
Protico. These three famous musicians were admitted
members in 1706, and from that time forward music
played a prominent part in the life of the Academy.
No one under the age of twenty-four was available for
membership, so that Handel never actually belonged to
the Academy; but he was a frequent guest at the meetings,
and took his full share in the musical performances.

Mr. E. J. Dent, in his admirable biography of Scarlatti, quotes an interesting description from Crescimbeni's
Arcadia of one of the Academy's music-meetings, which
gives a good idea of the kind of entertainment at which
Handel must often have assisted :—

"First came a sinfonia of Corelli, then two cantatas of
Pasquini to words by Gian Battista Felici Zappi (Tirsi).
After this came a duet by Scarlatti, also to words by

Zappi, followed by an instrumental piece of some sort. Scarlatti was at the harpsichord, but managed at the same time to observe that Zappi was in process of thinking out a new poem. He begged Zappi to produce it; Zappi agreed to do so on condition that Scarlatti set it to music at once. Scarlatti assented, and 'no sooner had Tirsi finished his recital than Terpandro, with a truly stupendous promptness, began to transcribe the verses recited, with the music thereto; and when these had been sung, the souls of those present received of them so great delight, that they not only obliged the singer to repeat the song again and again, but also urged both poet and musician to display their skill afresh.' After some pressing Zappi and Scarlatti repeated their impromptu performance, and 'meanwhile every one was astonished to see how two such excellent masters, the one of poetry and the other of music, did contend; and this contention was so close that scarce had the one finished repeating the last line of the new air than the other ended the last stave of the music.'"

Handel left Rome some time in the autumn of 1707, and took his way northwards to Venice.

He may have passed through Florence on his way, but if so it is not likely that he stayed there very long.[1] Prince Ferdinand was at Pratolino all that autumn, busy with the production of Perti's *Dionisio*, which had been specially composed for him, and Handel probably pushed on to Venice as quickly as he could. The precise date of his arrival cannot now be discovered, but it is known that he was presented to Prince Ernest Augustus of

[1] It was by no means the universal custom in those days to travel from Rome to Venice *via* Florence. Both Misson and Blainville went from Venice to Rome by Ancona, Loretto, Foligno, and Terni.

Hanover on the occasion of this visit, and as the Prince arrived in Venice on 30th September, and departed at the end of November,[1] we know at any rate that the historians who have represented Handel as only arriving in Venice in time for the Carnival are wrong. In Venice Handel found himself in the home of opera. In Florence opera was the plaything of princes, and at Rome papal prejudice forbade it altogether, but at Venice it was beloved of rich and poor alike, and at that time no fewer than seven [2] theatres were devoted to its cultivation.

Handel doubtless visited all of them, and heard the operas of Lotti, Gasparini, Albinoni and other famous composers, and listened to the mellifluous tones of Senesino, who was then singing at the Teatro San Cassiano, but he wrote nothing himself.[3]

Why this was so, it is now hard to say. Perhaps, being a foreigner, he found the doors of the theatres closed to him, or it is possible that he regarded his visit

[1] *Briefe des Herzogs Ernst August zu Braunschweig-Lüneburg an T. F. D. von Wendt*, 1902.

[2] Misson, *New Voyage to Italy*, 1714, vol. i. pt. I.

[3] Handel's two visits to Venice have given grievous cause for stumbling to all his biographers.

The original Jeroboam the son of Nebat who made Israel to sin was Mainwaring, who, notoriously inaccurate as he was with regard to times and seasons, confused the two visits, and placed the production of *Agrippina* during the first instead of the second. This error has been reproduced by almost all Handel's subsequent biographers, despite the fact staring them in the face in all the records of Venetian operatic history that *Agrippina* was produced during the Carnival season of 1709–10. In the first volume of his biography of Handel, published in 1858, Chrysander followed Mainwaring's error, but many years afterwards he admitted his mistake. Unfortunately his recantation appeared in a periodical little read in England (*Vierteljahrsschrift für Musikwissenschaft*, vol. x. 1894), and passed almost unnoticed, so that modern writers on Handel have gone on light-heartedly copying the original blunder.

to Venice as a holiday, and did not care to undertake serious work. He seems, at any rate, to have enjoyed himself, and to have made friends with many useful and influential people. The story of his meeting with Domenico Scarlatti, who was at Venice at the time studying with Gasparini, is well known.

It took place at a masquerade, where Handel was persuaded to play the harpsichord. The beauty of his performance astonished the guests, and every one wondered who the masked musician could be who achieved such miracles of dexterity, until Scarlatti, who had probably heard from friends in Rome of Handel's accomplishments, cried out that it must be either the famous Saxon or the devil.

From that time forward Handel and Domenico were fast friends. They returned together from Venice to Rome, and often met in friendly rivalry in the palace of Cardinal Ottoboni or of some other musical magnate. It was at one of the meetings of the Cardinal's Academy that the famous contest between the two *virtuosi* took place, in which they were adjudged equal so far as the harpsichord was concerned, while on the organ Handel was admittedly superior. All his life long Domenico retained his respect and admiration for Handel, and in his later years he is said never to have mentioned Handel's name without crossing himself. It is not, however, recorded that Handel crossed himself at the name of Scarlatti.

Reference has already been made to Handel's meeting with Prince Ernest Augustus of Hanover. The Prince was the youngest brother of the Elector of Hanover, who a few years later became George I of England. From all accounts, he was a singularly amiable young man, and his correspondence shows him to have been a great lover of

music. Handel met him at a fortunate moment. The
Prince was having a dull time in Venice, for his two
companions, Baron von Pallandt and Kammerherr van
Fabrice,[1] seem to have spent most of their time in houses
of ill fame, and left their royal master to amuse himself
as best he could. Consequently Ernest Augustus made a
great deal of Handel, and ended by begging him to pay a
visit to Hanover when his Italian tour was over.

Another grandee who crossed Handel's path in
Venice was the Duke of Manchester,[2] who was an
ardent patron of music, and worked as hard as any man
of his time towards establishing Italian opera in England.

The Duke was Ambassador Extraordinary at Venice
from July 1707 to October 1708, and entered with the
utmost gusto into the musical life of the city.[3] He gave
Vanbrugh material help in choosing the singers for his
new opera-house in the Haymarket, and, to judge by
his correspondence, spent a good deal more of his time
in listening to the newest *virtuosi* and in shopping for
the Duchess of Marlborough than in transacting official
business. Where he first met Handel we do not know,
but he seems to have been struck by the young composer's talent, and at once invited him to London.
Handel's arrangements would not allow him to accept
the invitation forthwith, but there is no doubt that the
Duke's amiable suggestion first turned his thoughts in
the direction of England.

Meanwhile he was due back in Rome, where his

---

[1] It is worth while to mention the names of these egregious persons,
since it has often been stated that the Prince was accompanied by Baron von
Kielmansegg and Steffani.

[2] *Gentleman's Magazine*, vol. xxx. p. 24.

[3] Duke of Manchester, *Court and Society from Elizabeth to Anne*, vol. ii.

friends the Arcadians were eagerly awaiting him. The chronology of Handel's Italian journeys is distressingly vague, and we know not whether Handel stayed in Venice for the Carnival, or kept his Christmas in Rome. There is an old tradition that Handel spent a Christmas in Rome, and heard the *zampognari* or *pifferari*, as the shepherds of the Abruzzi are called, who at that season descend from the mountains and play their quaint bagpipe melodies in the streets of Rome. It has been argued that the superscription *pifa*, which occurs in the autograph of *The Messiah*, implies that the Pastoral Symphony is founded upon one of these shepherd melodies. More probably it is only an imitation of the traditional style, like Corelli's famous Christmas concerto or the lovely pastoral air in Scarlatti's Christmas oratorio, which is quoted by Mr. Dent in his life of the composer. Still, it would be pleasant to think that Handel had heard the *pifferari*, and had listened to the wild music that a hundred years later made so profound an impression upon the youthful Berlioz.

Whether Handel heard the *pifferari* or not, he was certainly back in Rome early in the spring, safely established in the palace of his friend the Marquis di Ruspoli. An autograph cantata in the British Museum is dated Rome, 3 March 1708, and in April he composed his first oratorio, *La Resurrezione*, which was soon followed by the allegorical cantata, *Il Trionfo del Tempo e del Disinganno*. Both saw the light in the palace of Cardinal Ottoboni. It was during a rehearsal of the latter that the famous scene occurred in which Corelli and Handel played such characteristic parts. Corelli, whose technique appears to have been but moderate,—witness the story which Burney tells, on the authority of Corelli's pupil

Geminiani, of the famous violinist's lamentable fiasco at a concert in Naples,—was struggling with a difficult passage in the overture, when the impetuous German snatched the violin from his hands and played it himself. All that the gentle Corelli said was: "But, my dear Saxon, this music is in the French style, of which I have no experience." The matter was settled by Handel's writing a fresh symphony in a less exacting style. Handel left Rome for Naples early in the summer. He was in Naples by the beginning of July, as we learn from the date upon the autograph of his trio, "Se tu non lasci amore." The tradition that he was accompanied upon his journey by Alessandro Scarlatti has no foundation in fact, since the latter was in Rome in October, and did not reach Naples until the end of the year.[1]

Naples was a whirlpool of political conflict when Handel arrived there. For some years the struggles for the Spanish Succession had disturbed its tranquillity. The Archduke Charles of Austria had been proclaimed King of Spain in 1705, and in 1707 the Austrian troops had occupied Naples. When Handel reached Naples in July 1708 the post of viceroy had just been given to Cardinal Grimani, a Venetian, whose government was little appreciated by the jealous Neapolitans. The city swarmed with Austrian soldiers, discontented for lack of pay, and on the look-out for anything that they could pick up. Street disturbances were frequent, and blood flowed freely. Nevertheless, in the palaces of the nobility life went on much as usual. There was no lack of festivity, and Handel and his music were as welcome here as they had been in Rome. According to Mainwaring "he had a palazzo at command, and was

[1] Dent, *Alessandro Scarlatti.*

provided with table, coach, and all other accommodations. . . . He received invitations from most of the principal persons who lived within reach of the capital, and lucky was he esteemed who could engage him soonest and detain him longest." Mr. Dent quotes from Conforto, a Neapolitan diarist of the early eighteenth century, a description of a musical party of the period, which gives a good idea of the kind of entertainment in which Handel must often have taken part: "Among other things, he (an extravagant nobleman) held at his house a most lively assembly with the choicest music, consisting of ten instruments and four of the best voices of this city, directed by the Maestro di Cappella, Alessandro Scarlatti; and to the large crowd of titled persons that attended he caused to be offered continuously an unspeakable quantity of meats and drinks of all kinds, with various fruits, both fresh and candied, as he did also for the large number of servants in attendance on them. His palace was all most nobly decorated, and all lit with wax torches as far as the courtyard; the sideboard consisted of two long tables of silver fairly and symmetrically disposed; and there was visible in the distance a most beautiful fountain, also of silver, which for seven continuous hours spouted perfumed water, about which fluttered a large number of live birds. There was also a pavilion of crimson damask, under which were fourteen superb *trionfi* of fruit, both fresh and candied, as well as other curious inventions. The which entertainment lasted some time after midnight, the ladies and gentlemen, according to their usual habit, after having filled their bellies and their bosoms with sweetmeats, and having had every pleasure of sight, taste, and hearing, not failing to scoff and make a mock of the solemn folly of the last new marquis." There was a branch of the Arcadian Academy at Naples, which greeted Handel with acclamation, and it is almost certain that he composed the pastoral cantata, *Aci, Galatea e Polifemo*, a work which has nothing save name in common with the better known *Acis and Galatea*, for one of the Academical gatherings. Society at Naples was more cosmopolitan than in Rome. Mainwaring says that Handel's chief patroness was a Spanish Princess, and it was no doubt for her that he wrote his one extant Spanish song with guitar accompaniment. For another friend he wrote a set of little French *chansons*, to say nothing of the numerous cantatas that flowed like water from his pen during the whole of his sojourn in Italy. But the most influential friend that Handel made in Naples was Cardinal Vincenzo Grimani, the Viceroy, who seems to have taken the composer under his special protection, and evidently smoothed the way for his return to Venice and for the production of *Agrippina*. Grimani was a Venetian, and his family owned the Teatro di San Giovanni Grisostomo, so that his influence threw open all doors to Handel, that had been closed before owing to the prevailing prejudice against foreigners. His amiability carried him still further. In his leisure moments he trifled not unsuccessfully with the muse, and he paid Handel the compliment of writing for him the libretto of *Agrippina*.[1] How long Handel stayed in Naples it is impossible

---

[1] A note in Bonlini's *Glorie della Poesia* has been strangely misinterpreted by Chrysander. Referring to *Agrippina* the author observes : " Questo drama, come pure *l'Elmiro, Re di Corinto* e *l'Orazio*, rappresentate più di venti anno sono su l'istesso teatro, vantano comune l'origine da una Fonte sublime." (This drama, as also *Elmiro, Re di Corinto* and *Orazio*, per-

to say, but he must have been back in Rome some time in the spring of 1709, since he undoubtedly made Steffani's acquaintance during his stay in Italy, and Steffani, who had been sent to the papal court on a diplomatic mission by the Elector Palatine, was only in Italy from October 1708 to June 1709.[1] Steffani was something very much more than a mere musician, indeed in some ways he was one of the most remarkable men of his time. He started life as a chorister in Venice, and rose by his own exertions to be one of the leading diplomatists of Europe. He had been Kapellmeister at Hanover since 1685, and was now on the look-out for a promising successor. He must have known Handel well by reputation, since his former pupil Sophia Charlotte, now Queen of Prussia, was one of the young composer's earliest patronesses. He probably met Handel beneath the hospitable roof of Cardinal Ottoboni, and seized the opportunity of suggesting that Handel should step into his shoes at Hanover. Handel jumped at the offer, and promised to make his way to Hanover directly he left Italy.

It was probably in the autumn of 1709 that Handel said good-bye to Rome, and turned his steps northward. It is not known by what route he travelled, but we may consider it at least probable that he went *via* Florence, in

formed more than twenty years before at the same theatre, boast a common origin from a sublime Fount.)

The "sublime Fount" is, of course, Cardinal Grimani, who wrote the libretti of *Elmiro, Re di Corinto* and *Orazio*, produced respectively at the Teatro San Giovanni Grisostomo in 1687 and 1688, as well as that of *Agrippina*, but Chrysander in the most fantastic manner tried to twist out of the words a reference to Florence, the cradle of opera, in order to justify his view of the chronology of Handel's Italian travels.

[1] Woker, "Aus den Papieren des Kurpfälzischen Ministers Agostino Steffani." (*Vereinsschrift der Görres-Gesellschaft*, 1885.)

order to say good-bye to his friends at the Medici court.
If so, he found them in sad trouble. The *Gran Principe*
Ferdinand had been for some time in failing health. His
constitution was undermined by youthful excesses, and
in the previous year he had been brought almost to
death's door by the ministrations of an English physician
from the fleet at Leghorn, who had subjected him to a
treatment more drastic than his constitution could stand.[1]

In August 1709 he had gone as usual to pass the
autumn at Pratolino, and had been struck down on the
1st of September by a series of epileptic fits. For some
time his life was in danger.[2] Prayers were offered up
in all the Florentine churches, and the anxiety in the
city was great.[3] By the end of the month, however,
Ferdinand seemed to be well on the way to recovery,
and a *Te Deum* of thanksgiving, "with solemn and
exquisite music and rich symphonies, composed by the
first musicians of Florence and other foreign musicians,"[4]
was sung in the Church of the Annunziata.

If Handel stayed in Florence on his way to Venice,
it is quite possible that he was one of the foreign
musicians who helped to compose the *Te Deum*, especially as his old patron Gian Gastone was in Florence at
the time, and was actually present at the thanksgiving
service.[5] But we really know next to nothing of his
movements at this period.

[1] Galluzzi, *Istoria del Granducato di Toscana*, Tom. iv. Libro 8.

[2] Settimanni, *Diario*, 1532–1737. (Archivio di Stato, Florence.)

[3] Portinari, *Diario*, 1700–20. (Biblioteca Marucelliana, Florence).

[4] Settimanni, *Diario*.

[5] Mr. P. Robinson, in his *Handel and his Orbit*, has propounded a theory
that in the spring or summer of 1709 Handel visited the shores of the lake of
Como, stayed with friends at Urio and Erba, two villages in the neighbourhood, and there composed the *Te Deum* and *Magnificat*, hitherto ascribed

In due course Handel arrived at Venice, and the credentials that he brought from Cardinal Grimani made the production of *Agrippina* at the Teatro di San Giovanni Grisostomo an easy matter. There is an apparent discrepancy between the various records of its production. The libretto is dated 1709, and Allacci, followed by Wiel, gives 1709 as the date of production. Bonlini, on the other hand, followed by Ademollo, says 1710. The ambiguity arises from the fact that *Agrippina* was produced in what was called the Carnival season of 1710, and in Bonlini's catalogue all the operas produced during that season are grouped together under the date 1710. But the Carnival season actually began on December 26th, and as *Agrippina* comes first in Bonlini's list of the Carnival operas we may take it for granted that it was chosen to open the season. It may therefore be taken as a settled fact that *Agrippina* was produced on the 26th of December 1709. The scene must have been brilliance and gaiety itself. The opening of the Carnival was the great day of the year in Venice. The city was crowded with strangers from every country in Europe, and the theatres were crammed from floor to ceiling. The Teatro di San Giovanni Grisostomo was one of the handsomest

respectively to obscure contemporary composers named Urio and Erba, of which he made extensive use in later works. Mr. Robinson's singularly cogent and luminous reasoning may be said to have established the Handelian authorship of both works, though no actual evidence is forthcoming as to the date and place of their composition. It is quite possible that Handel left Rome with Steffani at the end of April 1709, and travelled with him *via* Florence to Venice, where he arrived on the 13th of May (Woker, *Aus den Papieren Agostino Steffanis*). Steffani stayed for a few days at the palace of the Elector of Hanover, and then returned to Düsseldorf. Handel may have accompanied Steffani to Venice, which would give some colour to Mainwaring's story of their having met there, and then gone to stay with his friends near Como.

in Venice. It had been built about thirty years before, in the richest and most luxurious taste of the *barocco* period. Its decorations were getting a little dingy, but at night, when thronged with a brilliant audience, and illuminated by the hundreds of wax tapers which the ladies brought with them to enhance their charms, it still contrived to make a brave show. The boxes were occupied by richly bejewelled ladies with their attendant cavaliers, for it was the fashion just then in Venice for a woman when she went to the opera to wear all the jewellery she could lay her hands upon. The pit and gallery were densely packed with gondoliers, who were admitted gratis, and enlivened the performance with sympathetic cries of delight and personal remarks of a remarkably intimate nature addressed to the singers. *Agrippina* went, in the expressive Italian phrase, to the stars. The audience waxed tumultuous in their enthusiasm as the evening wore on. Cries of " Long live the Saxon ! " rent the air, while the gondoliers in the gallery called down benedictions on every singer in turn, in such phrases as " Blessed be the father that begat thee," and " Blessed be the mother that bare thee." Meanwhile the young nobles in the boxes caught the infection. Leaning over the balustrade towards the stage in a frenzy of artistic rapture, they cried, " Cara, I throw myself headlong at your feet," and similar extravagances, while hastily written sonnets hurled upon the stage testified to the inspiring influence of Handel's music, and to the irresistible charms of his singers.[1] Handel was the hero of the hour, and every *calle* in Venice rang with his praises.

Among the singers who took part in the opera were Francesca Durastanti (Agrippina), who afterwards sang

[1] Blainville, *Travels*, vol. i. chap. lxxviii.

under Handel in London ; Boschi, a tremendous bass with a compass of two octaves and a half, who had sung in Naples in Handel's *Aci, Galatea e Polifemo*; and his wife, who appeared as Ottone. The principal *castrato* in the cast was Valeriano Pellegrini, who took the part of Nero. Pellegrini, or Valeriano as he was generally called, was a favourite singer of Johann Wilhelm, the Elector Palatine, at whose court he was generally to be found. Valeriano seems to have scored a great success in *Agrippina*. Giorgio Stella, another of the Elector's singers, writing from Venice to his patron on the 10th of January 1710 says: " I meant to send you the songs from the opera that is being played at the San Cassiano theatre, but I could not get hold of them. I am not sending the songs of the San Giovanni Grisostomo opera, as I suppose that Valeriano will send them. He is much applauded there, as he is a great artist."[1] *Agrippina* ran uninterruptedly for twenty-seven nights, a thing rare in the annals of Venetian opera, if not unprecedented, and soon brought all Venice to Handel's feet. His friend, the Duke of Manchester, was no longer in Venice, and Prince Ernest Augustus had also gone home, but there were plenty of other distinguished foreigners amusing themselves in the city of the lagoons.

Among them was one of the leading lights of the Hanoverian court, Baron Kielmansegg, the Elector's Master of the Horse, and the husband of the lady who enjoyed the reputation of being her sovereign's favourite mistress. Kielmansegg had probably heard of Handel from Prince Ernest Augustus and Steffani, and he was doubtless flattered to find that a fellow-German was the

[1] Einstein, " Italienische Musiker am Hofe der Neuburger Wittelsbacher." (*Sammelbände der Internationalen Musikgesellschaft*, Jahrg. ix. p. 407.)

hero of the hour in Venetian salons. At any rate, he made friends with Handel, and probably took him back to Hanover when he left Italy in the spring of 1710. In Hanover Handel was warmly welcomed by Steffani, to whose kind and friendly behaviour he afterwards paid a warm tribute in a conversation with Sir John Hawkins, which the latter records in his history: " When I first arrived at Hanover I was a young man. I understood somewhat of music, and—putting forth his broad hands and extending his fingers—could play pretty well on the organ. He received me with great kindness, and took an early opportunity to introduce me to the Princess Sophia and the Elector's son, giving them to understand that I was what he was pleased to call a virtuoso in music. He obliged me with instructions for my conduct and behaviour during my residence in Hanover, and being called from the city to attend to matters of a public concern, he left me in possession of that favour and patronage which himself had enjoyed for a series of years."

Handel received the appointment of Kapellmeister on the 16th of June 1710,[1] at an annual salary of 1000 thalers, but his stay in Hanover was a brief one. It seems to have been an understood thing that he was to finish his *Wanderjahre* before settling down to his work, and he soon obtained leave of absence. His first visit was to his mother at Halle, and after a short stay there he proceeded to Düsseldorf, where he was warmly welcomed at the court of the Elector Palatine. Johann Wilhelm was a typical German princeling of the eighteenth century. The Versailles tradition had dazzled him, and his starving people had to pay for the follies and ex-

[1] Fischer, *Opern und Concerte im Hoftheater zu Hannover*, 1899.

4

travagances of his court at Düsseldorf. In many ways he was a man of cultivation and refinement. The famous picture gallery of Düsseldorf bore witness to the correctness of his artistic taste. Music was another of his passions. The opera at Düsseldorf was one of the most brilliant in Germany, and the Elector's private band was specially admired by Blainville, who visited Düsseldorf in 1705. Even that seasoned traveller was dumbfounded at the magnificence of the Electoral court. " Balls, operas," he wrote, " comedies, concerts of music, festivals, all are equally splendid, all of which diversions we shared regularly during the month we were there." About Johann Wilhelm himself he wrote with some hesitation : " The Prince is of a middle stature, square-built, has a wide large mouth, and his under-lip very thick and turned up. He is about forty-six years of age, very courteous and affable, but not of a very equal temper, being so easy as to be the dupe of the first rogue that has the courage to put upon him, especially in matters that he imagines may contribute to his grandeur, for he is ambitious beyond all bounds." A neat little character-sketch follows of the Electress Anna Maria, who was a daughter of Cosmo III, the Grand Duke of Tuscany : " She is tall and easy, of a genteel shape, very fair in her complexion for an Italian lady, has black eyes, large and well cut. Her hair is of the same colour; she has a pretty mouth, only her lips are a little too thick. Her teeth are white as ivory, but her voice is a little too masculine, and she laughs too loud. She is about thirty-seven, and has never had any children. They say here that she is extremely jealous of her husband, to such a degree, that she has not unfrequently exposed herself to insults, by following him in the night veiled with a mantle, to find out his gallantries. There is nothing

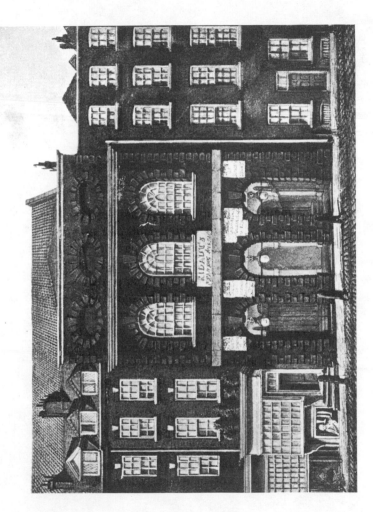

THE QUEEN'S THEATRE

astonishing in this, considering that she was educated in a country where jealousy prevails to madness, and all the world knows that the Elector is no enemy to gallantry."[1] Johann Wilhelm and his wife must both have known all about Handel,—the Elector from Steffani, with whom he maintained a close correspondence, and Anna Maria from her brothers Ferdinand and Gian Gastone,—and they welcomed him to Düsseldorf with open arms. Johann Wilhelm would gladly have kept Handel at his court, but that being impossible, he sped him on his way to England, presenting him on his departure from Düsseldorf with a service of plate. Handel journeyed to England through Holland, arriving in London in the late autumn of 1710.

[1] Blainville, *Travels in Holland, Germany, Italy, etc.*, vol. i. chap. viii.

CHAPTER IV

HANDEL'S FIRST VISIT TO ENGLAND, 1710–1711

IT would be interesting to know what were Handel's first impressions of London. It must necessarily have struck him as very different from anything he had yet seen, and he felt no doubt that he had left equally far behind him the tranquil respectability of Halle and Hamburg and the culture and vivacity of Rome and Florence. In the early eighteenth century travel and education had not swept away racial barriers. Society was not yet cosmopolitan. Each country had its own prejudices and peculiarities, and London in those days differed as much from Paris, as Paris now differs from Constantinople. London in 1710 was a compact city of some five hundred thousand inhabitants, about the present size of Birmingham. On the west it reached as far as Bond Street, on the north to Russell Square, and on the east to Whitechapel Church. Beyond these limits meadows and fields extended to the neighbouring villages, such as Kensington, Hampstead, and Ilford. Within the city the tumult, dirt and disorder were such as we moderns can scarcely realise. There were laws directing householders to keep the streets clean in front of their houses, but no one paid any attention to them. The streets were ankle-deep in mud and encumbered with heaps of refuse, which it seemed to be no one's business to clear away. In the middle of the eighteenth century no great surprise was expressed at the discovery of the body of a murdered infant, after several days' search, on a dunghill in Drury Lane. The crowd in the principal streets was overpowering, but though contemporary complaints of the noise are common, I suspect that in this respect our modern motor-buses could give points to the waggons of Queen Anne's time. At night, however, we have unquestionably the advantage. The few miserable oil-lamps that illuminated the streets in those days served but to make darkness visible, or to help the dreaded Mohocks to escape the interference of the watch. As to the Mohocks, it is probable that the horrors of their nocturnal exploits were considerably exaggerated, but even if we allow a margin for embroidery they remain sufficiently serious. We may doubt, for instance, whether it was a common pastime for these gentry to force an unarmed man to fight, and to kill him in the middle of the street, or to thrust a woman into a barrel and roll her down Ludgate Hill, though both feats are recorded as being favourite Mohock practices; but the issue of a proclamation referring to "the great and unusual Riots and Barbarities, which have lately been committed in the Night time in the open Streets," proves that the nocturnal dangers of London were far from being merely the figments of diseased imagination. But the truth was that public opinion was only just being aroused to the indecorum of this kind of thing. At a time when duels were openly fought in Lincoln's Inn Fields or in the meadows of Bloomsbury, the appeal to force struck no one as an offence against civilisation. If the horrors of the Mohock frolics were somewhat exaggerated by Gay and other writers of the time, there was no necessity for embroidering the exploits of the professional thieves who lurked in the quieter streets for unprotected wayfarers. To what lengths their audacity could go, Lady Cowper's *Diary* sets forth : " Friday night Mr. Mickelwaite was set upon by nine Footpads, who fired at his Postilion without bidding him stand just at the end of Bedford Row, in the road which goes there from Pancras Church to Gray's Inn Lane. His servants and he fired at them again, and the Pads did the same, till all the Fire was spent, and then he rode through them to the Town, to call for Help, it being dark, which they seeing they could not prevent, ran away. Near that Place, under the dead Wall of Gray's Inn Garden, a Gentlewoman, coming Home with her son about half an hour after ten of Saturday Night, two men met them, one of whom struck the Lanthorn out of her Son's Hand, and ran away with his Hat and Wig. She cried out ' Thieves ! ' and they shot her immediately through the Head, and are not yet discovered." [1] Nearly half a century later the streets were still dangerous. Horace Walpole wrote in 1750 : " I was sitting in my own dining-room [in Arlington Street] on Sunday night ; the clock had not struck eleven, when I heard a loud cry of ' Stop thief ! ' A highwayman had attacked a post-chaise in Piccadilly within fifty yards of this house ; the fellow was pursued, rode over the watchman, almost killed him, and escaped." On the other hand, in certain social matters, such as the twopenny post and the " Flying Coaches," the England of Queen Anne's time set an excellent example to foreign countries. The growth of club and coffee-house life, which was a feature of this period, also tended to soothe the ferocious manners of the day. Theatres were

[1] *Diary of Lady Cowper*, 1716.

to some extent under a cloud, owing largely to Queen Anne's personal disapproval of the stage, and in respect of opera Handel found London just as far behind the humblest German or Italian capital as it is to-day—a more complete condemnation cannot be conceived!

Until a few years before Handel's arrival there had been no opera at all in London. In 1705, however, an attempt was made to acclimatise in England the form of art which had been the delight of Italy for a hundred years. Clayton's *Arsinoe* was produced at Drury Lane "after the Italian manner, all sung." The opera was given in English, and the singers were all English, though at the first performance, according to the advertisement, Signora de l'Épine gave "several entertainments of singing before the beginning and after the ending of the Opera." *Arsinoe* broke the ice, and London soon woke up to the fact that the new form of entertainment was worth cultivating. Marcantonio Bononcini's *Camilla*, also given in English, was the next success. It was produced in 1706, and in the same year Sir John Vanbrugh opened his new Queen's Theatre in the Haymarket (" By Beauty founded, and by Wit designed," as the prologue gracefully phrased it, in compliment to Lady Sutherland, who laid the foundation stone) with Giacomo Greber's *Loves of Ergasto*, an Italian opera Englished by P. A. Motteux. *Ergasto* was a failure, and was followed by Vanbrugh's *Confederacy*. The new theatre, however, was too large for comedy, and Vanbrugh determined to persevere with opera. He tried to bring Bononcini to England, and his friend and patron, the Duke of Manchester, whose position as Ambassador Extraordinary at Venice placed him at the very heart of the operatic world, exhausted all the arts of diplomacy in his endeavours to win from the court of

Vienna permission for the popular composer to visit London.[1] Failing Bononcini himself, the English *dilettanti* had to content themselves with his music, and *Camilla* was revived in 1707. Meanwhile opera was becoming the fashion, though the absurd plan of giving the words, Hamburg fashion, partly in English and partly in Italian was still followed. Writing early in 1708 to the Duke of Manchester, who was quite as greedy for operatic as for political news, Vanbrugh declares that "the town cries out for a new man and woman of the first rate to be got against next winter from Italy." Manchester, as usual, was Vanbrugh's good angel. He discovered the desiderated "new man," and brought him in triumph to England in the handsome person of Nicolini, who appeared in the autumn of 1708 in Scarlatti's *Pirro e Demetrio*, and took London by storm. He was *mutatis mutandis* the Caruso of the hour, and his doings were catalogued by journalists with respectful awe. He was as good an actor as he was a singer, and even Steele, who from his position in the theatrical world had excellent reasons for grudging opera its popularity, did him full justice in this respect. His famous fight with the lion in *Hydaspes* furnished the *Spectator* and the *Tatler* with an admirable target for the arrows of their satire. Hitherto all the operatic performances in London had been either English or bilingual, but in 1710 the town, as Addison observed, tired of understanding but half of the entertainment, determined for the future to understand none of it, and *Almahide* was performed in Italian alone, followed by Bononcini's *Etearco*, also given without any admixture of English. London was thus ripe for Handel. Addison and Steele had in vain exhausted their powers of ridicule.

[1] Duke of Manchester, *Court and Society*.

Italian opera was firmly established in the good graces of society. The new composer, fresh from his triumphs in Italy, was received with open arms, and speedily received a commission from Aaron Hill to compose an opera for the Queen's Theatre in the Haymarket, whither the Drury Lane operatic company had migrated in 1708. *Rinaldo* was written in a fortnight to a libretto by Giacomo Rossi, who complained that he could not turn his verses out quickly enough to keep pace with the fervid flow of Handel's inspiration. *Rinaldo* was produced with great success on the 24th of February 1711, and was performed fifteen times before the close of the season, which came to an end on the 2nd of June. It is incorrect to say, as many of Handel's biographers have done, that *Rinaldo* was performed fifteen times without interruption. On the contrary, its run was broken by revivals, given "at the desire of several ladies of quality," of *Hydaspes, Almahide, Pirro e Demetrio,* and *Clotilda,* the attractions of the last-named being enhanced by a "Water-scene" which, according to the advertisements, "by reason of the Hot Weather," played for the greater part of the evening. *Rinaldo* itself underwent a certain amount of modification. After it had run for a month, some dances were introduced by M. du Breil and Mademoiselle la Fève, "just arrived from Bruxelles."

The success of *Rinaldo* alarmed the advocates of English opera, of whom the spokesmen were Addison and Steele. Steele, who was a patentee of Drury Lane and the owner of a concert-room in York Buildings, saw his audiences drifting away to the Haymarket. Addison was still smarting from the failure of his English opera *Rosamond,* which, set to music by Clayton, had achieved a run of three nights a few years before. The two essayists joined forces for the purpose of crushing *Rinaldo*, and the *Spectator* and *Tatler* did all that they could to render it absurd and odious in the eyes of their readers. One of the most famous of the *Spectator's* attacks upon *Rinaldo* relates to the sparrows that were let loose in the theatre during the performance of the air " Augelletti che cantate." For the sufferings of the unfortunate birds themselves the distinguished essayist manifested little enough sympathy, though, as he said, "instead of perching on the Trees and performing their parts, these young actors either get into the Galleries or put out the Candles," but he professed great anxiety lest the poor little creatures should remain in the theatre and become a general nuisance. "It is feared," he observes, "that in other plays they may make their Entrance in very wrong and improper Scenes, so as to be seen flying in a Lady's Bed-Chamber, or perching upon a King's Throne, besides the Inconveniences which the Heads of the Audience may sometimes suffer from them." The dragons in *Rinaldo* and the *mise-en-scène* generally speaking, which seems to have been unusually elaborate, came in for their share of ridicule, and it is worth noting that it was the *Spectator* which started the accusation against Handel, often afterwards repeated, of revelling in noise for its own sake. At the close of one of the *Spectator* essays ridiculing *Rinaldo* there is a burlesque advertisement of a supposed new opera, *The Cruelty of Atreus*, in which "the scene wherein Thyestes eats his own Children is to be performed by the famous M. Psalmanazar, lately arrived from Formosa, the whole supper being set to Kettle-drums." But *Rinaldo* rose superior to Addison's raillery. It was revived in 1712, with Nicolini still in the principal part, and was given again in 1715 and 1717. Even so late as 1731 it had not exhausted its popularity. Nor were its triumphs confined to England. It was performed at Hamburg with great success in 1715, and at Naples in 1717.

During his stay in London, Handel's duties at the opera-house seemed to have monopolised him almost entirely. He gave no concerts, but it is highly probable that he played at the houses of some of the great *dilettanti* of the day. We have a glimpse of him at Sir John Stanley's, who was uncle to little Mary Granville, afterwards the well-known Mrs. Delany. The latter writes in her autobiography: "In the year 1710 I first saw Mr. Handel, who was introduced to my uncle Stanley by Mr. Heidegger. We had no better instrument in the house than a little spinet of mine, on which that great musician performed wonders." The friendship so begun lasted all Handel's lifetime. In later years Handel was a frequent visitor at Mrs. Delany's house, and would play to her for hours at a time. Musical life in London was of course very different from what it is now, but still concerts were given from time to time, and it is a little curious that Handel did not think it worth while to give one himself, especially as personal popularity was evidently much harder to win in England than in Italy. The success of *Agrippina* in Venice raised the composer at once to the rank of a hero, but in London, even after the triumph of *Rinaldo*, Handel often found life something of a struggle. The following advertisement from the *Daily Courant* gives a specimen of the sort of concert that was popular in London at the time: "For the benefit of Signiora Lody on Tuesday, 24th April 1711, at Hume's Dancing School in Frith Street, Soho, will be a Consort of Vocal and Instrumental Musick; a new Cantata with a solo on the Harpsichord, performed by Mr. Babell

Junior, with a Variety of Concertos and other pieces composed and performed by Mr. Corbett and other of the best Masters, beginning at 7 o'clock." Handel himself may not impossibly have attended this very concert, since *Rinaldo* was that week performed on Wednesday the 25th instead of the usual Tuesday,—Tuesday and Saturday were the ordinary opera nights,—and if so it was in all likelihood the playing of Babell, who was the most noted performer upon the harpsichord in London, that drew from him the observation that when he first went to London there were very few good composers there but plenty of good players.

But the most famous concerts in London at that time were the weekly *réunions* of Thomas Britton, the small-coal man, which took place every Thursday in a loft "not much higher than a Canary Pipe, with a window but very little bigger than the Bunghole of a Cask,"[1] over his coal-cellar in Clerkenwell. Britton's career was a remarkable one, especially at a time when music was a slave to the odious and degrading system of patronage, and most musicians lived in a slough of complacent flunkeydom. Britton plied his sooty trade by day, hawking coal about the streets of London. In the evening, washed, clothed and in his right mind, he gathered his friends about him, and discoursed sweet music, being himself a notable performer upon the viol da gamba. Gradually his concerts became famous. The leading lights of musical London, Dr. Pepusch, Banister the violinist, John Hughes the author of *The Siege of Damascus*, who was a musician as well as a poet, and many others, took their parts in sonatas and concertos. Britton became the fashion. Visitors to London were taken to make his acquaintance as a matter

[1] Ward, *Secret History of Clubs*, 1709.

of course.   Thoresby, the diarist, records a visit, when he
heard "a noble concert of music, vocal and instrumental,
the best in town."[1]   Matthew Prior sang of him :—

> "Though doom'd to small coal, yet to arts allied ;
> Rich without wealth, and famous without pride."

Duchesses crawled up the crazy ladder leading to his
concert room, which was celebrated by the doggerel poet
Ned Ward, a near neighbour and intimate friend of
Britton's :—

> " Upon Thursdays repair
> To my palace, and there
> Hobble up stair by stair ;
> But I pray ye take care
> That you break not your shin by a stumble.[2]

Thither Handel often repaired, according to Hawkins,
playing both harpsichord and organ, and directing the
performance, to the delight of the audience, who, as Ward
vivaciously observed, were "willing to take a hearty Sweat
that they might have the Pleasure of hearing many notable
Performances in the charming Science of Musick."

Handel left London for Hanover soon after the conclusion of the opera season, on the 2nd of June 1711.   On
his way he stopped at Düsseldorf, where his old friend
and patron the Elector Palatine was as delighted as ever
to welcome him.   How long Handel stayed at Düsseldorf
cannot now be ascertained, but it is plain that he must
have begun to be a little anxious as to what the Elector
of Hanover would think of his prolonged absence, for a
couple of letters from the Elector Palatine, dated the 17th
of June, have recently come to light,[3] one addressed to the

[1] Ralph Thoresby, *Diary*, vol. ii.
[2] Ward, *Secret History of Clubs*, 1709.
[3] *Zeitschrift der Internationalen Musik-Gesellschaft*, Bd. viii. p. 277.

Elector of Hanover and the other to the old Electress Sophia, in which he apologises for keeping Handel "a few days," and explains that he is only doing so in order to show him some instruments, and get his opinion about them. Presumably the apology was accepted, and Handel settled down to his quiet life at Hanover without any uncomfortable questions being asked about his long holiday. At that time there was no opera at Hanover, and his energies were confined to chamber music. He had at his disposal an orchestra of eighteen musicians, for whom he probably wrote some of his hautboy concertos. He also composed a set of thirteen chamber duets, some German songs and a few harpsichord pieces.[1] The duets were written for the Princess Caroline, wife of Prince George, the Elector's son, afterwards George II. They show the influence of Steffani, who was an acknowledged master of the *genre*. Caroline of Ansbach was one of Handel's best and kindest friends, and he repaid her regard with warm gratitude and admiration. It is more than probable that they met as children at Berlin, for, when Handel visited the Prussian court as a juvenile prodigy in 1696, Caroline was actually living in Berlin under the care of her guardian, the Elector Frederick, and his wife, Sophia Charlotte. Caroline imbibed Sophia Charlotte's artistic tastes, and was always a devoted patron of music. She seems to have been no mean performer too. Leibniz, who heard her sing a duet with the Hereditary Princess of Cassel, said that she sang very correctly and had a marvellous voice,[2] and the Archduke Charles, who used to play her accompaniments, lost his heart so completely to the fair musician that, but for her

[1] Fischer, *Opern und Concerte im Hoftheater zu Hannover.*
[2] *Correspondence*, vol. iii. p. 105.

objections to the Roman Catholic religion, she might have been Empress of Germany.[1] The records of this period of Handel's career are sadly meagre, but we know from a letter of his written in July to Andreas Roner, a German musician who lived in London, that he spent some of his spare time in working at English ; and a message to John Hughes, with a request for a poem to set to music, shows that he retained friendly recollections of his friends in London.[2] In the autumn of 1711 he paid a visit to his relatives at Halle, and on November 23 stood godfather to his sister's daughter, Johanna Frederica, who was nominated as his residuary legatee in the will of 1750. After this we know nothing of his movements until a year later, when he obtained leave of absence from the Elector of Hanover on condition that he resumed his duties within a reasonable time. He left at once for London, where he arrived some time in the autumn of 1712.

[1] "Briefe der Königin Sophie Charlotte von Preussen." (*Publikationen aus den K. Preussischen Staatsarchiven*, vol. lxxix. p. 57.)

[2] Hughes, *Correspondence*, Dublin, 1773, vol. i. p. 39.

CHAPTER V

HANDEL'S SECOND VISIT TO ENGLAND
1712-1717

H ANDEL found changes in the musical world
of London. Since his departure opera had
languished, and the production in English of Galliard's
Calypso did little to restore the falling fortunes of the art.
Aaron Hill had given place to an adventurer named
MacSwiney, who now ruled the destinies of the Queen's
Theatre. For him Handel wrote a new opera, *Il Pastor
Fido*, to a libretto by Rossi, inferior in every way to that
of *Rinaldo*. *Il Pastor Fido* was produced on the 26th
November 1712, but in spite of the composer's popularity
it won little success. The public missed Nicolini, who
had left England in the summer, and the singing of his
successor, Valeriano Pellegrini, who had sung in Handel's
Agrippina three years before, did not make amends for
the absence of the favourite. *Il Pastor Fido* was only
given six times. Far greater success attended Handel's
Teseo, written to a libretto by Nicola Haym, which was
produced on January 10th, 1713. Its triumphant career
was hardly checked by the failure and flight of the
egregious MacSwiney, who, after *Teseo* had been given
twice, disappeared from the scene, leaving his bills un-
settled and his singers unpaid. The latter determined to

carry on the season as best they could, and as a matter of fact it endured until the 30th May, under the management of the famous "Swiss Count," Heidegger. *Teseo* was played twelve times, the last performance being a benefit for Handel, probably arranged to compensate him for MacSwiney's non-fulfilment of his liabilities. At this performance, Handel gave between the acts of the opera " an entertainment for the harpsichord," the forerunner of many similar displays of virtuosity.

Heidegger, who was one of the most prominent figures in London life during a large part of the eighteenth century, had so much to do with Handel that there is every excuse for lingering a moment over him and his fortunes. He was a native of Zurich, and appeared in London about the year 1708. His own story was that he came upon a diplomatic mission, but failing in his errand was compelled to enlist in the Guards. How he managed to win admittance to the councils of the Queen's Theatre is not known, but in 1709 he had a good deal to do with the production of *Thomyris*, and from that time forth he played a leading part in the management of opera in London. His engaging manners soon established him in the favour of the aristocracy, and he became a sort of *arbiter elegantiarum* in the world of art and fashion. The " Swiss Count," as he was always called, was an unusually ugly man, and his misshapen features furnished the wits of his time with an inexhaustible subject for mirth. The taste in humour of the eighteenth century was somewhat primitive, and Heidegger, whose business was to get on in life, threw self-respect to the winds, and encouraged every sort of joke at his own expense. He once laid a wager with Lord Chesterfield that, within a given time, his lordship would not be able to produce so hideous a

5

face in all London. After a strict search, an old woman was found, who at first sight was judged uglier even than Heidegger. The "Swiss Count," however, seized her head-dress, and putting it on himself was at once acclaimed the winner. Clever as he was, he was badly scored off on another occasion by the facetious Duke of Montagu, whose taste for practical joking was extensive and peculiar.[1] Montagu invited Heidegger to dinner, and, in concert with half a dozen other congenial spirits, made him so drunk that he was carried unconscious to bed. A cast of his face was then taken, and a wax mask constructed. At the next masquerade given by Heidegger at the opera-house a man was dressed up in a suit of his clothes, disguised in the mask, and smuggled into the orchestra. Heidegger was got out of the way under some pretext, and, on the entrance of George II and his mistress, the Countess of Yarmouth, his double bade the musicians strike up the well-known Jacobite tune, "Charlie over the water." The confusion and excitement were immense, but the King took the joke in good part and, when the real Heidegger flew back in consternation and was confronted by his double, laughed more than any one at the absurdity of the situation. Incidents such as this only served to increase Heidegger's popularity, and ere long he was able to retire to his house at Richmond with an ample fortune. "I was born a Swiss," he is reported to have said in a discussion as to the respective merits of the several European nations, "and came to England without

---

[1] He never seems to have outgrown it. In 1740 his mother-in-law, the old Duchess of Marlborough, wrote of him: "All his talents lie in things only natural in boys of fifteen years old, and he is about two-and-fifty; to get people into his garden and wet them with squirts, and to invite people to his country houses and put things into their beds to make 'them itch, and twenty such pretty fancies like these." *Private Correspondence*, vol. ii.

a farthing, where I have found means to gain five thousand
pounds a year, and to spend it. Now I defy the most
able Englishman to go to Switzerland and either to gain
that income or to spend it there."

During his first visit to London, Handel had made
many friends, who now contended for the honour of entertaining him. His first visit was to a Mr. Andrews, of
Barn-Elms in Surrey, who also possessed a town house
where Handel had a suite of apartments. Here he stayed
some months, moving to his friend Lord Burlington's
palace in Piccadilly before the end of the year. Handel's
life at Burlington House has been well described by
Hawkins: "Into this hospitable mansion was Handel
received, and left at liberty to follow the dictates of his
genius and invention, assisting frequently at evening
concerts, in which his own music made the most considerable part. The course of his studies during three years'
residence at Burlington House was very regular and
uniform; his mornings were employed in study, and at
dinner he sat down with men of the first eminence for
genius and abilities of any in the kingdom. Here he
frequently met Pope, Gay, Dr. Arbuthnot, and others of
that class; the latter was able to converse with him on
his art, but Pope understood not, neither had he the least
ear or relish for music—and he was honest enough to
confess it. When Handel had no particular engagements,
he frequently went in the afternoon to St. Paul's Church,
where Mr. Greene, though he was not then organist, was
very assiduous in his civilities to him; by him he was
introduced to, and made acquainted with, the principal
performers in the choir. The truth is, that Handel was
very fond of the St. Paul's organ, built by Father Smith,
which was then almost a new instrument. Brind was

then the organist, and no very celebrated performer. The
tone of the instrument delighted Handel, and a little
entreaty was at any time sufficient to prevail on him to
touch it; but after he had ascended the organ-loft it was
with reluctance that he left it, and he has been known,
after evening service, to play to an audience as great as
ever filled the choir. After his performance was over, it
was his practice to adjourn with the principal persons
of the choir to the Queen's Arms Tavern in St. Paul's
Churchyard, where was a great room, with a harpsichord
in it, and oftentimes an evening was there spent in music
and musical conversation."

Hawkins' facts are doubtless correct, but his chronology
seems to be a little shaky. The *noctes coenaeque deorum*
that he describes must belong to a later date. In 1712
Lord Burlington was only seventeen years old—rather an
early age for a youth, however precocious, to be entertaining a circle of wits. As a matter of fact, his acquaintance
with Gay does not seem to have begun till 1715, when the
poet celebrated his young patron in *Trivia*:[1]—

> "Yet Burlington's fair Palace still remains;
> Beauty within, without proportion reigns.
> Beneath his Eye declining Art revives,
> The Wall with animated Picture lives;
> There Handel strikes the strings, the melting strain
> Transports the Soul and thrills through every vein."

Burlington does not appear in Pope's correspondence
until 1718, when Pope wrote to Martha Blount: "I am
to pass three or four days in high luxury, with some
company, at my Lord Burlington's. We are to walk,
ride, ramble, dine, drink, and lie together. His gardens

[1] *Trivia* was published in January 1716. See Gay's *Works*, Muses
Library, vol. i. p. xxxvii.

are delightful, his music ravishing."[1] In the same year
Pope established himself at Chiswick "under the wing of
my Lord Burlington," with whom he was by that time on
intimate terms, if we may judge by Gay's *Journey to
Exeter*:—

> "While you, my Lord, bid stately piles ascend
> And in your Chiswick bowers enjoy your friend;
> Where Pope unloads the bough within his reach,
> The purple vine, blue plum, and blushing peach."

However, it is likely enough that Handel was staying
in Burlington House in the autumn of 1712. He may
very well have been invited thither by the Dowager
Countess, who was a great patroness of music, — the
English version of Gasparini's *Antiochus*, which was produced in 1711, was dedicated to her,—and the fact that
Teseo was dedicated to Lord Burlington implies some
kind of connection between Handel and the young
dilettante.

Rinaldo and *Teseo* gave Handel a position in the
musical world of London far more commanding than
that of any native-born composer, and there is nothing
surprising in his being chosen to write an ode in celebration of Queen Anne's birthday, or to compose the festival
Te Deum and *Jubilate* which were sung at the service
commemorating the Peace of Utrecht. It is possible,
too, that in the selection of Handel for so keenly coveted
a position we may trace the friendly influence of Lady
Burlington, who was one of the Queen's Ladies of the
Bed-Chamber. The Birthday Ode was performed on
the 6th of February 1713, probably in the Chapel Royal,
St. James's, and the Utrecht *Te Deum* and *Jubilate* at
St. Paul's on the 7th of July following. The Queen was

[1] Pope, *Works*, Elwin's edition, vol. ix. p. 264.

not well enough to be present at the latter service, but she heard Handel's music later at St. James's, and conferred upon him a pension of £200. Meanwhile, his duties at the court of Hanover summoned him in vain. The "reasonable time" for which he had received leave of absence had long since expired, yet still Rinaldo lingered in the enchanted gardens of Armida. Not only was Handel playing truant in the most unwarrantable fashion, but he was spending his time in the manner of all others most surely calculated to displease the Elector : accepting favours from Queen Anne, who lost no opportunity of showing her dislike of everything connected with Hanover, and celebrating the Peace of Utrecht, which the German confederate powers viewed with the utmost disapproval. It was no wonder, therefore, that when George I succeeded to the throne of England, on the sudden death of Queen Anne in August 1714, Handel did not dare to present himself at the court of St. James's, but waited quietly in the security of Burlington House to see what turn events would take. It was probably about this time that he wrote *Silla*, a work much slighter in scope than any of his previous operas, which may have been designed for a private performance at Burlington House, though no record of its production exists. The confusion which had reigned at the operahouse in the Haymarket since the flight of MacSwiney probably deterred Handel from contributing to its repertory, but in 1715 he once more tempted fortune with *Amadigi*, an opera conceived upon a scale at least as imposing as that of *Rinaldo*, and written to a libretto by Heidegger, who dedicated it to Lord Burlington in terms which make it certain that the music was composed by Handel at Burlington House. Nicolini, who had returned to England in 1714, appeared as the hero, and the part of Oriana was sung by the celebrated Anastasia Robinson, afterwards Countess of Peterborough, whose romantic love-story not long since formed the foundation of Mr. George Meredith's novel, *Lord Ormont and his Aminta*.

Amadigi was produced on the 25th of May, so late in the season that a long run was out of the question. Its success, however, was beyond dispute, and it received the compliment of parody at the theatres both of Drury Lane and Lincoln's Inn Fields. The scenery was so unusually elaborate that spectators were not allowed upon the stage, as had been customary, and a special by-law with regard to *encores* was issued by the management to this effect: "Whereas by the frequent calling for the songs again, the operas have been too tedious; therefore the singers are forbidden to sing any song above once; and it is hoped nobody will call for 'em, or take it ill when not obeyed."

Meanwhile, in spite of all that his friends could urge in his behalf, Handel was still an exile from court. King George, who liked going to the opera, and even condescended to act as godfather to the infant son of Mme. Durastanti, heard *Amadigi* but refused to pardon the composer. But a means of reconciliation was devised by Lord Burlington in conjunction with Handel's old friend Baron Kielmansegg, who was now the King's Master of the Horse and a personage of great consideration, though this was due less perhaps to his own merits than to the fact that his wife, "the Elephant," as she was nicknamed, shared with Mlle. Schulenburg—"the Maypole"—the King's most intimate favour.[1]

[1] It is now the fashion to regard Baroness Kielmansegg as a much maligned person, and a most determined attempt to whitewash her character

The river Thames was then, far more than now, one
of the main highways of London. It was still Spenser's
"silver Thames," and on a summer's day it must have
presented a picture of life and gaiety very different from
its present melancholy and deserted aspect. It was
peopled by an immense fleet of boats devoted solely to
passenger traffic, which were signalled by passing wayfarers from numerous piers between Blackfriars and
Putney, just as one now signals a hansom or taxi-cab.
Besides the humble boats that plied for hire, there were
plenty of private barges fitted up with no little luxury,
and manned by liveried servants. The manners and
customs of the boatmen were peculiar, and their wit-
combats, carried on in the rich and expressive vernacular
of Billingsgate, were already proverbial. However, no
one seems to have minded. On the water liberty reigned

has recently been made by her descendant, Baron Erich von Kielmansegg, in
his edition of the correspondence of Ernest Augustus, George I's youngest
brother. She was undoubtedly George's half-sister, being the daughter of
his father's mistress Countess Platen, but those who know what was the
standard of morality at the Hanoverian court will require a more cogent
argument than this to convince them, in the teeth of all contemporary opinion,
that George's relations with the Baroness were purely fraternal. Undoubtedly
she was extremely unpopular in England—more, it is to be feared, because
she was ugly, rapacious, and a foreigner than from any very exalted ideas upon
the subject of morality. There is a story that one day when she was driving
abroad, soon after her arrival in England, the mob became abusive, whereupon she put her head out of the window and cried in shocking English :
"Good people, why do you abuse us? We come for all your goods." "Ay,
damn ye," answered a fellow in the crowd, "and for all our chattels too."
Horace Walpole's description of this atrocious harpy is worth transcribing :
"I remember as a boy being terrified at her enormous figure. Two fierce
black eyes, large and rolling beneath two lofty arched eyebrows, two acres
of cheeks spread with crimson, an ocean of neck that overflowed and was
not distinguished from the lower part of her body, and no part restrained by
stays—no wonder that a child dreaded such an ogress !"

supreme. There was a tacit understanding that things
were there permitted which in the prosaic sobriety of the
streets would have savoured of indecorum. George I
liked the river. When the court was at Whitehall
water-parties to Richmond or Hampton Court were of frequent occurrence, and as often as not the royal barge
was accompanied by an attendant boat laden with
musicians.[1]

   Taking advantage of the King's taste for music, and
of the recognised aquatic licence already referred to,
Kielmansegg and Burlington bade Handel compose a
suite of gay dance movements, hired a competent orchestra,
and arranged that on the occasion of the next royal
water-party — possibly that mentioned by the *Flying
Post*, soon after the King's coronation, when George I
and his court rowed from Whitehall to Limehouse, and
"were diverted by a concert of music on board, which
was elegantly performed by the best masters and instruments"—Handel and his musicians should follow the
King's barge, discoursing the famous composition which
ever since has been known as the Water Music.[2] The

---

   [1] Aquatic serenades of this kind were popular at the time. There is a
description of one in Mrs. Delany's *Correspondence* (vol. i. p. 70): "Last
Wednesday I was all night upon the water with Lady Harriot Harley. We
went into the barge at five in the afternoon and landed at Whitehall Stairs.
We rowed up the river as far as Richmond, and were entertained all the time
with very good musick in another barge. The concert was composed of
three hautboys, two bassoons, flute allemagne, and young Grenoc's (*sic*)
trumpet.

   [2] The evidence to prove that the Water Music was composed in 1715 is
almost overwhelming. At the same time it is interesting to know that a very
similar performance took place two years later, which is recorded in the
Daily Courant of 19th July 1717: "On Wednesday evening (July 17) at
about eight the King took water at Whitehall in an open barge, wherein
were also the Duchess of Bolton, the Duchess of Newcastle, the Countess of

plot succeeded; the King was pleased, and asked the name of the composer, which gave Kielmansegg an opportunity of pleading his friend's cause. George was in a melting mood, and felt that Handel had endured exile from his sacred presence long enough. The composer was summoned from the neighbouring barge and duly forgiven.

Handel made his first appearance at a court concert shortly afterwards, at the special request of another old friend, Geminiani the violinist, who had recently established himself in London. Geminiani was notoriously difficult to accompany. Burney says that he lost the post of leader of the opera-band at Naples because " none

Godolphin, Madam Kilmanseck, and the Earl of Orkney, and went up the river towards Chelsea. Many other barges with persons of quality attended, and so great a number of boats, that the whole river in a manner was covered. A City Company's barge was employed for the music, wherein were fifty instruments of all sorts, who played all the way from Lambeth, while the barges drove ¦with the tide without rowing as far as Chelsea, the finest symphonies, composed express for this occasion by Mr. Hendel, which His Majesty liked so well that he caused it to be played over three times in going and returning. At eleven his Majesty went ashore at Chelsea, where a supper was prepared, and then there was another very fine consort of music, which lasted till two, after which His Majesty came again into his barge and returned the same way, the music continuing to play until he landed." Another account, in *The Political State of Great Britain*, mentions that the music was under the direction of Baron Kielmansegg. When Chrysander wrote the first volume of his biography of Handel in 1858 he followed the contemporary authorities in attributing the Water Music to the year 1715. In 1867, however, in his third volume, in discussing Handel's instrumental works he seems inclined to think that it was actually performed for the first time in 1717. Twenty years later (*Vierteljahrsschrift für Musikwissenschaft*, Jahrg. iii., 1887) he recanted his heresy, and returned to his original opinion. It is quite possible that the Water Music as we now know it was not all written for the same occasion. Its twenty-five numbers may very well represent Handel's share in numerous water-parties. It should be remembered that the Water Music was not published until 1740.

of the performers were able to follow him in his *tempo rubato*," and Tartini christened him "il furibondo Geminiani." He had written some new concertos, which he was anxious to perform, but he declared that nobody but Handel could play the harpsichord part. It was a case of no Handel, no concerto, and George I, nothing loth, gave way. Handel was thus fully reinstated in the royal favour, and the reconciliation was cemented by the King's allotting him a pension of £200, in addition to that already given him by Queen Anne. A few years later he received yet another pension of the same amount from the Princess of Wales, his old friend and patroness Caroline of Ansbach, on his appointment as music master to her little daughters. This £600 he continued to enjoy for the rest of his life.

When George I landed in England, he frankly confessed that he did not expect to stay long. The Jacobites were powerful and determined, and he took up his residence at St. James's in the full expectation of being turned out bag and baggage at no distant date. At first it seemed that his predictions were going to be fulfilled. The King himself made no secret of his dislike for England and everything English—even our oysters were so different from the stale ones to which he was accustomed at Hanover that they had to be kept for a day or two to suit his palate. He was unpopular, his mistresses were more unpopular still, and the crowd of hungry "Hanoverian rats," as the people called them, who settled upon the court and country and snatched all the best places from under the noses of English aspirants, brought the new dynasty into general disfavour. But as time passed on, his position grew more secure. The English people as a whole cared very little who ruled them, so long as they were let alone, and the Hanoverian dynasty was probably as good or as bad as another. The Jacobite rising of 1715 collapsed, the Septennial Act was passed, and in the summer of 1716 George thought he might allow himself a holiday and pay a visit to his beloved Hanover. On the eve of his departure he held a Drawing-room. " The King in mighty good humour," wrote Lady Cowper. " When I wished him a good journey and a quick return, he looked as if the last part of my speech was needless, and that he did not think of it." George set out for Hanover on 9th July 1716, accompanied by a numerous suite, including both his mistresses and his Kapellmeister Handel. Hanover received them with open arms, and George put aside the splendid dulness and wearisome etiquette of St. James's with delight, and settled down to his pipes and his beer and his snuffy clothes with the utmost relief.

Lady Mary Wortley Montagu, who stopped at Hanover for a short time on her way to Constantinople, found it very gay and very crowded. " The King," she wrote, " has had the goodness to appoint us a lodging in the palace, without which we should be very ill accommodated, for the vast number of English crowds the town so much, it is very good luck to be able to get one sorry room in a miserable tavern. . . . The King's company of French comedians play here every night. They are very well dressed, and some of them not ill actors. His Majesty dines and sups constantly in public. The court is very numerous, and his affability and goodness make it one of the most agreeable places in the world." The success of the French comedians seems to have left no room for opera, and Handel must have found time hang heavy on his hands. He amused himself by setting to music a poetical version of the story of the Passion by Barthold Brockes, a distinguished citizen of Hamburg, which had already been set by Keiser, and was subsequently set by Telemann and Mattheson.[1] He also found time for a visit to Halle, where his mother still lived. His old friend Zachow was dead, and his widow, who was left in poor circumstances, was thankful for the assistance that Handel generously gave. His travels extended as far as Ansbach, whither probably he went with some commission from the Princess of Wales. There he found an old college friend, Johann Christopher Schmidt, whom he induced to migrate to London and to live with him as his secretary and factotum. Schmidt had a son of thirteen in whom Handel took a friendly interest, paying for his schooling, and watching over him with almost paternal affection. In due time the boy, who anglicised his name into Smith,

---

[1] There is a good deal of uncertainty as to the genesis of Handel's *Brockes Passion*. Mattheson says in his *Ehren-Pforte* that it was "composed in England and sent by post to Hamburg in an uncommonly close-written score," but Mattheson's sketch of Handel's career is so thickly sown with inaccuracies that it is difficult to put much faith in any of his statements. It is at least probable that the fact of his being on German soil turned Handel's thoughts in the direction of German oratorio, and the eulogies of Keiser's setting of Brockes's *Passion*, which he must almost unavoidably have heard at Hanover, may very well have tempted him to pay his old rival out in his own coin for the impertinence of having re-set *Almira* ten years before. Mr. P. Robinson, in his recent work, *Handel and his Orbit*, inclines to the theory that Handel wrote his *Passion* for performance in England before the German-speaking King and his court. There has been a half-hearted attempt made in recent years to whitewash George I, and to present him as a highly moral and respectable person, but even his most devoted advocates have not ventured to claim much for him on the score of piety ; and the notion of the old reprobate sitting in the Chapel Royal, with the "Elephant" and the "Maypole" enthroned like cherubim, the one on his right hand and the other on his left, snuffling in concert over the Passion music, is, to borrow a phrase of Mr. Andrew Lang's, a little too steep !

succeeded his father as Handel's amanuensis, and later in his career won considerable fame as a composer.

King George left for England on the 5th of January 1717, and there is no reasonable ground for doubting that Handel went with him. There was nothing for him to do at Hanover, and his presence was urgently needed in London, where a revival of *Rinaldo* took place on the very day he left Hanover, while another of *Amadigi* was close at hand. He took with him his setting of the *Brockes Passion*, as it is usually called to distinguish it from the *John Passion* written in 1704, had it copied in London, and sent it to Hamburg, where it was performed in Lent 1717.

CHAPTER VI

CANONS AND THE ROYAL ACADEMY OF MUSIC, 1718–1726

JAMES BRYDGES, first Duke of Chandos, was the cynosure of his age. His splendour and extravagance, his generosity and ostentation, made him the talk of the town. As Paymaster to the British forces he had amassed an immense fortune, by means which Swift branded in the famous line—

"Since all he got by fraud he lost by stocks,"

and he signalised his retirement by building the magnificent palace of Canons, close to the village of Edgware, where he lived in regal state surrounded by crowds of lackeys and parasites. Everything at Canons was in the grand style. Pope, who satirised Chandos in his Epistle to Lord Burlington, made fun of the princely owner's megalomania:—

"To compass this, his building is a town,
His pond an ocean, his parterre a down,"

and ridiculed the tasteless magnificence that reigned in every corner. But humbler mortals bowed before splendour so profuse. Defoe's fluent vocabulary scarcely served to sing the praises of Canons.[1] "It is in vain," he wrote, "to attempt to describe the beauties of this

---

[1] *Tour in England*, 1725, vol. ii.

building; and as the Firmament is a glorious Mantle
filled with, or as it were made up of a Concurrence of
lesser glories the stars, so every part of this Building
adds to the beauty of the whole." The Duke, if not
himself a musician, fully appreciated the importance of
music in adding to the dignity of every kind of ceremony.
His private chapel at Canons was a masterpiece of its
kind, designed in imitation of the fashionable baroque
Italian style, and painted with sprawling cherubs by
Bellucci and Zamen,[1] and the music was worthy of its
shrine.   Pope of course sneered at it :—

> "And now the Chapel's silver bell you hear,
>   That summons you to all the pride of prayer;
>   Light quirks of music, broken and uneven,
>   Make the soul dance upon a jig to Heaven."

But Pope was notoriously ignorant of music, and other
authorities give a very different account. Defoe says:
"The Chapel is a singularity not only in its building and
the beauty of its workmanship, but in this also, that the
Duke maintains there a full Choir, and has the Worship
performed there with the best musick, after the manner
of the Chapel Royal, which is not done in any other
Nobleman's Chapel in Britain, no not the Prince of
Wales's, though heir apparent to the Crown.   Nor is this
Chapel only furnished with such excellent musick, but the
Duke has a set of them to entertain him every day at dinner."

It has often been said that when Canons was pulled
down, the chapel was left standing, and became the
parish church of Whitchurch, which still exists.   This,
like so many other Handelian traditions which have been
religiously copied by one biographer from another, is a
piece of pure romance.   The private chapel at Canons

---

[1] Pope, Letter to Aaron Hill, 5th February 1732.

"His Grace the Duke of Chandos's domestic Chapel, at his seat at Canons, Edgware, curiously adorned with paintings on the windows and ceilings, had Divine Worship performed in it with an Anthem on Monday last (29th August), it being the first time of its being opened." It is scarcely possible that the "Anthem" in question can have been *Esther*. Handel himself described his new venture into the realm of oratorio as a masque, and undoubtedly he intended that it should be performed with scenery, dresses, and action—in fact precisely as it was given in 1732 at Bernard Gates's house by the children of the Chapel Royal. The idea of performing an oratorio in ordinary concert form was a much later development. The libretto of *Esther*, which is an adaptation of Racine's famous drama, has been attributed to a certain Samuel Humphreys, who wrote a dull poem on Canons which he dedicated to the Duke of Chandos, and later in his career supplied Handel with the librettos of *Athaliah* and *Deborah*. It is more likely, however, that it was the work of Pope, who at any rate never denied the soft impeachment, though it is possible that Arbuthnot, to whom it is ascribed in some of the early text-books, had a hand in it. *Acis*, which was probably produced in 1721, was the work of Handel's old friend Gay. The Burlington circle thus had its share in the new development of Handel's genius, and it is not too much to assume that the idea of English oratorio took shape in the discussions around the hospitable board of Handel's earliest English patron.

Handel's association with Canons did not cut him off altogether from London life. Two of his letters written in 1719 are dated from London: the one a courteous refusal to contribute an autobiography to Mattheson's *Ehren-Pforte*, and the other an affectionate letter of sympathy to his brother-in-law Michaelsen, who had lost his wife a short time before. It was, too, during his residence at Canons that he was appointed music master to the daughters of his old friend Caroline, the Princess of Wales. There exists in the Buckingham Palace Library a copy by Smith of a set of "Lessons composed for the Princess Louisa," and it is more than possible that the famous *Suites de Pièces pour le Clavecin*, which were published in November 1720, owe their origin to the necessities of Handel's royal pupils. Many fair fingers must have itched to play the pieces that the illustrious young ladies were daily strumming in their schoolroom in Leicester Fields, and the musical pirates of the day were equal to the occasion. In his preface to the first edition, Handel observed that he had been "obliged to publish some of the following lessons, because surreptitious and incorrect copies of them had got abroad," adding with his habitual courtliness that he reckoned it his duty with his small talent to serve a nation from which he had received so generous a protection.

One of the pieces is the famous air with variations now universally known as "The Harmonious Blacksmith," which has probably occasioned the writing of more nonsense than any other musical composition in the world. The origin of the foolish nickname is unknown, but it certainly dates from long after Handel's time. The earliest known edition on which it appears was published in 1820. The title is obviously a publisher's catch-penny invention, like that affixed with the same wantonness to Beethoven's so-called "Moonlight" sonata. There is not a shadow of foundation for the absurd stories that have been fabricated in order to account for the name, but they have been copied and repeated so often by men who ought to have known better, that it is probably useless at this time of day to attempt to explode them. Follies of this kind die hard, and the legend of Handel's friend, the blacksmith of Edgware, with his hammer, anvil, and other appurtenances, baseless fabric of a vision as it is, will probably live until the cloud-capped towers of Handel's fame themselves dissolve and leave not a rack behind.

Handel lived a busy life at this time. He had duties in London as well as at Canons, and he must have learnt to know every tree on the Edgware Road by heart. Travelling in those days, though more tedious than at present, had a spice of excitement which is denied to us. Here, for instance, is a specimen incident of the time, recorded by the *Weekly Journal* of the 11th of February 1720, of which it is quite possible that Handel himself was a witness: "On Monday as the Duke of Chandos was riding to his beautiful house at Edgware, and being before his retinue some distance, two highwaymen came up and bid him deliver his money, but his servants coming in view fired their pistols, as did the highwaymen, but neither hurt or killed. One of the highwaymen quitted his horse and jumped over the hedge, and was followed by one of the Duke's servants, who knocked him down and took him, and the other was pursued to Tyburn and there taken. Both were committed to Newgate."

Early in 1719 the town, which had contrived to get through two years without an opera, save for an attempt at a season of English opera conducted by Owen MacSwiney at the Little Theatre in Lincoln's Inn Fields, suddenly awoke to a sense of its deprivation. The South Sea Bubble was in the heyday of its success, and company promoting was in the air. Following the fashion of the day, a number of the nobility and gentry put their heads together and founded the Royal Academy of Music, which, in spite of its high-sounding name, was only a company for the production of Italian opera at the King's Theatre in the Haymarket. The capital subscribed was £50,000, in 500 shares of £100, and the King headed the list with £1000. The company was ruled by a governor, deputy governor, and twenty directors. The first year the Duke of Newcastle was governor, Lord Bingley deputy governor, and the directors, of whom Lord Burlington was naturally one, were chosen from the finest flower of rank and fashion.

The Academy started with the brightest promise. Everything was to be the best of its kind. Handel naturally headed the list of musical directors, and with him were associated Giovanni Maria Bononcini, a brother of the Marcantonio whose *Camilla* had proved so much to the taste of London audiences, and Attilio Ariosti. Paolo Rolli and Nicola Haym were appointed poets to the establishment, and Heidegger was the stage manager. It was a curious fate that thus put Handel into the company of the two men with whom, if an oft-repeated legend is true, he had been thrust into rivalry in Berlin some years before. The omen was not favourable, but no gloomy forebodings troubled the sanguine promoters of the new scheme. Handel was at once dispatched to the Continent to enlist a new company of singers. He left London at the end of February 1719, journeying first to Düsseldorf, where he engaged Benedetto Baldassarri, and then proceeding to Dresden, where the opera was at that time particularly good. There he secured the services of Senesino, the most famous *castrato* of the age, a worthless man but a marvellous artist; of Signora Durastanti, who had sung in *Agrippina* at Venice in 1709; of Boschi, the well-known bass, and of several others. Business over, he turned to pleasure, and paid a

THE LANDING OF SENESINO

visit to his mother at Halle. While he was there he might, had fate been propitious, have made the acquaintance of Johann Sebastian Bach, who at that time graced the court of Prince Leopold of Anhalt-Cöthen. Bach, hearing that his famous contemporary was actually staying within forty miles, journeyed to Halle in order to meet him. But he had given Handel no warning of his intended visit, and when he reached Halle, he found that Handel had set out for England the day before. Bach's disappointment was doubtless great, but ours may be tempered by the reflection that had the two men met, no record of their conversation would probably have been preserved, or that if it had it would doubtless have been as little worthy of so unique an occasion as was the famous interview between Jackson and Nansen on the ice-floes of Franz Josef Land. They might, however, have compared notes as to their respective impressions of the court of Dresden, where Handel had just been presented with the handsome sum of a hundred ducats for playing the harpsichord to the King and Crown Prince; whereas Bach, who a year before had vanquished the French performer Marchand in single combat, was swindled out of his fee by a knavish courtier. Handel might have amused Bach, too, by telling him how his independent manners had shocked the aristocratic flunkeys at Dresden. A certain Count von Flemming, in particular, seems to have had his feelings sadly outraged. Writing to Melusine von Schulenburg,[1] who was a pupil of Handel's, he observes

---

[1] Melusine von Schulenburg was a daughter of George I's notorious mistress, the Duchess of Kendal. In 1733 she married the famous Lord Chesterfield, whose biographer, Dr. Maty, Principal Librarian of the British Museum, observes that "her amiableness of character, the accomplishments of her mind, her taste for the fine arts, and in particular for music, rendered her a fit companion for Lord Chesterfield." (*Miscellaneous Works of Lord Chesterfield*, 1777, vol. i. p. 71.)

querulously: " I tried to get a word with Mr. Handel, and
to pay him some civility for your sake, but I could do
nothing. I used your name in inviting him to come to
see me, but he was always out or else ill. To tell the
truth, I think he is a little mad!"[1]

Handel returned in due course to London, where about
this time he established himself in the house in Brook
Street, which remained his home for the rest of his life.[2] On
the 2nd of April 1720 the Royal Academy of Music opened
its campaign with Giovanni Porta's *Numitore*, a useful
stop-gap, which served to keep the subscribers amused until
the great novelty of the season, Handel's *Radamisto*, was
ready. The latter aroused an unusual amount of interest.
While the rehearsals were in progress it was the favourite
topic of the coffee-houses, and it drew an epigram from
the great Sir Isaac Newton. Dr. Stukeley, the celebrated
antiquary, records in his diary a meeting with the famous
philosopher, then in extreme old age: "*April* 18.—At the
Lincolnshire Feast, Ship Tavern, Temple Bar,—present,
Sir Isaac Newton. Upon my mentioning to him the
rehearsal of the opera to-night (*Radamisto*), he said he
never was at more than one opera. The first act he heard
with pleasure, the second stretched his patience, at the
third he ran away."[3] *Radamisto*, after a postponement
" by Royal Command," was finally produced with great
pomp and circumstance on the 27th of April. All London
turned out to do honour to the popular composer, and to
criticise the new singers. As a matter of fact, neither

---

[1] Opel, *Mittheilungen zur Geschichte der Familie Händel.*

[2] Handel's name first appears in the rate books of St. George's, Hanover
Square, in 1725, but some years ago Dr. W. H. Cummings, while examining
the house, discovered a fine cast-lead cistern, on the front of which was the
inscription, " 1721 G.F.H."

[3] William Stukeley, *Family Memoirs* [Surtees Society], vol. i. p. 59.

Senesino nor Durastanti sang in the original production of *Radamisto*, though both appeared in a revival of it a few months later.   An entry in Lady Cowper's diary gives a curt memorandum of the event.   " At night *Radamistus*, a fine opera of Handel's making.   The King there with his ladies.   The Prince in the stage-box.   Great crowd." The crowd was great indeed, and Mainwaring's description of the scene sounds like a prophetic vision of the riotous frenzy that accompanied the Jenny Lind furore more than a century later: " There was no shadow of form or ceremony, scarce indeed any appearance of order or regularity, politeness or decency.   Many, who had forced their way into the house with an impetuosity but ill suited to their rank and sex, actually fainted through the excessive heat and closeness of it.   Several gentlemen were turned back, who had offered forty shillings for a seat in the gallery, after having despaired of getting any in the pit or boxes."   *Radamisto* carried the opera on to the end of the season, and in the following autumn Senesino appeared for the first time in Bononcini's *Astarto*. Bononcini's pretty tunes and Senesino's marvellous voice[1] between them captivated the ear of the public. *Astarto* ran for something like thirty nights, and Bononcini became in public opinion a dangerous rival to Handel.

So high did party feeling run between the supporters of the two composers, that the directors of the Royal Academy finally hit upon a curious method of

---

[1] It is difficult for us moderns to realise what the voice of a *castrato* was like.   The expression used by Burney, of a song being " thundered out " by the voice of Senesino, proves it must have been something very different from anything that is now to be heard.   It must have had all the force of a tenor or bass voice, with the compass of a soprano or contralto.

settling the point of precedence. They persuaded the rival musicians to collaborate, and arranged to produce a new opera of which the third act was to be written by Handel, and the second by Bononcini, the first falling to the lot of Filippo Mattei, usually called "Pipo."[1] *Muzio Scevola*, the hybrid opera in question, was produced on the 15th of April 1721. Naturally enough, it won little success, indeed at the first performance the audience took much less interest in the music than in the news of the birth of the Duke of Cumberland, which was announced during the evening.[2] Nor did *Muzio Scevola* settle for a moment the controversy as to the respective merits of the rival composers, which raged indeed more fiercely after the production than before it. Meanwhile, the affairs of the Academy were not prospering. The audiences were good, but the enormous expenses swallowed up every penny of profit, and frequent calls were made upon the subscribers in order to cover the season's expenses. During the season of 1721–22, however, the tide turned, and a dividend of 7 per cent. was declared. The chief cause of this happy state of affairs was Bononcini, whose *Crispo* and *Griselda* scored great successes during the spring of 1722. Handel was less successful with his *Floridante*, which appeared on the 9th of December 1721, with Senesino in the principal part.

[1] An ambiguous passage in Mainwaring's *Memoirs* has given rise to a tradition, which has been copied by later writers, that the first act of *Muzio Scevola* was written by Attilio Ariosti. Contemporary evidence, however, makes it certain that Mattei was the composer. In Opel's *Mittheilungen zur Geschichte der Familie Händel*, a letter is quoted from Fabrice to Count von Flemming in which the question is settled beyond a doubt. "Chaque acte de cet opéra," he says, "est d'un compositeur différent, le premier par un nommé Pipo, le second par Bononcini, et le troisième par Hendell, qui l'a emporté haut à la main."

[2] See the letter already quoted in Opel's *Mittheilungen*.

His women singers did not do him justice. Durastanti was not a success. The English public thought her hard and masculine, and Anastasia Robinson was not musician enough to sing his music as it should be sung. In Bononcini's simpler strains she did well enough. A trifling little ballad like " Per la gloria " was well within her powers, and it was as the patient heroine of *Griselda*, in which this song occurs, that she is supposed to have completed her conquest of Lord Peterborough's susceptible heart.

But a singer was already on her way to England who was destined to restore to Handel his rightful supremacy, and to put a speedy end to Bononcini's shortlived triumph — the famous Francesca Cuzzoni. Meanwhile the autumn season had begun, and the wheels of Cuzzoni's chariot were lingering. Handel grew impatient, and sent his trusty lieutenant Sandoni in search of her. Sandoni's quest was successful. He brought Cuzzoni to England in triumph—as his wife. Why Sandoni married the most famous singer of the day is easy to comprehend, but why Cuzzoni married a humble accompanist is a more difficult problem to solve. Whatever may have been her reasons, she soon repented of them. She led Sandoni a woeful life for a few years, and then poisoned him. But this is to anticipate too much. Cuzzoni made her English début in Handel's *Ottone*, which was produced on the 12th of January 1723. She became at once the spoiled darling of the fashionable world, and retained her pride of place until her great rival Faustina appeared upon the scene in 1726, when a struggle for supremacy began to which the Handel-Bononcini controversy was mere child's play. Cuzzoni was a singularly unattractive woman. " She was short and squat," says Horace Walpole, "with a cross face, but fine complexion ; was not a good actress ; dressed ill, and was silly and fantastical." Her disposition did not belie her face. She had the temper of a fiend, and was as obstinate as a mule. But in Handel she met her match. He opened their acquaintance by observing in his gruffest tones, "Oh, Madame, je sais bien que vous êtes une véritable diablesse, mais je vous ferai savoir, moi, que je suis Béelzebub, le chef des diables." Encouraged by this greeting, she flatly refused to sing the beautiful air, "Falsa immagine," which Handel had set down as her opening song, whereupon he seized her round the waist and threatened to throw her out of the window. Cuzzoni owned herself beaten, sang the song, and in a moment had London at her feet. Her voice must have been wonderful, and her singing miraculous even for the eighteenth century. Burney speaks of a "native warble" which concealed the consummate art of her technique. "Her shake," he says, "was perfect, her high notes unrivalled in clearness and sweetness, and her intonation so just that she seemed incapable of singing out of tune." She charmed alike rich and poor, high and low. Mrs. Delany laughed at her nonsensical tricks, but adored her singing. "This morning," she wrote, "I was entertained with Cuzzoni. Oh! how charming! How did I wish for all I love and like to be with me at that instant of time. My senses were ravished with harmony." More epigrammatic and no less enthusiastic was a groom in the gallery, who, while Cuzzoni was singing a song in *Ottone*, cried out, "Damn her, she has got a nest of nightingales in her belly."

Cuzzoni had to the full the modern prima donna's talent for self-advertisement. She took good care that the public should be kept *au fait* with all her movements. When she presented her husband with a son and heir, the details of her confinement were the talk of the coffee-houses. Every one knew that she went to bed singing "La speranza," and bothered her husband into buying her a gigantic looking-glass and a black silk hood. But in spite of her follies she could be charming when she chose. Lady Bristol met her at a party, and was loud in her praises: "Cuzzoni was in high good humour. She sent for Whyburn with his lute, and sung for two hours like a nightingale. She has learnt two English ballads, which she makes the agreeablest thing you ever heard."[1]

The combination of Handel's music and Cuzzoni's voice dealt a severe blow to the Bononcini faction. Now that Handel had at his command a singer capable of doing justice to his music, his superiority was indisputable. In October 1722, Lady Bristol wrote to her husband: "Bononcini is dismissed the theatre for operas, which I believe you and some of your family will regret. The reason they give for it is his most extravagant demands."[1] Six months later, Mrs. Delany observed: "The young Duchess of Marlborough has settled upon Bononcini for his life £500 a year, provided he will not compose any more for the ungrateful Academy, who do not deserve that he should entertain them, since they don't know how to value his works as they ought, and likewise told him he should always be welcome to her table." Bononcini took the money, but apparently the quarrel was patched up, for he went on writing operas for the Academy. At any rate his *Farnace* and *Calfurnia* were both produced after this date, but his star was on the decline and the vogue of his music was over so far as the general public was

[1] *Letter Book of John Hervey, Earl of Bristol*, vol. ii.

concerned, though the compact little phalanx of his admirers supported him through thick and thin, and we read of concerts given by his patroness, the Duchess of Marlborough, at which only his music was performed.

People still chattered about the respective merits of the triumvirate. Gay wrote to Swift early in 1723: "As for the reigning amusement of the town, it is entirely music, real fiddles, bass viols and hautboys, not poetical harps, lyres and reeds. There's nobody allowed to say I sing, but an eunuch or an Italian woman. Everybody is grown now as great a judge of music as they were in your time of poetry, and folks that could not distinguish one tune from another, now daily dispute about the different styles of Handel, Bononcini and Attilio."[1]

About this time Byrom produced his celebrated epigram, which, familiar as it is, is too witty to be omitted:—

> "Some say, compar'd to Bononcini,
> That Mynheer Handel's but a ninny;
> Others aver that to him Handel
> Is scarcely fit to hold a candle.
> Strange, all this difference should be
> 'Twixt Tweedledum and Tweedledee!"[2]

---

[1] Swift, *Correspondence.*

[2] John Byrom was a facile and fluent writer of verse, and attained some degree of fame by his invention of a new system of shorthand. He seems actually to have written his famous epigram on the 22nd of February 1725, according to his *Journal* (published by the Chetham Society), in which occurs the entry: "Wrote some verses to Leycester about the Opera," on that date. It does not appear, however, to have been widely circulated until a few months later. On May 9 the *Journal* observes: "Mr. Leycester left my epigram upon Handel and Bononcini in shorthand for Jemmy Ord"; and on the 18th: "Mr. Leycester came there [to George's Coffee-House], and Bob Ord, who was come home from Cambridge, where he said he had made the whole Hall laugh at Trinity College, and got himself honour by my epigram upon Handel and Bononcini." By June 5 it had found its way into the newspapers.

Meanwhile, Handel continued his triumphant career with *Flavio* (14th May 1723), but his singers still gave him a good deal of trouble. Cuzzoni was by no means the only offender. For a quite insignificant part in *Flavio* he engaged a young English singer named Gordon, who seems to have entertained an uncommonly good opinion of his own musicianship. At any rate, one day when Handel was rehearsing with him the one song allotted to him in the opera, " Fato tiranno," he had the impertinence to criticise the composer's method of accompanying. This was more than Handel could put up with, and in a vigorous mixture of half a dozen languages he told Gordon to mind his own business. A quarrel ensued, and Gordon finished by declaring that if Handel persisted in accompanying him in that manner he would jump upon his harpsichord and smash it to pieces. " Oh," replied Handel, " let me know when you will do that, and I will advertise it; for I am sure more people will come to see you jump, than to hear you sing." *Giulio Cesare* (20th February 1724) was one of Handel's most brilliant masterpieces, in which Senesino's declamation of the accompanied recitative " Alma del gran Pompeo " was the talk of the town. Senesino won less honourable notoriety shortly afterwards by a quarrel with Anastasia Robinson, which ended in his being publicly horse-whipped by Lord Peterborough; and London had another hearty laugh over his abject plight one evening at the theatre when, as he was thundering out the words " Cæsar has no fear," a piece of the scenery fell from the flies upon the stage, which so terrified the poor little hero that he fell upon the boards and burst into a piteous flood of tears. People ridiculed the follies and vanities of the singers, but the worship of everything connected with

opera still continued, in spite of the protests of old-
fashioned critics, who denounced the degradation of
English society in no measured terms.

But we must hasten over the next few years, which
saw the production of Handel's *Tamerlano* (31st October
1724), *Rodelinda* (13th February 1725), and *Scipio* (12th
March 1726). All three operas were successful, and
provided triumphs for Cuzzoni and Senesino. For
Tamerlano Handel's company was strengthened by the
arrival in England of Borosini, of whom *Mist's Weekly
Journal* humorously observed: " It is commonly reported
this gentleman was never cut out for a singer." He was,
in fact, a tenor, and during his stay in England Handel
wrote several important parts for him—contrary to the
taste of the time, which favoured only soprani and
contralti, with an occasional exception in favour of a bass.
In *Rodelinda*, Cuzzoni's triumph was not only vocal, for
the brown silk gown trimmed with silver in which she
played the part of the heroine became the rage, and set
the fashion for the season. *Rodelinda* was one of Handel's
most popular operas. Byrom refers to it in some stanzas
addressed to an opera-loving friend:—

> " Dear Peter, if thou canst descend
> From *Rodelind* to hear a friend,
> And if those ravished ears of thine
> Can quit the shrill celestial whine
> Of gentle eunuchs, and sustain
> Thy native English without pain,
> I would, if 'tain't too great a burden
> Thy ravished ears intrude a word in." [1]

But in spite of individual successes the affairs of the
Academy were not prospering, and the directors deter-

[1] Byrom, *Letter to R. L., Esq.*

mined upon a magnificently audacious *coup*. They engaged Faustina Bordoni, Cuzzoni's only serious rival, and commissioned Handel to write an opera in which the two prima donnas were to appear together upon precisely equal terms. The task was one of extreme difficulty, but Handel undertook it with alacrity. He was in excellent spirits just then. He had become a naturalised Englishman on the 13th of February 1726, and the King had immediately appointed him Composer to the Chapel Royal[1] and Composer to the Court, offices which could only be held by British subjects. Bononcini seemed at last to be utterly crushed; and Handel felt powerful enough to face unmoved even the wrath of two jealous prima donnas.

---

[1] This appointment seems to have been purely honorary, and had nothing to do with the post of organist, which was held by Dr. Greene.

CHAPTER VII

FAUSTINA AND CUZZONI, 1726–1728

I F music has power to charm the savage breast, it
can also at times excite well-behaved and well-
educated people to excesses of savagery that would
disgrace a troglodyte. In the history of music there
are many famous quarrels, but none ever surpassed in
violence and acrimony the historic feud between Faustina
and Cuzzoni and their respective partisans. Cuzzoni
had the advantage of being first in the field, but though
her magnificent singing had won her many supporters
during the three years for which she had adorned the
London stage, she had estranged many of them by her
vanity and ill temper, and the engagement of Faustina
was no doubt partly intended to bring Cuzzoni to a
proper sense of her position. In *Alessandro* (5th May
1726) the two great singers appeared side by side.
Handel and his librettist had worked so cleverly together
that neither artist had anything to complain of. They
sang song for song throughout the opera. Each of them
sang a duet with Senesino, and they had one duet
together which was so skilfully composed that neither
of them could say which was singing the principal
part.

The applause was equally divided, and the audience

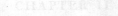

FRANCESCA CUZZONI SIGNORA
SANDONI FAUSTINA

CUZZONI AND FAUSTINA

left the theatre discussing the all‑important question
whether Cuzzoni or Faustina was the greater artist. In
a few days every tea-table in London was ringing with
the same question. The Handel-Bononcini controversy
was forgotten in the rivalry of the two prima donnas.
If any one had imagined that the arrival of Faustina
was going to resolve the discords of the musical world
he was sadly mistaken. She came bringing not peace
but a sword. London seemed to divide in a moment
into two parties. There was no middle course. Every
one had to be on one side or the other. Cuzzoni's chief
backer was Lady Pembroke, and the leader of the
Faustina faction was Dorothy, Lady Burlington, the
young wife of Handel's patron. Lady Walpole, who
must have been almost as good a diplomatist as her
husband, was one of the few who contrived to keep on
good terms with both sides. Faustina and Cuzzoni
actually met under her roof, but neither would consent
to sing in the presence of the other. At last, by a lucky
inspiration, Lady Walpole contrived to smuggle Faustina
into an adjoining room, under the pretext of showing her some china, and while her back was turned,
Cuzzoni, who fancied that her rival had fled, was
induced to sing. Later in the evening a similar piece of
diplomacy extracted a song from Faustina. Meanwhile
the newspapers had taken up the controversy, and
lampoons fanned the flame of faction. Doggerel verses
were passed from hand to hand, of which the following
is a specimen :—

> " At Leicester Fields I give my vote
>   For the fine-piped Cuzzoni ;
> At Burlington's I change my note,
>   Faustina for my money.

Attilio's music I despise,
   For none can please like Handel,
  But the disputes which hence arise,
    I wish and hope may end well." [1]

As a rule, the controversialists were not so amiable as
this anonymous poet. Many of them, in the good old-
fashioned seventeenth-century style, turned to the private
lives of the singers, and aspersions upon the morality of
the fair rivals were openly circulated, so gross in language
and suggestion that respectable newspapers refused to
publish them. It was not the fashion just then to be
mealy-mouthed, and the freedom of thought and expression displayed in "An Epistle from Signora F——a to
a Lady," to take but one instance, raises a mild curiosity
as to what the poems can have been like which the
virtuous *British Journal* considered too outspoken for its
chaste pages.

Handel's *Admeto*, which was produced on the 31st
of January 1727, raised the excitement to fever heat.
Both ladies had good parts in the new opera, and their
respective admirers seized the opportunity not only of
acclaiming their own favourite, but of trying to drown
the applause of the opposite faction. The production
of Bononcini's *Astyanax* on the 6th of May brought
matters to a head. Both parties turned up in force, and
Cuzzoni's first song was a signal for the tumult to
begin. The poor woman's voice was drowned by hisses,
groans and cat-calls. However, she had been warned
of what was going to happen, and stood her ground
manfully. When Faustina's turn came, the Cuzzonites
had their revenge. The theatre was turned into a bear-
garden, and the fine flower of English society behaved

[1] *Historical MSS. Commission*, Report xii. Appendix, pt. 9.

like a parcel of drunken pot-boys at Greenwich Fair. The presence of the Princess Amelia was no check on the disorder, and the evening ended in riot and confusion. Lady Pembroke, the leader of the Cuzzonites, seems to have realised that she and her party had let their feelings carry them rather too far. There is an interesting letter extant from her to Mrs. Clayton, afterwards Lady Sundon, who was Mistress of the Robes to the Princess of Wales, entreating that amiable person to explain the state of affairs to the Princess, who presumably was vexed at her daughter's having been treated with so little respect:—

"DEAR MADAM," the letter runs,—" I hope you will forgive the trouble I am going to give you, having always found you on every occasion most obliging. What I have to desire is, that if you find a convenient opportunity, I wish you would be so good as to tell Her Royal Highness that every one who wishes well to Cuzzoni is in the utmost concern for what happened last Tuesday at the Opera in the Princess Amelia's presence; but to show their innocence of the disrespect which was shown to Her Highness, I beg you will do them the justice to say that the Cuzzoni had been publicly told, to complete her disgrace, she was to be hissed off the stage on Tuesday. She was in such concern at this that she had a great mind not to sing, but I, without knowing anything that the Princess Amelia would honour the Opera with her presence, positively ordered her not to quit the stage, but let them do what they would—though not heard, to sing on, and not to go off till it was proper; and she owns now that if she had not had that order she would have quitted the stage when they cat-called her to such a degree in one song that she was not heard one note, which provoked the people that like her so much that they were not able to get the better of their resentment, but would not suffer the Faustina to speak afterwards. I hope Her Royal Highness would not disapprove of any one preventing the Cuzzoni's being hissed off the stage; but I am in great concern they did not suffer anything to have happened to her, rather than to have failed in the high respect every one ought to pay to a Princess of Her Royal Highness's family; but as they were not the aggressors, I hope that may in some measure excuse them."[1]

After this outburst the subscribers seemed to have been somewhat ashamed of themselves, but the close of the season on the 6th of June was marked by even more scandalous disturbances. This time the Princess of Wales herself was in the theatre, but nothing could check the insanity of the audience. The climax of the entertainment on this occasion was a personal encounter between Faustina and Cuzzoni, who, roused to fury by the excesses of their partisans, threw decency to the winds and attacked each other tooth and nail. Arbuthnot seized the opportunity of making bitter fun of the singers and their followers in *The Devil to pay at St. James's*.[2] After describing how " the two Singing Ladies pulled each other's Coifs " and scolded each other " like Billingsgates," he went on to make a severely practical suggestion. " In

---

[1] *Memoirs of Viscountess Sundon*, vol. i.

[2] Arbuthnot's latest biographer, Mr. G. A. Aitken, denies his authorship of this pamphlet, which, however, appears in the collected edition of his works.

the meantime, I humbly propose that since these Ladies are not to be reconciled by any other gentle Means, 'tis best that they should fight it out at Figg's or Stoke's Amphitheatre; that a subscription be opened for that purpose, and the best woman have the whole house." [1] The Homeric contest of the two singers naturally fired the doggerel poets to further efforts, but their epigrams

[1] Figg was a well-known prize-fighter, who taught boxing to the gilded youth of the day at an "academy" in the fields to the north of Oxford Street. He is immortalised by Hogarth in his *Rake's Progress*, and by Pope in one of his satires :—

> "See, where the British youth, engaged no more
> At Figg's or White's with felons or a w——e !"

Byrom, too, wrote an amusing set of verses on one of Figg's historic encounters, beginning—

> "Long was the great Figg by the prize-fighting swains
> Sole monarch acknowledged of Marybone Plains."

As to the notion of a feminine prize-fight, there was nothing in that to shock or even to surprise an eighteenth-century public. Contests of this sort were, if not an everyday occurrence, at any rate by no means uncommon. César de Saussure, who was in London in 1727, gives an elaborate and rather blood-curdling account of a prize-fight between two women, which evidently he thoroughly enjoyed, though he adds : "I consider that cock-fights are much more diverting." But at that time women took a far more prominent share in what are usually called "manly" exercises than is considered correct even in these days of golf and hockey. "I am told," writes Saussure, "that in Kew Green women and girls, scantily clothed, run races, the smock being the prize, hence the appellation 'smock runs.'" (Saussure, *England in the Reigns of George I and George II.*) Even in the depths of the country the same sports were practised. The vivacious Mrs. Bradshaw writes from Cheshire to her friend Mrs. Howard : "My lady Mohun and I have our rural pleasures too. The Colonel gave a smock for the young wenches to run for. The pleasure of the day ended with a prison base ; all the swains from the two neighbouring towns performed feats of activity, and ran against one another with little more than a fig leaf for their clothing, and we, being in a state of innocence, were not ashamed to show our faces." (*Suffolk Correspondence*, 1722.)

are scarcely worth the trouble of transcribing. This is perhaps the best of them :—

> " Old poets sing that beasts did dance
> Whenever Orpheus played ;
> So to Faustina's charming voice
> Wise Pembroke's asses brayed."

But for the moment the opera scandal was thrust into the background by events of wider importance. On 11th June, King George I died suddenly at Osnabrück, struck to the heart, it was whispered, by a warning of approaching doom sent to him by his injured and neglected wife, Sophia Dorothea, whom he had kept in close confinement for years in the fortress of Ahlden, to expiate her supposed adultery with Count Königsmark. Other authorities attribute his death to a surfeit of watermelons. The news reached England on the 14th, and on the following day George II was proclaimed King. The new King continued the pension already allotted to Handel by Anne and George I, and added a further pension of £200 in consideration of the composer's services as music master to the Princesses Amelia and Caroline. It is doubtful whether any salary was attached to the offices of Composer to the Court and to the Chapel Royal, which George I had conferred upon him when he became naturalised ; and the latter at any rate he seems to have shared with Maurice Greene, who used to blow the organ at St. Paul's for him in the old Burlington House days, but had now gone over to the Bononcini faction. It was probably in virtue of the former appointment that Handel wrote the minuets which were performed at the court ball on the 30th of October 1727, and composed the magnificent series of anthems for the

King's coronation on the 11th of October which, as
Rockstro justly says, have made that event a landmark in
the history of music. Handel had a tussle with the Archbishops of Canterbury and York over the selection of
words for these anthems. The worthy prelates had their
own ideas upon the subject, and wanted to dictate to
Handel what words he should set. But it needed more
than a couple of archbishops to browbeat Handel into
submission. "I have read my Bible very well," he cried,
"and shall choose for myself." And so he did, and with
excellent results, for his anthems strike just the right
note of regal splendour and magnificence, and seem to
sparkle with the glitter of the gleaming pageant. Saussure,
who gives one of the best extant descriptions of the
coronation, was evidently much impressed by them,
though anything but an expert. "During the whole
ceremony," he writes, "a band of the most skilful musicians,
together with the finest voices in England, sung admirable
symphonies, conducted by the celebrated Mr. Handel, who
had composed the Litany."

The King's Theatre opened again on 11th November
with a new opera by Handel, *Riccardo Primo, Re
d'Inghilterra,* but the days of the Royal Academy were
numbered. The scandals of the previous season had
alienated the sympathies of all respectable people. Old
subscribers fell off, and no new ones were forthcoming.
It was hoped that *Riccardo* would draw the town by
reason of its popular and patriotic subject, but the houses
were poor. Mrs. Delany thought it "delightful," but she
was compelled to add: "I doubt operas will not survive
longer than this winter. They are now at their last
gasp; the subscription is expired, and nobody will renew
it. The directors are always squabbling, and they have

so many divisions among themselves that I wonder they have not broke up before." [1]

More disastrous to the Academy even than its own internal dissensions was the rivalry of *The Beggar's Opera*, which had been produced early in 1727 at the Little Theatre in Lincoln's Inn Fields, and at once took London by storm. Every one was laughing at Gay's jests, coarse as they often were, and humming the charming old folk-songs so cleverly arranged by Dr. Pepusch. In vain Arbuthnot thundered against the degradation of popular taste, in vain Carey scarified the "Newgate Pastoral," as Swift called it, with ridicule. The beauty of the music and the freshness of the libretto won all hearts. Even Mrs. Delany, who deplored the empty houses in the Haymarket, and declared that "The English have no real taste for music, or they could not neglect an entertainment so perfect in its kind for a parcel of ballad singers," had to admit that *The Beggar's Opera* was very "comical and full of humour."

Gay wrote to Swift with ill-disguised triumph: "The outlandish (as they call it) opera hath been so thin of late that some have called that *The Beggar's Opera*; and if the run continues, I fear, I shall have a remonstrance drawn up against me by the Royal Academy of Music." A month later he added: "*The Beggar's Opera* hath been acted now thirty-six times, and was as full the last night as the first; and as yet there is not the least probability of a thin audience, though there is a discourse about the town that the doctors of the Royal Academy of Music design to solicit against it being played on the outlandish opera days."

The falling fortunes of the Academy roused its enemies

[1] Delany, *Correspondence*, vol. i.

to fresh efforts. Hostile pamphleteers launched anonymous pasquinades against Handel and his music. The
hand of Bononcini is plainly to be traced in *Advice to
the Composers and Performers of Vocal Musick*, which
was published in Italian and English in 1727, with its
spiteful references to composers who "overcharge and
encumber the composition with too many symphonies."

Handel alone was not to be cowed by the imminence
of disaster. He stood to his guns manfully, and produced
opera after opera in rapid succession. *Riccardo* was
followed by *Siroe* (5th February 1728), and *Siroe* by
Tolomeo (19th April 1728), but all in vain. *Tolomeo* was
only performed seven times, and on the 1st of June the
season came to an abrupt termination. The original
£50,000 was all spent, and there was no prospect of
raising any more, so there was nothing to be done but
to disband the company and close the doors of the
theatre.

CHAPTER VIII

HANDEL AS MANAGER, 1728-1732

THE collapse of the Royal Academy of Music was very far from destroying Handel's belief in the future of Italian opera in England. Probably he felt that the affairs of the Academy had been mismanaged, as indeed was almost inevitable when the broth was committed to the care of such an army of cooks, and he fancied that in proper hands opera might yet be a paying concern. At any rate he was ready to back his belief to the extent of his own savings, which were said to amount to ten thousand pounds. He joined forces with his old friend Heidegger, and took the King's Theatre. A partnership of five years was agreed upon, and the first season was to include fifty performances at a subscription of fifteen guineas a ticket. The enterprise was under the special patronage of Handel's old pupil, the Princess Royal.[1] Heidegger seems to have started operations by hastening abroad in search of new singers, but his efforts were unsuccessful, and he soon resigned the task of choosing a company to his partner. Handel probably left England in the autumn of 1728, and went straight to Italy, postponing his visit to his aged mother at Halle until his return journey. He went the round of Italy,

[1] *Shaftesbury Biographical Sketch.*
108

visiting in turn Rome, Milan, Venice, and other important musical centres, and hearing all the newest works of the newest composers. Handel's previous biographers are practically unanimous in stating that he made this journey in the company of his old friend Steffani, regardless of the fact that the latter had breathed his last at Frankfort on the 12th of February 1728.[1] At Rome Handel renewed his friendship with the hospitable Cardinal Ottoboni, and doubtless once more took part in his famous Wednesday performances of chamber music.

He also encountered another old friend, Cardinal Colonna, at whose house many years before, as the reader will remember, he played duets with a juvenile prodigy. Colonna seems to have endeavoured to bring about a meeting between Handel and the Chevalier de St. George, who was at that time resident in Rome, and was devoted to music, but Handel was wise enough not to prejudice his credit at the Hanoverian court by dallying with the Pretender. Handel's movements were followed with considerable interest by his English friends, and the musical world of London seems to have regarded his Italian tour as almost of national importance. Sir Lionel Pilkington wrote to a friend in April 1729: "Handel is doing his endeavour in Italy to procure singers, and I fancy his journey will be of more effect than Heidegger's; but I'm told Senesino is playing an ungrateful part to his friends in England, by abusing 'em behind their backs, and saying he'll come no more among 'em."[2] Abroad, too, all kinds of absurd rumours were circulated as to the methods employed by English managers to secure

[1] Woker, "Agostino Steffani." (*Vereinsschrift der Görres-Gesellschaft*, 1886.)

[2] *Hist. MSS. Commission*, 35.

Italian singers. Mattheson, who was always glad to do
Handel a bad turn, though in this case he did not
mention him by name, gave a currency to a ridiculous
story about a nun with a wonderful voice having been
abducted from a Milanese convent by emissaries of a
London impresario.[1]   Senesino doubtless did all that he
could to enhance his own value, but Handel was tired of
his conceit and impertinence, and made up his mind to
try to get on without him.   In his stead he engaged
another artificial soprano, Bernacchi ; and his new prima
donna was Signora Strada del Pò, whom Burney
describes as " a coarse singer with a fine voice," though it
is evident, from the music that Handel wrote for her, that
she was already mistress of a brilliant technique.   Strange
as it seems to us, who live in an age of tenor-worship,
nobody in the eighteenth century cared a jot about tenors
compared with the all-conquering *castrati*.   However,
Handel, who was nothing if not enterprising, determined
to strike out upon a new line, and engaged the best tenor
of the age, Annibale Fabri, together with his wife, who
excelled in male parts.   In March 1729 Handel was in
Venice, whence he wrote to his brother-in-law, Dr.
Michaelsen, promising to visit Halle on his way home.   A
little later, he received distressing news of his mother's
health.   He hastened to Halle to find her stricken with
paralysis and totally blind, but still able to move about
the house.   He stayed with her as long as he could, even
declining an invitation to meet Bach at Leipzig, so that
she might not lose a day of his society, and finally bidding
her farewell in the middle of June 1729.   She lingered
until the close of the following year, dying in her
eightieth year in all peace and honour, but he never saw

[1] Mattheson, *Musikalischer Patriot*.

her again.   On his way home Handel passed through
Hanover, and renewed memories of his youth by paying
a visit to Hamburg, where he engaged the bass singer
Riemschneider.   Handel reached London on the 1st
July and his new singers arrived in September, but the
season did not actually begin until the 2nd of December,
when Handel's *Lotario* was produced.   London had been
deprived of opera for eighteen months, and excitement
ran high with regard to the new "Academy," as it was
called.   Everybody was talking about the new artists,
and the privileged few who were admitted to the rehearsals had a great deal to say about their merits and
defects.   Mrs. Delany, who was one of these, wrote an
elaborate account of them to a musical friend :
"Bernacchi has a vast compass, his voice mellow and
clear, but not so sweet as Senesino, his manner better,
his person not so good, for he is as big as a Spanish
friar.   Fabri has a tenor voice, sweet, clear, and firm, but
not strong enough, I doubt, for the stage.   He sings
like a gentleman, without making faces, and his manner
is particularly agreeable.   He is the greatest master of
music that ever sang upon the stage.   The third is the
bass, a very good distinct voice, without any harshness.
La Strada is the first woman ;   her voice is without
exception fine, her manner perfection, but her person
very bad, and she makes frightful mouths.[1]   La Merighi
is the next to her ; her voice is not extraordinarily good
or bad.   She is tall, and has a very graceful person with
a tolerable face.   She seems to be a woman about forty ;
she sings easily and agreeably.   The last is Bertolli ; she
has neither voice, ear, or manner to recommend her ; but

---

[1] Burney says of her : "She had so little of a Venus in her appearance,
that she was usually called "The Pig."

she is a perfect beauty, quite a Cleopatra, that sort of complexion with regular features, fine teeth, and when she sings has a smile about her mouth, which is extremely pretty, and I believe has practised to sing before a glass, for she has never any distortion in her face." *Lotario* was not a success. Even so staunch a Handelian as Mrs. Delany did not altogether approve of it. "I never was so little pleased with one of Mr. Handel's operas in my life," she wrote. But she would not allow other people to criticise it. "The opera is too good for the vile taste of the town," she continued. "It is disliked because it is too much studied, and they love nothing but minuets and ballads; in short, the *Beggar's Opera* and *Hurlothrumbo* are only worthy of applause."

The Beggar's Opera was by this time a very old story, and none of its numerous sequels and imitations had won a tithe of its success. Gay, or rather his patroness, the Duchess of Queensberry, had got into trouble over *Polly*, a continuation of *The Beggar's Opera*, the production of which had been forbidden by the Lord Chamberlain. Like our muzzled dramatists of to-day, Gay thought to shame the censor by publishing his play, and the Duchess was so strenuous a canvasser, urging everybody she met to subscribe for a copy, even under the very nose of the King, that at last he forbade her to appear at Court. *Hurlothrumbo* was a spectacular piece by a dramatist named Samuel Johnson, which was produced in April 1729, and for many months drew all London to Lincoln's Inn Fields. Byrom, the author of the famous Handel-Bononcini epigram, gives an amusing account of the first night in a letter to his wife: "As for Mr. Johnson, he is at present one of the chief topics of talk in London. Dick's Coffee-House resounds *Hurlothrumbo* from one

end to the other. He had a full house and much good
company on Saturday night, the first time of acting; and
report says all the boxes are taken for next Monday, and
the quality, they say, expect an epilogue next time (there
being none last) from Mr. B——. It is impossible to
describe this play and the oddities, out-of-the-waynesses,
flights, madness, nonsense, comicalities, etc., but I hope
Johnson will make his fortune by it for the present. We
had seven or eight Garters, they say, in the pit; I saw
Lord Oxford and one or two more there, but was so
intent upon the farce that I did not observe many quality
that were there. We agreed to laugh and clap beforehand,
and kept our word from beginning to end. The night
after, Johnson came to Dick's, and they all got about him
like so many bees. They say the Prince has been told
of *Hurlothrumbo*, and will come and see it. . . . I shall
get Johnson to vary some passages in it, if I can, that
from anybody but himself would make it an entertainment
not quite so proper for the ladies, and I would have our
ladies here see it because they know the man. For my
part, who think all stage entertainments stuff and
nonsense, I consider this as a joke upon 'em all."
However, as Johnson was a friend and a fellow-
Lancastrian, Byrom consented to fulfil expectation, and
wrote an epilogue for the piece, in which occur the
lines:—

> "Handel himself shall yield to *Hurlothrumbo*,
> And Bononcini too shall cry : Succumbo."

Partenope, produced on the 24th of February 1730, was
more successful than *Lotario*, but on the whole the season,
which closed in June, was anything but brilliant, and
Handel had to take serious thought for the future.

8

The first thing to do was to reorganise his company. Bernacchi, whose singing, according to Mrs. Delany, did not suit English ears, was dismissed, and, in deference to popular taste, Senesino was engaged in his place.[1] Various other engagements were made, and the season opened on the 3rd of November with a revival of *Scipio*, in which Senesino took his old part of the hero. A novelty was forthcoming on the 2nd of February 1731, in the shape of *Poro*, with Senesino as the Indian king, Fabri as Alexander the Great, and Strada as Cleofide. Fortune now smiled upon Handel and his theatre, and the following season— during which *Ezio* (15th January 1732) and *Sosarme* (19th February 1732) were produced—was no less successful. But meanwhile Handel was winning triumphs in a very different field. It has often excited the surprise of historians that, after inaugurating what was practically a new form of art in *Esther* and *Acis and Galatea*, Handel returned complacently to opera, and apparently forgot all about his experiments in oratorio. The fact is, that Handel himself had no suspicion of the importance of these two works in the history of his artistic development. *Esther* and *Acis* were doubtless written for some special occasion, and Handel being an eminently practical man

---

[1] The English infatuation for Senesino seems to have surprised foreigners. Writing from Milan in 1734 Lord Harcourt says : "The English have quite lost their reputation of being judges in musick ever since the bad reception Bernacchi met with in England ; and although his voice may be perhaps a little worn out, nevertheless, to show how much he is esteemed in this country for his good taste, skill, and judgment in musick, he is called the Father of musick—which title he certainly well deserves, since 'tis he that has given the fine taste of musick (as the Italians express themselves) to the famous Farinelli, Carestini, etc. And on the other hand, to show the difference of the Italian and English taste, Senesino, who is so much admired in England, would not be able to get his bread in this country." *Harcourt Papers*, vol. iii. p. 27.

designed them in view of the forces that he had at his
disposal. The choir at Canons was first-rate, and for that
reason he assigned unusual importance to the choral parts
of both works. But nothing would have surprised him
more than to hear *Esther* or *Acis* described as an oratorio.
Both works were unquestionably intended for dramatic
performance. It was an accident that gave them the
special character which fitted them equally well for
stage or concert performance. Handel doubtless looked
upon them merely as *pièces d'occasion*, as a kind of holiday
task in the midst of the real business of his life, and he
must have been pleasantly surprised when Bernard Gates,
the master of the children of the Chapel Royal, asked
for leave to give a private performance of *Esther* at his
own house. Handel, no doubt, was flattered, and in due
course the performance took place. The fact that it was
given on Handel's birthday, 23rd February 1732, indicates
the friendly and intimate character of the entertainment.
The choir boys sang their parts capitally, the company
present was charmed, and it was speedily arranged that
the performance should be repeated at the Crown and
Anchor Tavern in the Strand under the ægis of the
Academy of Ancient Music, an institution in which
Handel took a special interest. *Esther* was given twice
at the Crown and Anchor before crowded audiences, and
its fame spread far and wide. Princess Anne heard of it
and, with her usual enthusiasm for the music of her
beloved master, expressed a very earnest desire to see it.
She suggested a performance at the opera-house, but the
Bishop of London, Dr. Gibson, stepped in and put his
veto upon the scheme of acting a Biblical drama in a theatre.
He had no objection, however, to a performance without
dramatic action, a decision which was pregnant with fate

for Handel's future. Meanwhile, the chatter about *Esther* had brought another Richmond into the field, and an announcement duly appeared to the effect that a performance of *Esther*, "as it was composed for the Most Noble James, Duke of Chandos," would be given at the Great Room in Villiers Street, York Buildings, on the 20th of April 1732. Nebulous as the copyright laws are nowadays, they seem to have been even more indefinite in the eighteenth century, or Handel of all men in the world never have sat down under such an aggressive piece of piracy as this. However, he soon replied with a counter-announcement that "by his Majesty's Command," *Esther* would be given at the King's Theatre in the Haymarket on the 2nd of May "by a great number of Voices and Instruments." Very significant as a document in the history of oratorio is the note at the end of the advertisement : "*N.B.*—There will be no acting on the Stage, but the house will be fitted up in a decent manner for the audience. The Musick (*i.e.* the performers) to be disposed after the manner of the Coronation Service." *Esther* was much revised and enlarged for this performance, and the fact that the text-book bore the legend, "The additional words by Mr. Humphreys," is a sufficient proof that that egregious poetaster was not the author of the original poem. *Esther*, we are told by Colman, was a great success. The entire royal family was present at the first performance, and the crowd was so great that many persons, who had bought tickets, were unable to get into the theatre, and their money was returned to them. The oratorio was given six times in all, and always before packed houses. Handel always suffered much at the hands of pirates, and at this period they seem to have been exceptionally active. Hardly was the success of

Esther established in the teeth of unprincipled competition, when the same scurvy trick was played in connection with *Acis and Galatea*. This time the offender was Thomas Arne, the father of the well-known composer, who was running a season of English opera at the Little Theatre in the Haymarket. Handel had already permitted, or at any rate not objected to, a single performance of *Acis*, given for the benefit of a singer named Rochetti at Rich's theatre in Lincoln's Inn Fields, but it was too much to see his property filched from under his very nose and then exhibited at his own door. Arne's impudent piracy compelled him to assert his rights, and he announced a performance of *Acis* on the 10th of June 1732, which was designed to compensate his opera subscribers for the fact that only forty-nine performances, instead of the promised fifty, had been given during the preceding season.[1] In view of this revival he remodelled his score in a drastic manner, borrowing several numbers from his Neapolitan serenata, *Aci, Galatea e Polifemo*, and adding some new songs. As regards the performance, he followed the precedent already laid down in *Esther*. "There will be no action on the Stage," said the advertisement, "but the Scene will represent in a picturesque manner a rural prospect with rocks, groves, fountains and grottoes, among which will be disposed a Chorus of Nymphs and Shepherds, the habits and every other decoration suited to the subject." Strada and Senesino sang the principal parts, and the work was received with so much favour that it was performed four times. During the next few years it was often repeated, in many cases with alterations both in words and music, until about the year 1740 it assumed the final shape with English words in which it has won world-wide renown.

[1] *Shaftesbury Biographical Sketch.*

CHAPTER IX

STRUGGLES AND DEFEATS, 1732–1737

WHEN the autumn season of 1732 began, Handel's position seemed unassailable. He ruled the musical destinies of London with a rod of iron. He had proved himself incomparable in opera and oratorio alike. His enemies lay crushed beneath his feet. So little did he fear the competition of his erstwhile rival Bononcini, that he had contemptuously allowed him the use of the Opera-house for the performance of a serenata on the 24th of June. But destiny had her revenge in store. Handel was an autocrat, and though his sway was grateful to those who could appreciate good music, his masterful bearing made him enemies among small and great. In the old days of the Royal Academy of Music he occupied a more or less subordinate position. He had a board of directors over him, to whom he was bound to submit. But during his own management he reigned supreme. He brooked no rival near his throne. The subscribers had to be content with what he gave them. He permitted no remonstrance or complaint. He chose the singers and the operas, and those who cavilled at the entertainment he provided might go elsewhere. The result was not, on the whole, surprising. Handel had many staunch supporters, but among his subscribers a spirit of revolt was astir. The aristocracy of England was not accustomed to be treated in this manner. Who was this upstart German who dared to dictate to them? They paid the piper, and they had the right to call for the tune. Handel no doubt was not conciliatory, indeed, his enemies called him overbearing. Neither side would yield an inch, and it was generally felt that a crisis was at hand. Meanwhile, the opera season opened as usual in November, with Senesino and Strada still at the head of affairs, and on the 23rd of January 1733 a new opera, *Orlando*—one of Handel's finest works — was produced. *Orlando* was too good for the subscribers, but it triumphed in the teeth of opposition, and was given sixteen times during the season. But Handel had another string to his bow. He had learned that oratorio was at least as marketable an asset as opera, and for the future he proposed to run the two in double harness. The beginning of Lent was therefore the signal for the production of a new oratorio, *Deborah*, which was given for the first time on the 17th of March for Handel's benefit, outside the ordinary series of opera subscription performances. On this occasion several new features were introduced. The house was "fitted up and illuminated in a new and particular manner," which was well enough, but what was less well was that the prices of admission were doubled, the tickets for the pit and boxes being a guinea, and for the gallery half a guinea. Handel seems to have made up his mind that oratorio, which just then was the more popular form of entertainment, should pay for the deficiencies of opera. The excuse given for the raised prices was the "extraordinary expense" of the production,[1] but there is no doubt that this new piece of imposi-

---

[1] *Shaftesbury Biographical Sketch.*

tion, as it was generally considered, was a severe trial even to Handel's admirers, and his enemies of course made capital out of it. The fact that the performance was given upon one of the "opera days" further incensed the subscribers, and the high prices militated against the success of *Deborah*, in spite of the patronage of the King, who came with all the royal family to the performance on the 31st of March. The situation became more strained than ever. The air was full of rumours, and the newspapers of satirical squibs. The well-known and often reprinted letter which appeared in *The Craftsman* of the 7th of April 1733, though of course primarily a lampoon directed against Walpole and his unpopular Excise Bill, represents pretty accurately the attitude of Handel's enemies. In several points the Walpole cap does not fit Handel at all, as in the attack on Walpole's brother, Sir Horatio, but the squib would have lost its point if it had not had at least a general application to the Handel squabbles, so that it is still worth reprinting as a specimen of the kind of abuse to which Handel had to submit.

SIR,—I am always rejoiced, when I see a spirit of Liberty exert itself among any sect or denomination of my countrymen. I please myself with the hopes that it will grow more diffusive, some time or other become fashionable, and at last useful to the publick. As I know your zeal for Liberty, I thought I could not address better than to you the following exact account of the noble stand lately made by the polite part of the world in· defence of their Liberties and Properties against the open attacks and bold attempts of Mr. H——l upon both. I shall singly relate the fact and leave you, who are better able than I am, to make what inferences or applications may be proper.

" The rapid rise and progress of Mr. H——l's power and
fortune are too well known for me now to relate. Let it
suffice to say that he was grown so insolent upon the
sudden and undeserved increase of both, that he thought
nothing ought to oppose his imperious and extravagant
will. He had for some time govern'd the Operas and
modell'd the Orchestre without the least control. No
Voices, no Instruments, were admitted, but such as
flatter'd his ears, though they shock'd those of the
audience. Wretched Scrapers were put above the best
Hands in the Orchestre. No Musick but his own was to
be allowed, though everybody was weary of it, and he
had the impudence to assert that there was no Composer
in England but himself.

" Even Kings and Queens were to be content with whatever low characters he was pleased to assign them, as it
was evident in the case of Seignior Montagnana, who,
though a King, is always obliged to act (except an angry,
rumbling song or two) the most insignificant part of the
whole Drama. This excess and abuse of power soon
disgusted the town; his Government grew odious, and
his Opera grew empty. However, this degree of unpopularity and general hatred, instead of troubling him, only
made him more furious and desperate. He resolved to
make one last effort to establish his power and fortune by
force, since he found it now impossible to hope for it from
the goodwill of mankind. In order to this, he formed a
Plan, without consulting any of his Friends (if he has any),
and declared that at a proper season he would com-
municate it to the publick, assuring us at the same time
that it would be very much for the advantage of the
publick in general and of his Operas in particular. Some
people suspect that he had settled it previously with

Signora Strada del Pò, who is much in his favour; but all that I can advance with certainty is that he had concerted it with a brother of his own, in whom he places a most undeserved confidence. In this brother of his, heat and dulness are miraculously united. The former prompts him to do anything new and violent, while the latter hinders him from seeing any of the inconvenience of it. As Mr. H——l's brother, he thought it was necessary he should be a Musician too, but all he could arrive at after a very laborious application for many years was a moderate performance upon the Jew's Trump. He had for some time play'd a *Parte Buffa* abroad, and had entangled his brother in several troublesome and dangerous engagements in the commissions he had given him to contract with foreign performers, and from which (by the way) Mr. H——l did not disengage himself with much honour. Notwithstanding all these and many more objections, Mr. H——l, by and with the advice of his brother, at last produces his project, resolves to cram it down the throats of the Town, prostitutes great and awful names as the patrons of it, and even does not scruple to insinuate that they are to be the sharers of the profit. His scheme set forth in substance that the late decay of Operas was owing to their cheapness and to the great frauds committed by the Doorkeepers; that the annual Subscribers were a parcel of Rogues, and made an ill use of their tickets, by often running two into the Gallery; that to obviate these abuses he had contrived a thing that was better than an Opera call'd an Oratorio, to which none should be admitted but by Permits or Tickets of one Guinea each, which should be distributed out of Warehouses of his own and by Offices of his own naming, which officers would not so reasonably be supposed to cheat in the collection of guineas as the Doorkeepers in the collection of half-guineas; and lastly, that as the very being of Operas depended upon him singly, it was just that the profit arising from hence should be for his own benefit. He added indeed one condition, to varnish the whole a little, which was that if any person should think himself aggrieved, and that the Oratorio was not worth the price of the Permit, he should be at liberty to appeal to three Judges of Musick, who should be obliged within the space of seven years at farthest finally to determine the same, provided always that the said Judges should be of his nomination, and known to like no other Musick but his.

"The absurdity, extravagancy, and opposition of this scheme disgusted the whole town. Many of the most constant attenders of the Operas resolved absolutely to renounce them, rather than go to them under such exhortation and vexation. They exclaim'd against the insolent and rapacious Projector of this Plan. The King's old and sworn servants of the two Theatres of Drury Lane and Covent Garden reap'd the benefit of this general discontent, and were resorted to in crowds, by way of opposition to the Oratorio. Even the fairest breasts were fired with indignation against this new imposition. Assemblies, Cards, Tea, Coffee, and all other female batteries were vigorously employ'd to defeat the Project and destroy the Projector. These joint endeavours of all ranks and sexes succeeded so well that the Projector had the mortification to see but a very thin audience in his Oratorio ; and of about two hundred and sixty odd, that it consisted of, it was notorious that not ten paid for their Permits, but on the contrary had them given them, and money into the bargain for coming to keep him in countenance.

"This accident, they say, has thrown him into a deep Melancholy, interrupted sometimes by raving fits, in which he fancies he sees ten thousand Opera Devils coming to tear him in pieces; then he breaks out into frantick, incoherent speeches, muttering *Sturdy beggars, assassination*, etc. In these delirious moments, he discovers a particular aversion to the City. He calls them all a parcel of Rogues, and asserts that the honestest Trader among them deserves to be hang'd. It is much question'd whether he will recover; at least, if he does, it is not doubted but he will seek for a retreat in his own Country from the general resentment of the Town.—I am, Sir, your very humble Servant,

"P——LO R——LI

"P.S.—Having seen a little Epigram, lately handed about Town, which seems to allude to the same subject, I believe it will not be unwelcome to your readers:—

'Quoth W——e to H——l, shall we two agree
And excise the whole Nation?
                    H.—Si, caro, si.

Of what use are Sheep, if the Shepherd can't shear them?
At the Haymarket I, you at Westminster.
                    W.—Hear him!

Call'd to order, their Seconds appear in their place
One fam'd for his Morals,[1] and one for his Face.[2]
In half they succeeded, in half they were crost:
The Excise was obtain'd, but poor *Deborah* lost.'"

Plainly there was a strong personal feeling against Handel and his methods, but, after all, hard words break no bones, and the controversy might have ended in smoke, had not a redoubtable antagonist entered the field

[1] Lord Hervey.   [2] Heidegger.

against the composer, no less a personage than the heir
to the throne, Frederick, Prince of Wales.

Frederick was at that time the most popular man in
England. He had landed in England four years before
at a propitious moment. The hopes founded upon the
new reign had already declined. England was cured of
any illusions she may have entertained with regard to
George II. Vain and spiteful, mean and avaricious, the
new King soon estranged the sympathies of court and
society. Frederick, on the other hand, had many points
in his favour. His manners were charming, and he spoke
English more than tolerably. He had inherited much of
his mother's intelligence, he had a taste for art and literature, and had himself been known to trifle not unsuccessfully with the muse. He was generous and extravagant,
although in a continual state of impecuniosity. He liked
walking about the streets unguarded, and had a bow and
a smile for every one he met. To the common people his
taste for sport particularly endeared him. He loved horse
racing and was an enthusiastic cricketer, indeed it is said
that the abscess which ultimately caused his death was
occasioned by a blow from a cricket-ball.[1] But his surest
passport to the nation's favour was his known hostility to
the King and Walpole. His father unquestionably treated
him badly. He kept him short of money, and would not
allow him a separate establishment. In revenge Frederick
threw himself into the arms of the Opposition, and played
no insignificant part in the defeat of Walpole over the
Excise Bill. Within the walls of St. James's Palace the
flame of family feud burnt still hotter. Frederick was
always at daggers-drawn with his two elder sisters, Anne
and Amelia. Anne was the musician of the family, and

[1] A. E. Knight, *The Complete Cricketer*.

when Handel, whose pupil she had been, took the King's Theatre she persuaded the King and Queen to subscribe for a box, and to patronise the performances very often. This gave the Prince a good opportunity of annoying his sister, and of affronting the King and Queen. He was something of a musician himself, and took violin lessons from Dubourg. Probably he knew as well as any one that Handel was a far better composer than any of his rivals, but to suit his own purposes he pretended to despise Handel's music, and he carried his perversity so far as to combine with several of the influential subscribers in founding a rival enterprise at Lincoln's Inn Fields with Porpora as leading composer.[1] The scheme seems to have been hatched some time in the spring of 1733, and on the 15th of June a meeting was summoned at Hickford's Great Room in Panton Street to discuss the plan of the campaign. Handel's enemies were accomplished strategists. They contrived to seduce the greater part of his company from their allegiance. Senesino, whose conceit and rapacity had always made him a difficult subject to manage, revolted first, and his defection was followed by that of Montagnana and the others. Heidegger seems also to have severed his connection with Handel about this time. Only Strada remained faithful to her old impresario. For the moment, however, Handel had to turn his attention from the squabbles of pampered opera singers and the intrigues of offended aristocrats, and hastened to Oxford to conduct a series of performances of his oratorios. Ever since the Revolution Oxford had been a hotbed of Jacobitism, and the new Vice-Chancellor, Dr. Holmes, a staunch Hanoverian, had made up his mind to do something to bring about a better understanding between the Court

[1] Hervey, *Memoirs*, i. 320.

and the University.   He determined to make a beginning
by inviting Handel, who was known to be a *persona grata*
to the King and Queen, to give the Oxford Jacobites a taste
of his music during the annual festivities of Commemoration, or, as it was then called, the Public Act, and to receive
the degree of Doctor of Music.   The second part of the
scheme went agley, for when Handel found that the degree
would cost him £100, he lost his temper and declared he
was not going to throw his money away to oblige a parcel
of blockheads;[1] but the oratorios came off in due course,
and the occasion was rendered historical by the production
of *Athaliah* on July 10.   Handel had a popular success at
Oxford, but the Jacobite dons looked askance at the
Whig composer.   A passage in the diary of Thomas
Hearne, the antiquary, who was a Fellow of Edmund
Hall, throws an amusing sidelight upon the opinion of
Handel and his music held by the dry-as-dust Oxford
pundits.   Hearne, whose devotion to "monkish manuscripts" was sung by Pope,[2] cared little about music and
concerts, which, according to him, only "exhausted gentlemen's pockets and were incentives to lewdness."   He had
to admit Handel's "great skill," but he was indignant at
having to give five shillings for his ticket, and a shilling
for a book of words "not worth a penny," and in his heart
of hearts he resented the action of the Vice-Chancellor in
forbidding a company of strolling players to come into
Oxford, while "Handel and his lousy crew, a great number

---

[1] The Abbé Prévost gave his readers a different explanation of the fact
that Handel did not take his degree, and one slightly less in keeping with
Handel's character : "M. Handel s'est rendu à Oxford, mais on a été surpris
de lui voir refuser les marques de distinction qu'on lui destinait.   Il n'y avait
que cette modestie qui pût être égale à ses talents."   *Le Pour et le Contre*,
i. 123.

[2] Pope, *Moral Essays*, iv.

of foreign fiddlers," were admitted to the sacred precincts
of the Sheldonian Theatre.[1]

The undergraduates, too, for once agreed with the
dons in complaining of Handel's excessive charges. In a
squib of the period, Mr. Thoughtless, a Merton "blood,"
bewailing his impecuniosity, cries : " In the next place,
there's the furniture of my room procured me some
tickets to hear that bewitching music, that cursed
Handel, with his confounded Oratio's (*sic*); I wish him
and his company had been yelling in the infernal shades
below."[2]

Handel returned to London to find the operatic
quarrel raging more fiercely than ever. Luckily, though
peers and proctors joined forces against him, he had
plenty of trusty friends left, who rallied manfully to his
standard. Arbuthnot riddled the opposition with light
artillery in *Harmony in an Uproar*, a squib published under
the pseudonym of " Hurlothrumbo Johnson."[3] Handel
is on his trial, and the judge proceeds to detail the various
charges which he has to answer :—

" Imprimis, you are charg'd with having bewitch'd us
for the space of twenty Years past, nor do we know where
your Inchantments will end, if a timely stop is not put to
them, they threatening us with an entire Destruction of
Liberty and an absolute Tyranny in your Person over the
whole Territories of the Haymarket.

" Secondly, you have most insolently dar'd to give us
good Musick and sound Harmony when we wanted and

---

[1] Hearne, *Reliquiæ Hearnianæ*.

[2] *The Oxford Act : A New Ballad-Opera*, London, 1733.

[3] Arbuthnot's latest biographer, Mr. G. A. Aitken, denies his authorship
of this pamphlet, in spite of its inclusion in the collected edition of his works
published in 1751.

Thou tunefull Scarecrow, & thou warbling Bird,
No shelter for your Notes these Lands afford
This Town protects no more the Sing Song Strain
Whilst Balls & Masquerades Triumphant Reign.
Sooner than midnight revels ere shou'd fail
And ore Ridottos Harmony prevail.
That Cap (a refuge once) my Head shall Grace
And Save from ruin this Harmonious face)

CUZZONI, FARINELLI AND HEIDEGGER

desir'd bad, to the great Encouragement of your Operas
and the ruin of our good Allies and Confederates the
Professors of bad Musick.

"Thirdly, you have most feloniously and arrogantly
assum'd to yourself an uncontroul'd Property of pleasing
us, whether we would or no, and have often been so bold
as to charm us, when we were positively resolv'd to be out
of Humour."

Then come more special charges, in which we can
discern a sly hit at the "Academics" of the day, the
learned professors who maintained that nobody could
compose unless he had taken a degree at Oxford or
Cambridge.

"First then, Sir, have you taken your Degree? Boh!
Ha, ha, ha! Are you a Doctor, Sir? A fine Composer
indeed and not a Graduate! . . . Why, Doctor Pushpin
(Pepusch) and Doctor Blue (Greene) laugh at you and
scorn to keep you company. . . . I understand you have
never read Euclid, are a declar'd Foe to all the proper
Modes and Forms and Tones of Musick, and scorn to be
subservient to or ty'd up by Rules or have your Genius
cramp'd. Thou Goth and Vandal to just Sounds! We
may as well place Nightingales and Canary birds behind
the Scenes, and take the wild Operas of Nature from them
as allow you to be a Composer."

But the time for words was over. The combatants
were already on the *terrain*, and the duel was to be fought
à outrance. Handel snatched a brief holiday after his
visit to Oxford, and, accompanied by his friend Schmidt,
took a hasty trip to the Continent in search of new singers.
In Italy he heard Farinelli, then a young man and comparatively unknown, and Carestini. Unfortunately for
his pocket he preferred the latter, whom he at once

9

engaged and brought back with him to England.[1]   He
opened his season on the 30th of October, the King's
birthday, and was honoured by the presence of the court,
even the Prince of Wales being compelled by etiquette to
put in an appearance.   A few weeks later his new *castrato*,
Carestini, made his appearance.

Carestini was undoubtedly a very great singer, but he
had the misfortune in his earlier days to be eclipsed by
Senesino, and in his later by Farinelli.   His voice, originally
a soprano, had sunk by this time to "the fullest, finest,
and deepest counter-tenor that has perhaps ever been
heard."[2]   Hasse said of him that whoever had not heard
Carestini was unacquainted with the most perfect style of
singing.   He was a great success in London, the more so
as Senesino's voice was distinctly not what it had been.
Arbuthnot, indeed, rudely speaks of the latter as "almost
past his Business."[3]

The rival company—the Opera of the Nobility, as it
pompously called itself—opened its season in the Lincoln's
Inn Fields Theatre on the 29th of December 1733 with
Porpora's *Ariadne*.   Handel replied with an *Ariadne* of
his own, produced on the 26th of January 1734, and so the
struggle went on.   Carestini was Handel's trump card,
but his other singers were nothing very much to boast of.
Lady Bristol tells us all about them in a letter to her
husband: "I am just come home from a dull empty
opera (*Caio Fabrizio*, a pasticcio), tho' the second time.
The first was full to hear the new man (Carestini), who I
can find out to be an extream good singer.   The rest are
all scrubbs, except old Durastanti, that sings as well as
ever she did."[4]   Party feeling ran high between the two

---

[1] Hawkins, *History*, v. 318.   [2] Burney, *History*, iv. 369.
[3] *Harmony in an Uproar*, 39.   [4] *Letter Book of John Hervey*, iii.

opera-houses and their supporters. Everybody who had
a grudge against the court went to Lincoln's Inn Fields
in order to curry favour with the Prince. The King and
Queen cared little about music, but they were very much
annoyed at Frederick's behaviour, which they regarded as
a personal slight. They made a point of patronising
Handel as much as possible, and, as Lord Hervey says,
"sat freezing constantly at the empty Haymarket Opera."
Unfortunately for Handel, the King was at that time
extremely unpopular, and the presence of the court at his
theatre by no means implied full houses.

"The affair," Hervey continues, "grew as serious as
that of the Greens and the Blues under Justinian at
Constantinople. An anti-Handelian was looked upon as an
anti-courtier, and voting against the court in Parliament was
hardly a less remissible or more venial sin than speaking
against Handel or going to the Lincoln's Inn Fields Opera.
The Princess Royal said she expected in a little while to
see half the House of Lords playing in the orchestra at
the latter house in their robes and coronets; and the
King—though he declared he took no other part in this
affair than subscribing £1000 a year to Handel—often
added at the same time that 'he did not think setting
oneself at the head of a faction of fiddlers a very honourable
occupation for people of quality, or the ruin of one poor
fellow so generous or so good-natured a scheme as to do
much honour to the undertakers, whether they succeeded
or not; but the better they succeeded in it, the more he
thought they would have reason to be ashamed of it.'"[1]

Meanwhile Handel's old enemy, Bononcini, had disappeared from the scene, accused of having palmed
off a madrigal of Lotti's upon the Academy of Ancient

[1] Hervey, *Memoirs*, i. 320.

Music as a work of his own. The matter was much discussed at the time, and Bononcini had every opportunity
given him of justifying his action. He preferred, however,
to remain silent, so the case was given against him, and
he left England for ever, disappointed and disgraced.

The great social excitement of the year was the
marriage of the Princess Royal to William, Prince of
Orange. The match could hardly be called a brilliant
one, since the Prince was not of royal rank, was as
poor as a church mouse, and deformed into the bargain.
Princess Anne did not pretend to care about him, and
the King and Queen snubbed him unmercifully. When
he arrived at St. James's Palace, Anne was surrounded
by a bevy of her favourite opera singers, and refused to
leave the harpsichord in order to greet her fiancé. However, the marriage was popular throughout the country,
partly as a guarantee for the Protestant succession, and
partly because of the magic that still hung round the name
of Orange. The wedding took place on the 14th of March.
Handel wrote an anthem for the occasion, or rather
compiled one, for the work in question, " This is the day,"
was made up entirely of selections from his earlier works.
The Princess's marriage gave birth to yet another work,
the serenata *Parnasso in Festa*, which was performed the
day before the wedding, at the Haymarket Theatre, before
the King and all the Royal Family. This also was largely
a compilation, being taken principally from *Athaliah*,
which having only been given at Oxford was not yet
familiar to London audiences.

In Anne, Handel lost a friend whose enthusiasm was
only equalled by her indiscretion. She was devoted to
her old preceptor and his music, yet by stirring up the
Prince of Wales against him she indirectly inflicted upon

him the severest injury that he ever had to endure. Yet Handel owed much to her. The frequent grants "to the undertakers of the Opera to discharge their debts" which appear in the *Treasury Papers* during Handel's tenancy of the King's Theatre, may be traced to her amiable influence. She trained her sisters, too, to be thorough-going Handelians—though Amelia was much more at home on horseback than in her box at the opera, and the gentle Caroline never pretended to be the musician that Anne was. Nevertheless, we find Handel still drawing his £200 a year as their music master some years after Anne's marriage.[1] But court favour could not ensure Handel against ill-luck and the injuries of determined enemies. His lease of the Haymarket Theatre expired in July 1734, and before he could renew it, his rivals, by a clever piece of sharp practice, stepped in and secured the theatre for themselves. Worse still, they strengthened their company by the addition of the famous Farinelli, the most prodigiously gifted singer of the age, who had already turned the heads of all the amateurs on the Continent, and was shortly to throw Senesino, Carestini, and all the rest into the shade, so far as England was concerned. But Handel never knew what it was to be beaten. He accepted the inevitable, and hastened to secure the new theatre in Covent Garden which had been built a few years before by John Rich. His mana-gerial worries do not seem to have affected his spirits in the least. We have a pleasant glimpse of him at a musical party at Mrs. Delany's about this time. "Mr. Handel was in the best humour in the world," wrote the hostess to her sister. "He played lessons and accompanied Strada and all the ladies that sung, from seven o'clock till

[1] *Treasury Papers*, 1736.

eleven. I gave them tea and coffee, and about half an hour after nine had a salver brought in of chocolate, mulled white wine, and biscuits. Everybody was easy and seemed pleased."[1] Meanwhile Handel's plans were slightly modified by the claims of his old friend Anne, now Princess of Orange, who had been spending the summer in England, and wanted to hear some music before rejoining her husband at the Hague. So, to oblige her, Handel took the theatre in Lincoln's Inn Fields, and opened a short season there on the 5th of October 1734, relying chiefly upon *Ariadne* and *Il Pastor Fido*, which had been revived with great success during the previous season in a much revised and altered form. In November he moved to the far more convenient theatre in Covent Garden, signalising his arrival in his new quarters by the production of a ballet, *Terpsichore*, played as a prologue to *Il Pastor Fido*, in which the French *ballerina* Mlle. Sallé, who had already danced herself into the favour of London audiences in Rich's pantomimes at Lincoln's Inn Fields, made her appearance. He also produced a pasticcio selected from his own works, entitled *Orestes*. These were followed by a new opera, *Ariodante* (8th January 1735). Carestini was still with Handel, but even the magic of his mellifluous voice was powerless in the face of the brilliant galaxy of talent which the opposition had assembled at the King's Theatre. Farinelli, Senesino, Cuzzoni, and Montagnana formed, indeed, a combination that was hard to beat—and harder still to pay, as the aristocratic directors found ere long to their cost.

The Farinelli furore soon reached the borders of positive insanity. "On aimait les autres," wrote the Abbé

[1] Delany, *Correspondence*, vol. i.

Prévost, "pour celui-ci, on en est idolâtre; c'est une fureur."[1] His singing entranced even a jealous rival like Senesino, who, when they first appeared together, burst into tears at the conclusion of Farinelli's first song, and, forgetful of all else, ran across the stage and threw himself into Farinelli's arms. What his audiences thought of him may be summed up in the famous exclamation wrung from a too impressionable dame, and afterwards immortalised by Hogarth in "The Rake's Progress": "One God, one Farinelli!" But the enthusiasm of his English admirers took a more practical form. The Prince of Wales gave him a gold snuff-box set with diamonds and rubies, containing a pair of diamond knee buckles and a purse of a hundred guineas; and society followed suit to such purpose that though Farinelli's salary was only £1500, he contrived during his stay in London to make no less than £5000 a year. On his return to Italy he built a villa with the proceeds of his trip to England, which he not inaptly christened the "English Folly." In the face of the general infatuation for Farinelli, Handel and his "scrubbs" were helpless, and his enemies triumphed over his defeat. In a private letter of the 27th of December 1734 in the *Throckmorton Papers* we read: "I don't pity Handel in the least, for I hope this mortification will make him a human creature; for I am sure before he was no better than a brute, when he could treat civilised people with so much brutality as I know he has done."[2]

With the approach of Lent, Handel turned his energies in the far more profitable direction of oratorio. With his second-rate company he could scarcely hope to compete with the brilliant operatic performances at the

[1] *Le Pour et le Contre*, v. 204.
[2] *Historical MSS. Commission*, Appendix to 3rd Report.

Haymarket, but in oratorio he was supreme, and Porpora's attempt to rival him on his own ground by producing his oratorio *David* only recoiled on his own head. During Lent *Esther* was given six times, *Deborah* thrice, and *Athaliah* five times—a sufficient proof that London was steadily learning to cultivate a taste for the new art-form.

An interesting feature of this year's oratorio season was the intoduction of organ concertos between the acts, as they were still called. Handel's fingers had not lost their old cunning, and his performance was extremely popular. Mrs. Delany wrote of it to her mother: "My sister gave you an account of Mr. Handel's playing here for three hours together. I did wish for you, for no entertainment in music could exceed it, except his playing on the organ in *Esther*, where he performs a part in two concertos, that are the finest things I ever heard in my life." [1]

Another event of the season worth recording is the first appearance under Handel's standard of the famous tenor, John Beard. Beard had sung as a boy in the performance of *Esther* given in 1732 at Bernard Gates's house by the choristers of the Chapel Royal. He is referred to in a letter of Lady Élizabeth Compton's, dated the 21st of November 1734. "A Scholar of Mr. Gates, Beard, who left the Chapel last Easter, shines in the opera of Covent Garden, and Mr. Handel is so full of his Praises that he says he will surprise the Town with his performance before the Winter is over." [2] Beard seems only to have sung minor rôles until 1736, when he took the principal tenor part in *Alexander's Feast*. He

---

[1] Delany, *Correspondence*, vol. i.
[2] *Historical MSS. Commisson*, Report xi. Appendix, pt. 4.

afterwards sang in many of Handel's oratorios, notably in
Israel in Egypt, Samson, and *Jephtha.*

When Lent was over, Handel returned to opera, and in
Alcina (16th April 1735) scored one of the most brilliant
successes of his career, though the dances, with which
the opera was liberally besprinkled, were not well received, and Mlle. Sallé, who seems to have quite outlived
her popularity, was actually hissed.[1] Mrs. Delany writes
of *Alcina* with special enthusiasm : "Yesterday morning
my sister and I went to Mr. Handel's house to hear the
first rehearsal of the new opera *Alcina.* I think it is the
best he ever made, but I have thought so of so many, that
I will not say positively 'tis the finest, but 'tis so fine
I have not words to describe it. Strada has a whole
scene of charming recitative — there are a thousand
beauties. Whilst Mr. Handel was playing his part,
I could not help thinking him a necromancer in the
midst of his own enchantments." Handel had, of course,
the usual trouble with his singers. Carestini grew restive
under his dictatorship, and refused to sing the lovely air
"Verdi prati." "You dog!" cried the composer, "Don't
I know better as yourself what is good for you to sing?
If you will not sing all the songs what I give you, I will
not pay you a stiver." Carestini sang the song, and with
it scored one of his most brilliant triumphs, but he never
forgave the composer, and left the company at the end of
the season. Deprived of his leading man, and unable at
the moment to find an adequate substitute, Handel was
reduced to silence. He thought it was wiser to keep his
theatre closed, than to open it in a despairing attempt
to compete with his invincible rivals in the Haymarket.
In the following year, however, he entered the lists with

[1] Prévost, *Le Pour et le Contre,* vi. 35.

a new choral work, *Alexander's Feast*, which was produced on the 19th of February with overwhelming success. Musical criticism figures so rarely in the newspapers of the day, that the *London Daily Post's* observations are worth recording: "There never was upon the like occasion so numerous and splendid an audience at any theatre in London, there being at least thirteen hundred persons present; and it is judged that the receipt of the house could not amount to less than £450. It met with general applause, though attended with the inconvenience of having the performers placed at too great a distance from the audience, which we hear will be rectified the next time of performance." The success of *Alexander's Feast* must have cheered Handel more than a little, but hard work and the incessant worries of a managerial life had already begun to tell seriously upon his health. During the past few years he had paid several visits to Tunbridge Wells, but the baths there had done him little good, and he was troubled by presages of approaching calamity.

The marriage of the Prince of Wales to Princess Augusta of Saxe-Gotha roused him to fresh activity. He wrote a new wedding anthem, "Sing unto God," which was duly performed at the ceremony in the Chapel Royal on the 27th of April 1736, and he opened a short opera season on the 5th of May, the principal interest of which centred in the production of *Atalanta* on the 12th of May. *Atalanta*, being written to celebrate the Royal marriage, was of an appropriately festive character. It ended with a nuptial chorus in the Temple of Hymen, and a display of fireworks. *Atalanta* seems to have won the Prince of Wales's heart, or, more probably, the departure of the Princess Royal removed his only reason for objecting to Handel's music.

At any rate, from this time forth he was a cordial supporter of the Covent Garden opera, while the King, who was determined, whatever happened, never to be on the same side as his son, discontinued his support. The opposition at the King's Theatre, not to be outdone by Handel, produced a marriage cantata, *La Festa d'Imeneo*, by Porpora; but in spite of Farinelli's singing it fell lamentably flat, and was only given two or three times. The truth was that Farinelli had already outstayed his welcome. He had been the wonder of an hour, but the fickle public was getting tired of him and of the rubbishy operas in which he sung, and was on the look-out for a new excitement.

"When I went out of Town last autumn," wrote Mrs. Delany to Swift, "the reigning madness was Farinelli; I find it now turned on *Pasquin*,[1] a dramatic satire on the times. It has had almost as long a run as the *Beggar's Opera*, but in my opinion not with equal merit, though it has humour."

With the opening of the autumn season, Handel's hopes rose high. The Haymarket opera was on its last legs. Senesino had already gone home, and Farinelli was beginning to think about taking his departure. Handel now had the Prince and Princess of Wales on his side, and his company was strengthened by the accession of several new and promising recruits. Mrs. Delany was in high spirits: "At the Haymarket," she wrote, "they have Farinelli, Merighi,—with no sound in her voice, but thundering action, a beauty with no other merit,—and one Chimenti, a tolerable good woman with a pretty voice, and Montagnana who roars as usual! With this band of singers and dull Italian operas, such as you almost fall

[1] By Henry Fielding.

asleep at, they presume to rival Handel, who has Strada, that sings better than ever she did, Gizziello,[1] who is much improved since last year, and Annibali,[2] who has the best part of Senesino's voice and Carestino's, with a prodigious fine taste and good action. . . . Mr. Handel has two new operas ready, *Arminius* and *Giustino*. He was here two or three mornings ago, and played to me both the overtures, which are charming."[3]

Handel worked with the courage of despair. His expenses had been heavy, and with the advent of his new singers would be heavier still, but hope sprang eternal in his breast. The approaching collapse of the Haymarket opera, which was an open secret, nerved him to fresh efforts. During the spring of 1737 he produced no fewer than three new operas, *Arminio* (January 12), *Giustino* (February 16), and *Berenice* (May 18), besides revising his thirty-year-old Italian oratorio, *Il Trionfo del Tempo*, for the Lenten performances. No constitution, however Herculean, could stand such a strain, and the inevitable breakdown came in the middle of April. By the end of the month Handel was a little better, and the *London Daily Post* was able to announce that " Mr. Handel, who had been some time indisposed with the rheumatism, is in so fair a way of recovery that it is hoped he will be able to accompany the opera of *Justin* on the 24th of May." He contrived to pull himself together, but before the end of the season came another collapse. This time it was useless to disguise the fact that the malady was paralysis,

---

[1] Gioachino Conti, called Gizziello after his master Gizzi. He had a high soprano voice, and his style was remarkable for delicacy and refinement. He made his English début in *Atalanta*.

[2] Domenico Annibali, a contralto who came to London from Dresden.

[3] Delany, *Correspondence*, vol. i.

which completely crippled his right hand, complicated by
serious brain trouble.[1] The mighty Handel was reduced
to a state bordering upon childishness, and it was only
with the greatest difficulty that his friends could induce
him to start for Aix-la-Chapelle, where it was hoped that
the sulphur baths would cure him. By the side of this
grievous affliction the final failure of his operatic enterprise
seemed a trifle. A failure it was, disastrous and complete.
When Covent Garden closed its doors on the 1st of June,
Handel was a bankrupt. The savings of a lifetime,
amounting to £10,000, were scattered to the winds, and
his creditors—artists and tradesmen alike—had to be
satisfied with bills. To the credit of mankind be it
recorded, that in all cases, save that of Signor del Pò,
Strada's husband, they were accepted, and in due time
redeemed. It was a poor consolation to Handel that in
ruining him his opponents had ruined themselves. The
Haymarket opera struggled on for ten days longer, when
the unexpected departure of Farinelli brought matters to
a sudden and ignoble collapse. The rival enterprises had
devoured each other, and the town turned with a sigh of
relief from their futile struggles to the broad humours of
The Dragon of Wantley, in which the pompous inanity
of grand opera was mercilessly parodied. The somewhat
obvious fun of Henry Carey's burlesque delighted the
King, who kept poor dying Queen Caroline from her bed
by his interminable descriptions of the dragon's antics,[2]
and Lampe's vivacious music extorted an approving smile
even from Handel, overwhelmed as he was with debt and
disaster.[3]

The end was perhaps inevitable, nor in the interests

---

[1] *Shaftesbury Biographical Sketch.*
[2] Hervey, *Memoirs*, iii. 295.   [3] *Wentworth Papers*, p. 539.

of art much to be deplored. Opera in England then, as
now, was an exotic. It had no root in the affections of
the general public ; it merely catered for the whimsies of
a pleasure-seeking aristocracy. None save a very select
few pretended to think that the entertainment was anything more than a social festivity. The beaux and belles
of the day went to hear Senesino and Farinelli, just as
our modern grandees go to hear Melba and Tetrazzini, and
cared little or nothing what music they listened to. The
flame of partisanship burnt fiercely for a while. People
quarrelled passionately over rival houses and rival singers,
but the very excesses into which their frenzy led them
brought about a speedy reaction.

Sensible people like Mrs. Delany realised very soon
that all the strife and partisanship did not imply any real
interest in music. "Our operas," she wrote to Swift,
"have given much cause of dissension. Men and women
have been deeply engaged, and no debate in the House of
Commons has been urged with more warmth. The dispute
of the merits of the composers and singers is carried to so
great a height, that it is much feared by all true lovers
of music that operas will be quite overturned. I own I
think we make a very silly figure about it."[1] Nothing is
so healthy for the cause of art as discussions and debate
or even a good hand-to-hand fight, when the difference
of opinion springs from genuine interest and enthusiasm.
But the operatic wars of the eighteenth century were
merely the squabbles of idle children over their play-
things. A new toy caught their eye, and their once
cherished puppets were cast upon the dust-heap. The
mournful part of the business from our point of view is
that one of the puppets was a man of genius.

[1] Delany, *Correspondence*, vol. i.

But Handel emerged uninjured, if breathless, from the struggle. The mire of aristocratic intrigue had not sullied his garments. Even in that murky atmosphere the flame of his genius burnt clear and pure. Whoever had cause to blush, he had none. He had worked loyally in the cause of art through all dangers and difficulties, and he could look back upon those anxious years of toil and endeavour without shame or regret. He had cast his pearls before swine, and had seen them trampled under foot. He had learned his lesson in a hard school, and had paid dearly for it. At last it was over, and the experience that he had bought at so ruinous a price was in the end to lead him to a wider immortality than any that could be conferred by the fickle favour of courts and courtiers.

CHAPTER X

ECCE CONVERTIMUR AD GENTES! 1737–1741

AIX-LA-CHAPELLE made a new man of Handel; indeed, he recovered his health so rapidly under the genial influence of the waters, that the good people of the place were inclined to believe that a miracle had been wrought on behalf of their famous visitor. While he was at Aix, Handel seems to have made the acquaintance of some honest burghers from the city of Elbing, near the Baltic coast. Elbing was preparing to celebrate the five-hundredth anniversary of her foundation, and Handel, whose speedy recovery had had the effect of putting him into an unusually amiable frame of mind, consented to join forces with a local musician in composing a cantata for the occasion. Records of the work exist, but the music has unfortunately disappeared.[1]

Another story, told by Coxe in his *Anecdotes of Handel*, seems to refer to Handel's "cure" at Aix, though it is difficult to make it fit in with the facts. Frederick the Great was on his way to the baths, and hearing that Handel was there sent a messenger to say that he wished to see him. Presumably the message was couched, or at least delivered, in what Handel considered insolent terms,

---

[1] Doering, " Die Musik im Preussen." (*Monatshefte für Musikgeschichte,* i. 155.)

at any rate his back was up in a moment, and he left the place a few days before the arrival of the King. The only objection to this interesting anecdote is that Frederick was not at Aix nor anywhere in its neighbourhood in the year 1737. His only visit to Aix, which he thought "le pays le plus sot que je connaisse," took place in September 1741, while Handel was writing *The Messiah* in London. It is certainly a pity that Frederick never happened to meet Handel. He was himself a musician, and the man who silenced the chatter of his courtiers with the words: "Gentlemen, the great Bach has arrived," could hardly have failed to appreciate Handel.

Handel left Aix in October, and returned to England *via* Flanders. In Lord Shaftesbury's *Biographical Sketch* there is an anecdote relating to the journey which has not, I think, been printed before: "His recovery was so complete that in his return thence to England he was able to play long voluntaries upon the organ. In one of the great towns of Flanders, where he had asked permission to play, the organist attended him, not knowing who he was, and seemed struck with Mr. Handel's playing when he began. But when he heard Mr. Handel lead off a fugue, in astonishment he ran up to him, and embracing him said, 'You can be no other but the great Handel.'"

Handel reached London early in November, "greatly recovered in health."[1]

He arrived only just in time to add his private sorrow to the general grief of the nation at the death of Queen Caroline, who expired after a short illness on the 20th of November. No English sovereign was ever more widely or genuinely mourned. Over her coffin king and clodhopper mingled their tears. George II showed his

---

[1] *London Daily Post*, 7th November 1737.

10

sorrow in peculiarly characteristic fashion, but of its sincerity there cannot be a doubt. Though his infidelities had been notorious, his respect for Caroline's talents and his admiration of her virtues had never wavered. On her death-bed she entreated him to marry again. "Non, non," he whimpered, "j'aurai des maîtresses." "Mon Dieu," she replied, remembering her own exper·ences, "cela n'empêche pas."

The King was inconsolable for many months after her death, and seems to have been a prey to strange superstitions. Duchess Sarah tells an odd story of his behaviour at the card-table: "Some queens were dealt to him, which renewed his trouble so much, and put him into so great disorder, that the Princess Amelia immediately ordered all the queens to be taken out of the pack."[1] The King's thoughts ran upon ghosts and vampires. Lord Wentworth gives a curious illustration of his superstitious terror: "Saturday night between one and two o'clock, the King waked out of a dream very uneasy, and ordered the vault, where the Queen is, to be broken open immediately, and have the coffin also opened; and went in a hackney chair through the Horse Guards to Westminster Abbey, and back again to bed. I think it is the strangest thing that could be."[2]

Handel was not troubled by the King's childish fancies, but his grief was scarcely less profound. Caroline was one of his oldest friends. He had met her first when they were children together at the court of Berlin. He had learnt to know her better at Hanover, and since they had been in England she had always been his staunchest patroness and supporter. He poured forth his sorrow in

---

[1] *Correspondence of Sarah, Duchess of Marlborough*, vol. ii.

[2] *Wentworth Papers*, p. 538.

the marvellous strains of the Funeral Anthem, "The ways of Zion do mourn," which was performed at the ceremony in Westminster Abbey, on the 17th of December, a noble tribute to a great and good woman, which for sublimity of thought and expression Handel himself rarely surpassed.

Handel's recent experiences in the arena of Italian opera were not calculated to make him anxious to return to the fray. But beggars cannot be choosers; his debts were still unpaid, and his creditors were pressing. When therefore he was approached by Heidegger,[1] who had gathered together the wreck and remnant of the two companies that had failed in the summer, and with characteristic energy had started a season at the King's Theatre, he felt it his duty to enter into negotiations with his quondam partner. After some deliberation it was agreed that for a consideration of £1000 Handel should supply Heidegger with two new operas, and should arrange a pasticcio from his earlier works. It must have been gall and wormwood to Handel to be forced once more into business relations with the man who had behaved so badly to him at a time when he most needed friends, but Handel was nothing if not conscientious, and he felt that his own feelings must give way. The operas were dashed off at lightning speed, and duly produced,

---

[1] Heidegger is usually supposed to have been responsible for the season, as the advertisements relative to the subscription that appeared in the newspapers were signed by him, but Lord Shaftesbury's *Biographical Sketch* distinctly says that Handel composed *Faramondo* and *Serse* "for the gentlemen at the Haymarket," so it is probable that Heidegger was backed by a board of aristocratic directors similar to that presided over by Lord Middlesex in 1741. Lord Middlesex himself does not appear to have begun to dabble in management until 1739, when Mrs. Delany mentions that he was "chief undertaker" of a season of concerts at the Haymarket Theatre.

Faramondo on the 7th of January, and *Serse* on the 15th of April 1738. The pasticcio was *Alessandro Severo*, which with a few new songs and a new and very fine overture was given on the 25th of February.

Heidegger's company included some good singers. Caffarelli, a contralto, was the most famous of them; but Francesina, a youthful soprano with a pretty voice and what Burney calls "a lark-like execution," and Marchesini, called La Lucchesina, were both of them artists of high quality. Montagnana, with his thundering bass voice, was also engaged. Caffarelli was thought by many critics to be superior to Farinelli, but he did not make much of a success in London. He is said to have been in bad health during his sojourn here, and he came at an unfortunate time—when society had been sated with Italian opera, and was weary of the endless quarrels and rivalries which seemed to be its inevitable accompaniment.[1]

The season was a calamitous one, and the only time that the theatre was full was on the 20th of March, when Handel was constrained by his friends to take a "benefit." It is easy to understand how distasteful to a man of his independent spirit it must have been to accept a favour of this kind, but circumstances forbade him to stand upon his dignity. Del Pò, who was still one of his principal creditors, was more insistent than ever, and even threatened the composer with a debtors' prison. The

---

[1] Caffarelli's insolence and conceit caused him to be as heartily disliked as Farinelli was beloved for his amiability. He lived to a good old age, and retained his voice almost to the last. Burney heard him at Naples in 1770, when he was sixty-seven. "Though his voice was thin," he remarks, "it was easy to imagine, from what he was still able to do, that his voice and talents had been of the very first class." He was then living in a sumptuous house of his own building, over the door of which was inscribed the legend, "Amphion Thebas, ego domum."

VAUXHALL GARDENS, WITH ROUBILIAC'S STATUE OF HANDEL

"benefit" had the effect of stopping his greedy mouth. It realised a large sum of money, according to Burney £800, according to Mainwaring £1500, but at any rate enough to stave off the more pressing claims and to give the composer time to look around him. Another graceful compliment was paid to his genius about this time, in the erection of a marble statue of him by the rising young sculptor Roubillac, or Roubiliac, as he is usually called in English, in Vauxhall Gardens, a popular place of resort, which had been opened in 1732, where Handel's music was often performed.[1]

After the close of the opera season on the 5th of June, Handel probably left London. Between the 23rd of July and the 27th of September he was engaged upon the composition of *Saul*, the libretto of which is believed to have been the work of Charles Jennens,[2] who later adapted Milton's *L'Allegro ed il Penseroso* for Handel, and furnished him with the text of *The Messiah*. Handel had a sincere regard for Jennens, and often stayed at his country house at Gopsall in Leicestershire. If Jennens wrote *Saul*, it is likely enough that he invited Handel to spend the summer with him, the advantage to librettist and composer alike of being under the same roof being undeniable. Jennens was one of those men whose character is very difficult to reconstruct from contemporary

---

[1] This statue, after passing through many hands, is now the property of Mr. Alfred Littleton, the head of the firm of Novello & Co. It stands in the entrance hall of Messrs. Novello's beautiful new place of business in Wardour Street.

[2] A letter of Handel's to Jennens is extant, written in 1735, acknowledging the receipt of an oratorio of which he writes: "What I could read of it in haste gave me a great deal of satisfaction." There is no reason for doubting that the work referred to was *Saul*, the next in order of Handel's oratorios, the authorship of which was never acknowledged.

evidence.   He was rich, generous and eccentric, and had
an excellent conceit of himself.   He was surrounded by
parasites who flattered him and often lured him into
making a fool of himself by writing about things that he
did not understand, as, for instance, in his controversy with
Dr. Johnson and George Steevens about Shakespeare.
At the same time he was a staunch friend and a benevolent and hospitable neighbour, besides being a man of
considerable culture.   During his quarrel with Steevens a
friend of his wrote: " I assert that Mr. Jennens is a man
of abilities; is conversant in the Polite Arts; that he
understands Musick, Poetry and Painting.   I appeal to
the catalogue of his Pictures, which bear all the living
testimony that Pictures can bear of original and intrinsic
merit.   His taste in Musick is still less disputable—the
compilation of *The Messiah* has been ever attributed to
him.   Handel generally consulted him, and to the time of
his death lived with him in the strictest intimacy and
regard.   Was Handel so mean and despicable as to offer
incense at the shrine of Ignorance?"[1]   Jennens loved
display.   In his youth the splendour of his household
earned him the nickname of "Solyman the Magnificent."
All through his life he made a point of doing things in
the grand style.   If he wanted to go from his town house
in Great Ormond Street to call on his printer in Red
Lion Passage, he must needs travel with four servants
behind his carriage.   When he alit, a footman walked
before him up the paved passage, to kick oyster-shells
and other impediments out of his way.   At Gopsall
Handel had the advantage of tranquillity, comfort and
congenial society, for Jennens was a bachelor like himself.
It is perhaps worth noting that fifty years after Handel's

[1] Nichols, *Literary Anecdotes of the Eighteenth Century*, vol. iii.

death a tradition existed to the effect that some at any rate of his oratorios were composed at Gopsall. A local parson contributed the following note to Nichols's *Literary Anecdotes*: "I know not whether you are aware that there is a probability, I think almost an immediate proof, that Handel's oratorios took their rise in this county. The rich Mr. Jennens of Gopsall was a man of great piety, beneficence and taste in the fine arts. He built a magnificent house, and in it a beautiful chapel, in which he read prayers to his family daily. Handel (who, you know, loved good living) was often his guest, as also Dr. Bentley of Nailston, his neighbour, nephew of the great Bentley. I have heard that the idea of the oratorios was Mr. Jennens's, and Dr. Bentley furnished the words." If Dr. Bentley, who by the way was a scholar of some consideration and his famous uncle's literary executor,[1] had any hand in the production of *Saul*, the world has good reason to be grateful to him; and still more so if he was in any way responsible for *Israel in Egypt*, which Handel began four days after he had finished *Saul*. It would be interesting to know what first led Handel to undertake the composition of his gigantic epic, so different in aim and structure from any of his previous works. It is plain that originally he had no idea of writing anything in the received oratorio form. He began with what is now the second part, the autograph of which is headed "Moses'

---

[1] He was christened Richard after his uncle, but is often confused with another of the great Bentley's nephews, Thomas, whom Pope attacked in the *Dunciad*:—

"Bentley his mouth with classic flattery opes
And the puff'd orator bursts out in tropes."

Thomas Bentley was a friend of Byrom's, and wrote him amusing letters from abroad, which are published in Byrom's *Remains*.

Song, Exodus, chapter xv." Apparently he intended something in the nature of an anthem, but the subject fascinated him, and when he had finished the second part, he wrote the first part as a kind of prelude. *Saul* and *Israel* were both produced during the following year at the King's Theatre, which Handel hired from Heidegger for his oratorio concerts—*Saul* on January 16, and *Israel* on April 4, 1739.

In the case of *Saul*, Handel, who like many other great composers was accused by his contemporaries of a passion for mere noise, took pains to add a special touch of dignity to the famous Dead March. "I hear," wrote young Lord Wentworth to his father, "that Mr. Handel has borrowed from the Duke of Argyll a pair of the largest kettle-drums in the Tower; so to be sure it will be most excessive noisy with a bad set of singers. I doubt it will not retrieve his former losses."[1] *Saul*, however, was on the whole a success, being given six times during the season. *Israel*, on the other hand, seems to have been above the heads of the audiences of that day. After the first performance, it was only thrice repeated, and in a form altered to fit it more harmoniously to the taste of the day, according to the advertisement : "shortened and intermixed with songs." It must have been a bitter pill to Handel to be compelled to mutilate his great work to suit the artistic depravity of London audiences. The songs introduced were not the adaptations of Italian airs to Biblical words that are now occasionally given in performances of the oratorio, but popular airs from his earlier works and some new Italian songs apparently written for the occasion, which were thrust into *Israel* without the semblance of any appropriateness. A further

[1] *Wentworth Papers*, p. 543.

alteration was the introduction of the Funeral Anthem, which was performed at the beginning of the oratorio, the words being altered so as to apply to the death of Joseph. In spite of these almost cynical concessions to popular taste, *Israel* did not please. A few voices, however, cried in the desert. Two anonymous admirers poured forth their enthusiasm in letters to the *London Daily Post*,[1] but the general public was not to be beguiled.

By the middle of April the new oratorios seem to have exhausted their powers of attraction, and Handel fell back upon a different kind of entertainment. On the 26th an advertisement appeared in the *London Daily Post* to this effect: "On Tuesday next, 1st May, will be performed, at the King's Theatre in the Haymarket, a dramatical composition called *Jupiter in Argos*, intermixed with choruses, and two concertos on the organ." What *Jupiter in Argos* exactly was is now difficult to determine. The autograph has disappeared, all save the last leaf, which is preserved in the Fitzwilliam Library at Cambridge, and bears the inscription: "Fine dell' opera *Jupiter in Argos*, April 24, 1739. G. F. Handel." Although Handel called it an opera, the terms used in the advertisement point rather to its being something of the same kind as *Parnasso in Festa*, which was still far from having lost its popularity. Probably it was a pasticcio, hastily put together to meet the emergency, but no proof of its having been actually performed can be adduced.

If the season as a whole had turned out a failure, it is hardly fair to lay all the blame upon London society. The political excitement of the time was unfavourable to music or to art of any kind. War was in the air, and

[1] See Appendix B.

Bellona elbowed Polyhymnia from the field. John Bull had awoke from his long sleep, and wanted to go out and fight somebody.

Walpole and his peace policy had ruled the roost for thirty years. He had made England the greatest commercial nation in the world; he had doubled her income, and given her peace and prosperity. But in a moment he and his benefits were forgotten. The lust of war descended upon the nation, and all peaceful interests bent before the storm of martial ardour.

The "Patriots," as the Opposition called themselves, were always on the look out for sticks wherewith to beat Walpole. They found one ready to their hand in the supposed aggression of our historic enemy, Spain. We were, as usual, entirely in the wrong. In defiance of the Treaty of Utrecht, our traders had for years been carrying on a roaring trade—largely in slaves—with the Spanish colonies. In vain the Spanish authorities had endeavoured to put some check upon this vast system of smuggling. From time to time brushes with our privateers occurred, and now and then Englishmen found their way into Spanish prisons. After all, Spain was only asserting her just rights, if occasionally in a high-handed and arbitrary manner. But it was easy for Pulteney and his "Patriots" to make out a case against her. Popular passion was fanned by the usual trickery, and the excitement reached its height when a master mariner named Jenkins was produced at the bar of the House of Commons. Jenkins had a thrilling story to tell. Some years before, his vessel had been boarded off Havana by Spanish revenue officers. Innocent as a babe as he was, he had been shamefully maltreated. He had been hanged at the yard-arm and cut down half-dead. He had been slashed with cutlasses and his left ear had been torn off by a Spanish miscreant, who flung it in his face, bidding him carry it home to King George. "In that supreme moment," concluded Jenkins with dramatic solemnity, "I commended my soul to God and my cause to my country." The phrase flew like wild-fire through the country The war fever seized all classes alike. Walpole vainly struggled for peace. The country was against him, and it was a case of yielding to their will or resigning office. He chose the former, and declared war with Spain.

London threw its cap into the air, and roared huzza! with all its thousand throats. The city blazed with flags and pennons, and bells rang defiance from every steeple. Throngs of vengeance-breathing heroes paraded the streets, and the Prince of Wales joined with the mob at Temple Bar in drinking success to the campaign. While the frenzy reigned, Handel sat gloomily in his empty theatre. It was useless to struggle against the tide of popular feeling. We who remember the opening days of the Boer War can fully realise the situation. There was nothing to be done but wait till the martial enthusiasm of the country had expended itself in idle vapouring, and society returned once more to its ordinary avocations.

In the autumn, Handel, whose losses of late had been severe, clipped the wings of his ambition and moved to the theatre in Lincoln's Inn Fields, where, on the 17th of November 1739, he produced his setting of Dryden's *Ode for St. Cecilia's Day*, which seems to have pleased his patrons, since it was repeated several times during the season in conjunction with either *Alexander's Feast* or *Acis and Galatea*. Doubtless its success would have been greater than it was, but during that winter the elements fought against Handel, and owing to an exceptionally

severe frost he was compelled to close his theatre from
the 20th of December to the 21st of February.   It is easy
to believe that in Handel's days theatres were very far
from being the cosy luxurious temples of amusement
that they now are, and the Lincoln's Inn Fields theatre
was notoriously ill built and uncomfortable.   Handel did
all that he could.   His advertisements in the *London
Daily Post* are almost pathetic: "Particular care has been
taken to have the House surveyed and secured against
the cold, by having curtains placed before every door,
and constant fire will be kept in the House till the time of
performance."   But it was useless to expect people to brave
the terrors of an Arctic temperature in order to listen to
good music.   Even in favourable weather it was as much
as he could do to scrape together an audience, and when
the frost set in, the case was hopeless.   For some reason
best known to the clerk of the weather, the winters in the
eighteenth century were decidedly more severe than they
are in our days, or at any rate people made far more fuss
about them.   Owing to the arches of old London Bridge
getting choked with ice, it was by no means uncommon
for the Thames "above bridge" to be frozen so hard that
a "Frost Fair," or "Blanket Fair" as it was sometimes
called, could be held upon it.   When this happened, as it
did in the winter of 1739–40, London gave itself up to
a kind of impromptu carnival.   The Thames for the time
being was a debatable land, over which none of the
recognised authorities cared to exercise any jurisdiction.
Everybody did what he liked, and the fun was as fast as
it was furious.   It was the right thing for the aristocracy
to come down and join in the people's sports at "Frost
Fair."   Charles II set the fashion in the great frost of
1684, and in 1716 George II, then Prince of Wales,

FROST FAIR ON THE THAMES

followed his example. In 1740 the frozen Thames was a little town of tents and booths. Coaches plied between Lambeth and London Bridge, and every form of festivity and diversion was practised, the roasting of oxen being of course a special feature. As usual, merriment and misery went hand in hand, for the distress among the lower classes must have been very severe. But London was prosperous and charitable, and there are many records of benevolent endeavour to relieve the pressing necessities of those whom the frost had robbed of employment.

It would have needed a harder frost even than that of 1740 to check the flow of Handel's inspiration. While London was disporting itself upon the icebound Thames he was busily setting to music a strange libretto, concocted by his friend Jennens out of Milton's *L'Allegro* and *Il Penseroso*. Not content with boiling down the two poems into a singularly inharmonious whole, he added a *coda* of his own, entitled *Il Moderato*, in which the virtues of moderation are celebrated in numbers which would sound awkward and ungainly in any company, and by the side of Milton's sonorous lines seem doubly pedestrian. The libretto, however, inspired Handel, who wrote to it some of the most romantic and picturesque music that he ever composed. Handel's *L'Allegro* in its turn inspired a nameless bard, who, after hearing it performed, burst into verse of the following quality:—

> " If e'er Arion's music calmed the floods,
> And Orpheus ever drew the dancing woods,
> Why do not British trees and forests throng
> To hear the sweeter notes of Handel's song ?" [1]

Unfortunately for Handel not only did the British trees and forests refuse to throng to his concerts, but the

[1] *Gentleman's Magazine*, May 1740.

British lords and ladies as well. The aristocratic cabal against him and his music was as bitter and as powerful as ever, and at the Lincoln's Inn Fields theatre empty benches were the rule rather than the exception. But his pluck was inexhaustible. During the next season he dropped sacred oratorio altogether, save for a single performance of *Saul*, and offered his patrons only works of a lighter cast. In his determination to succeed he even fell back upon his old love, Italian opera. Despite the fact that to those who remembered Faustina, Cuzzoni, Senesino, and the great singers of the past, his company must have seemed, to borrow Lady Bristol's graceful expression, "a set of scrubbs," he produced a two-act operetta, *Imeneo* (22nd November 1740), with the composition of which he had amused himself two years before in the intervals of writing *Saul,* and wrote a new opera, *Deidamia*, to a libretto by his old enemy Rolli, which was performed for the first time on the 10th of January 1741. All was in vain. Serious music was a drug in the market. *The Beggar's Opera, The Dragon of Wantley*, and their thousand and one successors had revolutionised popular taste in music, just as Hogarth had revolutionised it in art. Handel owned himself defeated, and his defeat was embittered by the apologetic attitude taken up by some who called themselves his friends. On the 4th of April 1741, the *London Daily Post* published a portentous rigmarole singed J. B., in which a kind of attempt is made to recommend Handel to the good graces of the aristocratic ignoramuses who had been doing their best to ruin him. "I wish," writes the amiable J. B., "that I could persuade the gentlemen of figure and weight, who have taken offence at any part of this great man's conduct (for a great man he must be in the musical world, whatever misfortunes may now, too late, say to the contrary), I wish I could persuade them, I say, to take him back into favour, and relieve him from the cruel persecution of those little vermin, who, taking advantage of their displeasure, pull down even his bills as fast as he has put them up, and use a thousand other little acts to injure and distress him."

What Handel thought—and probably said—of a begging letter of this kind can be better imagined than described. Nothing was farther from his thoughts than apologies or concession. He had given his best to England, and England would have none of it. But he had another string to his bow. In the hour of his defeat he bethought him of the sister isle, whence warm invitations from many good friends had often reached him. The people of his choice would have none of him, and he turned in despair to the Gentiles. He shook the dust of London from his feet, and prepared for a visit to Dublin.

CHAPTER XI

HANDEL IN IRELAND, 1741–1742

WILLIAM CAVENDISH, fourth Duke of Devonshire and Lord Lieutenant of Ireland, was one of those amiable and accomplished peers immortalised by the muse of Sir William Gilbert, who spend their existence in doing nothing in particular and doing it very well. His sole claim to immortality rests upon the fact that he invited Handel to Dublin. The rest of his blameless and respectable career has faded into the shadows of the past. His Lord Lieutenancy seems on the whole to have been a success. He was rich, and spent his money generously. He built a quay in Dublin and beautified the city in other ways. It probably did not lie within his power to do much towards ameliorating the lot of the deeply injured and suffering people whom he ruled—the Home Government kept too tight a hand upon him for that. As to his private life, his obsequious biographer records with proper enthusiasm that "he generally conversed with his friends and neighbours with that cheerfulness and condescension, that bespoke the truly great man"; but a pleasanter idea of what the man really was is given in a story of Sir Robert Walpole's brother Horatio, who, when asked what he thought of Devonshire House, replied: "Why, I think it something like the master; plain and good without, but one of the best inside houses in Britain."[1]   Whatever were his faults or virtues, the Duke appreciated Handel, and it was in response to a definite invitation from Dublin Castle that Handel started for John Bull's other island.

He left London during the first week of November 1741, carrying with him his completed *Messiah*, which he had begun on the 22nd of August and finished on the 14th of September.   Burney, as a boy of fifteen, saw him at Chester, and his story, though it has often been quoted before, is too good to be omitted :—

"When Handel went through Chester on his way to Ireland in the year 1741, I was at the public school in that city and very well remember seeing him smoke a pipe over a dish of coffee at the Exchange Coffee-House; for, being extremely anxious to see so extraordinary a man, I watched him narrowly as long as he remained in Chester; which, on account of the wind being unfavourable for his embarking at Parkgate, was several days.   During this time he applied to Mr. Baker the organist, my first music master, to know whether there were any choirmen in the Cathedral who could sing at sight, as he wished to prove some books that had been hastily transcribed by trying the choruses which he intended to perform in Ireland.   Mr. Baker mentioned some of the most likely singers then in Chester, and among the rest a printer of the name of Janson, who had a good bass voice and was one of the best musicians in the choir.   A time was fixed for the private rehearsal at the Golden Falcon, where Handel was quartered; but alas ! on trial of the chorus in *The Messiah*, 'And with His stripes we are healed,' poor Janson, after repeated attempts, failed so egregiously that

[1] Grove, *Lives of the Dukes of Devonshire*, 1764.

II

Handel let loose his great bear upon him, and, after swearing in four or five different languages, cried out in broken English: 'You scoundrel, did you not tell me that you could sing at sight?'

"'Yes, sir,' says the printer, 'and so I can, but not at first sight.'"

The contrary winds still continuing, Handel left Chester and proceeded to Holyhead, whence he contrived at last to cross to Dublin. He arrived at his destination on the 18th of November,[1] and established himself in a house in Abbey Street. His company of singers and players soon began to assemble. Maclaine, the organist, he had brought with him. Signora Avolio arrived on the 24th. Mrs. Cibber was already in Dublin, where for some time past she had been turning everybody's head as Polly Peachum in *The Beggar's Opera*. His old friend Dubourg the violinist was already established in Dublin. Handel opened his season on the 23rd of December with a performance of *L'Allegro, Il Penseroso ed il Moderato*, together with the usual allowance of concertos, given in the recently built hall in Fishamble Street.[2] A report of

[1] "Last Wednesday the celebrated Dr. Handel arrived here in the Packet Boat from Holyhead, a Gentleman universally known by his excellent Compositions in all kinds of Musick, and particularly for his *Te Deum*, *Jubilate*, Anthems, and other compositions in Church Musick (of which for some years past have principally consisted the Entertainments in the Round Church, which have so greatly contributed to support the Charity of Mercer's Hospital), to perform his Oratorios, for which purpose he hath engaged the above Mr. Maclaine (mentioned in the preceding paragraph) his Wife and several others of the best performers in the Musical Way." *Faulkner's Journal*, 21st November 1741.

[2] Fishamble Street is situated in a quarter which, though now fallen from its high estate, was at that time highly fashionable. Neal's Music Hall was first opened to the public on 2nd October 1741. Many years afterwards it was converted into a theatre. In 1850 it was, according to Rockstro, "a neglected old building with a wooden porch." It has now totally disappeared.

the proceedings only appeared in *Faulkner's Journal*: "Last Wednesday, Mr. Handel had his first oratorio at Mr. Neal's Musick Hall in Fishamble Street, which was crowded with a more numerous and polite audience than ever was seen upon the like occasion. The performance was superior to anything of the kind in the kingdom before, and our nobility and gentry, to shew their taste for all kinds of genius, expressed their great satisfaction and have already given all imaginable encouragement to this grand musick." Handel's satisfaction equalled that of his audience, and a few days later he wrote in high spirits to Jennens :—

DUBLIN, *29th December* 1741

"S^r.—It was with the greatest Pleasure I saw the Continuation of your kindness by the Lines you was pleased to send me, in order to be prefix'd to your Oratorio *Messiah*, which I set to Musick before I left England. I am emboldened, Sir, by the generous Concern you please to take in relation to my affairs, to give you an account of the Success I have met here. The Nobility did me the honour to make amongst themselves a Subscription for 6 Nights, which did fill a Room of 600 Persons, so that I needed not to sell one single ticket at the Door, and without Vanity the Performance was received with a general Approbation. Sig^ra. Avolio, which I brought with me from London, pleases extraordinary. I have found another Tenor Voice which gives great Satisfaction, the Basses and Counter Tenors are very good, and the rest of the Chorus Singers (by my Direction) do exceedingly well. As for the Instruments they are really excellent, Mr. Dubourgh being at the Head of them, and the Musick sounds delightfully in this charming Room, which puts me in good Spirits (and my Health being so good) that I exert myself on my Organ with more than usual success.

"I open'd with the *Allegro, Penseroso, and Moderato*, and I assure you that the words of the Moderato are vastly admired. The Audience being composed (besides the Flower of Ladies of Distinction and other People of the greatest Quality) of so many Bishops, Deans, Heads of the Colledge, the most eminent People in the Law, as the Chancellor, Auditor General, etc. etc., all which are very much taken with the Poetry, so that I am desired to perform it again the next time. I cannot sufficiently express the kind treatment I receive here, but the Politeness of this generous Nation cannot be unknown to you, so I let you judge of the satisfaction I enjoy, passing my time with honour, profit and pleasure. They propose already to have some more performances, when the 6 nights of the Subscription are over, and my Lord Duke the Lord Lieutenant (who is always present with all his Family on those Nights) will easily obtain a longer Permission for me by His Majesty, so that I shall be obliged to make my stay here longer than I thought. One request I must make to you, which is that you would insinuate my most devoted Respects to my Lord and my Lady Shaftesbury ; you know how much their kind protection is precious to me. Sir William Knatchbull will find here my respectful Compliments. You will increase my Obligations if by occasion you will present my humble service to some other Patrons and friends of mine. I expect with impatience the Favour of your News concerning your Health and Welfare, of which I take a real share. As for the news of your Operas I need not trouble you, for all the Town is full of their ill success by a number of Letters from your quarters to the People of Quality here, and I can't help saying but that it furnishes great Diversion and laughter.

"The first Opera [1] I heard myself before I left London, and it made me very merry all along my journey, and of the second Opera, called *Penelope*,[2] a certain nobleman writes very jocosely, 'Il faut que je dise avec Harlequin, notre Pénélope n'est qu' une Sallope,' but I think I have trespassed too much on your Patience.

"I beg you to be persuaded of the sincere veneration and esteem with which I have the Honour to be, Sir, your most obliged and most humble servant,

"GEORGE FRIDERIC HANDEL"

All through the winter Handel continued to give concerts at regular intervals, the original six subscription concerts being followed by six others. His repertory, besides *L'Allegro*, included *Alexander's Feast*, the *St. Cecilia Ode*, *Esther*, and *Hymen*, the latter a revised version of the opera *Imeneo*, described as a "new serenata." The Lord Lieutenant left for London on the 16th of February, but Handel was now firmly established in the good graces of Dublin society, and needed no court patronage to ensure the acceptance of his works.

On the 27th of March 1742 the following notice appeared in *Faulkner's Journal*: "For Relief of the Prisoners in the several Gaols, and for the Support of Mercer's Hospital in Stephen's Street, and of the Charitable Infirmary on the Inn's Quay, on Monday the 12th of April will be performed at the Musick Hall in

---

[1] *Alessandro in Persia*, a pasticcio, produced October 31. The opera season at the King's Theatre was now managed by the Earl of Middlesex, with Galuppi as musical director.

[2] By Galuppi.

Fishamble Street, Mr. Handel's new Grand Oratorio, called *The Messiah*, in which the Gentlemen of the Choirs of both Cathedrals will assist, with some Concertos on the Organ, by Mr. Handell. Tickets to be had at the Musick Hall, and at Mr. Neal's in Christ Church-yard at half a Guinea each. *N.B.*—No person will be admitted to the Rehearsal without a Rehearsal ticket, which will be given gratis with the Ticket for the Performance when payed for."

The rehearsal duly took place on the 8th, and was thus recorded by *Faulkner's Journal*:—

"Yesterday Mr. Handel's new Grand Sacred Oratorio, called *The Messiah*, was rehearsed at the Musick Hall in Fishamble Street to a most Grand, Polite, and Crowded Audience; and was performed so well, that it gave universal Satisfaction to all present; and was allowed by the greatest Judges to be the finest Composition of Musick that ever was heard, and the sacred Words as properly adapted for the occasion.

"*N.B.*—At the desire of several persons of Distinction, the above Performance is put off to Tuesday next. The doors will be opened at Eleven, and the Performance begin at Twelve. Many Ladies and Gentlemen who are well-wishers to this Noble and Grand Charity, for which this Oratorio was composed, request it as a favour, that the Ladies who honour this performance with their Presence, would be pleased to come without Hoops, as it will greatly encrease the Charity, by making Room for more company."

A further advertisement published on the morning of the performance entreated gentlemen to come without their swords for the same reason.

On Tuesday, the 13th of April 1742, the first perform-ance of *The Messiah* took place. On the ensuing Saturday the following report appeared in *Faulkner's Journal*:—

" On Tuesday last Mr. Handel's Sacred Grand Oratorio, *The Messiah,* was performed in the New Musick Hall in Fishamble Street ; the best Judges allowed it to be the most finished piece of Musick. Words are wanting to express the exquisite Delight it afforded to the admiring crowded Audience. The Sublime, the Grand, and the Tender, adapted to the most elevated, majestick and moving Words, conspired to transport and charm the ravished Heart and Ear. It is but Justice to Mr. Handel that the World should know he generously gave the Money arising from this Grand Performance, to be equally shared by the Society for relieving Prisoners, the Charitable Infirmary, and Mercer's Hospital, for which they will ever gratefully remember his Name ; and that the Gentlemen of the two Choirs, Mr. Dubourg, Mrs. Avolio and Mrs. Cibber, who all performed their Parts to Admiration, acted also on the same disinterested Principle, satisfied with the deserved Applause of the Publick, and the conscious Pleasure of promoting such useful and extensive Charity. There were above 700 People in the Room, and the Sum collected for that Noble and Pious Charity amounted to about £400, out of which £127 goes to each of the three great and pious Charities."

The only other contemporary account of the first performance of *The Messiah* with which I am acquainted was furnished to Burney by an Irish doctor named Quin, who was living in Dublin during Handel's visit. Of Handel he wrote :—

" He was received in that kingdom by people of the first distinction with all possible marks of esteem as a man, and admiration as a performer and composer of the highest order. *The Messiah,* I am thoroughly convinced, was performed in Dublin for the first time, and with the greatest applause.[1] Mrs. Cibber and Signora Avolio were the principal performers. These, with the assistance of the choristers of St. Patrick's Cathedral and Christ Church, formed the vocal band ; and Dubourg, with several good instrumental performers, composed a very respectable orchestra. There were many noble families here, with whom Mr. Handel lived in the utmost degree of friendship and familiarity. Mrs. Vernon, a German lady who came over with King George I, was particularly intimate with him, and at her house I had the pleasure of seeing and conversing with Mr. Handel, who, with his other excellences, was possessed of a great stock of humour ; no man ever told a story with more. But it was requisite for the hearer to have a competent knowledge of at least four languages, English, French, Italian and German, for in his narratives he made use of them all."

In spite of these records some uncertainty still exists as to the singers who took part in the first performance of *The Messiah,* and the mystery has by no means been dispelled by the discovery in 1891 of the only known copy of the original word-book of the oratorio, with the names of the singers written in pencil by the side of the songs that they sang. One interesting point, at any rate, is made clear by this document—the identity of the male soloists, whom Dr. Quin declares to have been taken from the choirs of the two cathedrals. They were James Baily (tenor), William Lambe and Joseph Ward (altos), John Hill and John Mason (basses). The first four belonged to the choirs of both cathedrals, but Mason was a Vicar Choral of Christ Church alone.

---

[1] In Burney's time there was some uncertainty, now completely dispelled, as to whether *The Messiah* had not been performed in London during the previous year.

With regard to the female soloists, the word-book raises
difficulties rather than settles them. Dr. Quin and
Faulkner's Journal agree in saying that Signora Avolio
and Mrs. Cibber took part in the performance, but in the
word-book not only is there no mention of Signora Avolio,
but against several of the soprano numbers the name
"McLean" is pencilled, referring presumably to the wife
of Maclaine the organist, who is known to have accompanied her husband to Ireland. It is true that "McLean"
does not seem to have sung all the soprano solos. Her
name is only written against the recitatives "There were
shepherds," "Thy rebuke hath broken His heart," and
the air, "I know that my Redeemer liveth," so that it is
possible that Signora Avolio may have sung "Rejoice
greatly," "Come unto Him,"[1] and "How beautiful are
the feet," against which no name is pencilled in the word-
book.

It is possible, of course, that the notes in this word-
book may refer to the second performance of *The Messiah*
on the 3rd of June, not to the first at all, and this theory is
supported by the fact that the printer seems accidentally
to have omitted the recitative, "Unto which of the
angels," and a slip of paper containing the words of the
omitted number and of the following chorus has been
pasted into its right place. No record of this performance

---

[1] We already knew from the Dublin MS. that at the first performance of *The
Messiah* the air "He shall feed his flock" was, as is now customary, divided
between the contralto and the soprano, not, as in the autograph, given to the
soprano alone. This is confirmed by the word-book, in which Mrs. Cibber's
name is written against the opening words of the song. Mrs. Cibber also
sang "If God be for us," presumably in a transposed edition, and "He was
despised." With reference to her singing of the latter air there is a tradition
that Dr. Delany, who was present at the first performance, was so much
affected that he cried aloud : "Woman, for this thy sins be forgiven thee."

has survived, and it is legitimate therefore to suppose that at the first performance Signora Avolio found her part too heavy, and at the second arranged to share the soprano solos with Mrs. Maclaine. But the evidence of the word-book must not be taken too seriously. The pencil notes were doubtless hastily jotted down, and may very likely be inaccurate ; indeed the attribution of the tenor air, " Thou shalt break them," to the alto Lambe seems almost impossible.

The incidents of Handel's stay in Dublin after the production of *The Messiah* may be briefly summed up. *Saul* was performed on the 25th of May, and *The Messiah* repeated on the 3rd of June. This was the last of Handel's own performances, though he probably took part in Signora Avolio's benefit concert on the 16th of July, and in Mrs. Arne's concert on the 21st of July, at which a great deal of his music was performed.

It was doubtless at one or other of these entertainments that the incident occurred which was mentioned by Burney as an instance of Handel's quickness of wit. "One night," he writes, "when Handel was in Dublin, Dubourg (a well-known violin player of that time) having a solo part in a song and a close [1] to make *ad libitum*, he wandered about in different keys a good while, and seemed indeed a little bewildered and uncertain of his original key ; but at length coming to the shake which was to terminate this long close, Handel to the great delight of the audience cried out loud enough to be heard in the most remote parts of the theatre, " You are welcome home, Mr. Dubourg." [2]

Handel left Dublin on the 13th of August and returned

[1] We should now call it a *cadenza*.
[2] Burney, *Commemoration*.

to London, whence on the 9th of September he addressed
the following letter to his friend Jennens :—

"DEAR S^r·—It was indeed your humble Servant
which intended you a Visit on my way from Ireland to
London, for I certainly would have given you a better
account by word of Mouth, as by writing, how well your
Messiah was received in that country, yet as a Noble
Lord and not less than the Bishop of Elphin[1] (a Nobleman very learned in Musick) has given his Observations
in writing on this Oratorio, I send you here annexed the
contents of it in his own words. I shall send the printed
Book of *The Messiah* to Mr. J. Steel for you.

"As for my success in general in that generous and
polite Nation, I reserve the account of it till I have the
honour to see you in London. The report that the
Direction of the Opera next winter is committed to my
care, is groundless. The gentlemen who have undertaken
to meddle with Harmony cannot agree, and are quite in a
confusion. Whether I shall do something in the Oratorio
way (as several of my friends desire) I cannot determine
as yet. Certain it is, that this time 12-month I shall
continue my Oratorios in Ireland, where they are going to
make a large subscription already for that purpose.

"If I had known that my Lord Guernsey[2] was so near
when I passed Coventry, you may easily imagine, Sir,
that I should not have neglected of paying my Respects
to him, since you know the particular Esteem I have for

---

[1] Edward Synge, a prelate who enjoyed the probably unique advantage of
being the son of an archbishop, and the grandson, great-nephew, and brother
of bishops.

[2] Afterwards the Earl of Aylesford, a relative of Jennens, to whom he
bequeathed his books and pictures.

his Lordship.   I think it a very long time to the month
of November next, when I can have some hopes of seeing
you here in Town.   Pray let me hear meanwhile of your
Health and Welfare, of which I take a real share, being
with an uncommon Sincerity and Respect, S^r, your most
obliged humble servant,

"GEORGE FRIDERIC HANDEL"

In spite of his promise, Handel never revisited Ireland.
How it happened that what seems to have been a settled
arrangement was thrown over is not known.   Possibly the
subscription was not after all taken up with the enthusiasm
that was expected, or he may have thought that the
future looked more promising in London.   At any rate
his Irish visit remains a unique episode in his career, a
moment of brilliant sunshine in the midst of gathering
clouds and threatening storms, on which he must have
often looked back with vain regret in the troublous times
that were soon to come.

CHAPTER XII

THE SECOND BANKRUPTCY, 1742-1745

WHEN Handel returned to London he found his position materially improved. His triumphs abroad had won him consideration at home. His flight to Ireland had been sung by no less celebrated a bard than Pope. Pope knew little and cared less about music, but he was under no illusions as to his ignorance, and was content to accept the opinion of an expert. He asked his friend Arbuthnot what was Handel's real value as a musician. "Conceive the highest that you can of his ability," replied the doctor, "and they are much beyond anything that you can conceive." Pope laid the words to heart, and a scathing passage in the *Dunciad* pilloried Handel's enemies for all time. The genius of Italian opera, "by singing Peers upheld on either hand," is pleading her cause before the throne of Dulness :—

> " 'But soon, ah soon, Rebellion will commence
> If Music meanly borrows aid from sense.
> Strong in new arms, lo ! Giant Handel stands
> Like bold Briareus with a hundred hands ;[1]
> To stir, to rouse, to shake the soul he comes,
> And Jove's own Thunders follow Mars's Drums.
> Arrest him, Empress, or you sleep no more——'
> She heard, and drove him to the Hibernian shore."

[1] A note of Pope's own explains the pun in this passage, which has sometimes been misinterpreted. "Mr. Handel," he says, "had introduced

Handel came back with a new oratorio, *Samson*, in his pocket, which he had written, all save the concluding air and chorus, immediately after *The Messiah* in September and October 1741. In October 1742 he put the finishing touch to it, but it was not produced until the 17th of February 1743. The libretto was by Newburgh Hamilton, who, in his dedication to the Prince of Wales, makes an interesting reference to the odious persecution which Handel still had to endure from a certain set among the aristocracy: "As we have so great a genius amongst us, it is a pity that so many mean artifices have been lately used to blast all his endeavours, and in him ruin the art itself; but he has the satisfaction of being encouraged by all true lovers and real judges of musick; in a more especial manner by that illustrious person, whose high rank only serves to make his knowledge in all arts and sciences as conspicuous as his power and inclination to patronize them."

Samson was from the first one of the most popular of Handel's oratorios. Even Horace Walpole, who made fun of everything and everybody, had to own that it was a success.

A few days after the first performance he wrote:—

"Handel has set up an Oratorio against the Opera, and succeeds. He has hired all the goddesses from the farces, and the singers of 'Roast Beef' from between the acts at both theatres, with a man with one note in his voice, and a girl without ever an one, and so they sing and make brave hallelujahs, and the good company

a great number of hands and more variety of instruments into the orchestra, and employed even drums and cannons to make a fuller chorus; which proved so much too manly for the fine gentlemen of his age that he was obliged to remove his music into Ireland."

encore the recitative, if it happens to have any cadence
like what they call a tune."

Walpole's criticisms on Handel's singers were to a
certain extent justified. The girl without a note was
evidently Mrs. Cibber, whose voice Burney, one of her
great admirers, had to admit was "a mere thread," while
even so enthusiastic a Handelian as Mrs. Delany
confessed that Beard (the man with one note) had "no
voice at all." [1] Beard, however, was not only a first-rate
artist, but a man of real culture and refinement, besides
being totally without the vanity to which tenors are
usually supposed to have a prescriptive right. Miss
Hawkins says of him: "His lowly appreciation of
himself—only one of his many virtues!—was shown when
in hearing Harrison, at one of the grand commemorations
of Handel, then in fine voice sing 'Oft on a plat,' he said
to my father, who happened to sit next to him, 'I never
sang it half so well.'" [2] His marriage to Lady Henrietta
Herbert a few years before had been a nine days' wonder
in the fashionable world. Lady Mary Wortley Montagu
wrote wickedly about it to a friend: "Lady Harriet
Herbert furnished the tea-tables here with fresh tattle for
the last fortnight. I was one of the first who was informed of her adventure by Lady Gage, who was told that
morning by a priest, that she had desired him to marry
her the next day to Beard, who sings in the farces at
Drury Lane. He refused her that good office, and
immediately told Lady Gage, who (having been unfortunate in her friends) was frightened at this affair, and
asked my advice. I told her honestly, that since the
lady was capable of such amours, I did not doubt if this
was broke off she would bestow her person and fortune

[1] *Correspondence*, ii. 271.　　　[2] *Anecdotes*, 1822.

on some hackney-coachman or chairman; and that I really saw no method of saving her from ruin, and her family from dishonour but by poisoning her; and offered to be at the expense of the arsenic, and even to administer it with my own hands, if she would invite her to drink tea with her that evening. But on her not approving that method, she sent to Lady Montacute, Mrs. Durich, and all the relations within reach of messengers. They carried Lady Harriet to Twickenham, though I told them it was a bad air for girls.[1] She is since returned to London, and some people believe her married; others, that she is too much intimidated by Mr. Waldegrave's threat to dare to go through this ceremony; but the secret is now public, and in what manner it will conclude I know not. Her relations have certainly no reason to be amazed at her constitution, but are violently surprised at the mixture of devotion that forces her to have recourse to the church in her necessities, which had not been the road taken by the matrons of her family." Lady Henrietta, in spite of the objurgations of her family, lived happily with Beard until 1753. After her death he married a daughter of Rich, the famous Harlequin and theatrical manager.

Meanwhile, *Samson* pursued its successful career. "The Oratorios thrive abundantly," wrote Horace Walpole; "for my part they give me an idea of Heaven, where everybody is to sing, whether they have voices or not." Miss Catherine Talbot, the adopted daughter of Dr. Secker, Archbishop of Canterbury, and one of the famous "Blue Stocking" gang, took it much more seriously. "I heard *Samson* in one of the College Halls," she wrote from Oxford to her friend Elizabeth Carter,

---

[1] Because Pope, her quondam admirer and inveterate enemy, lived there.

"and I believe to the full as finely as it ever was in town. I really cannot help thinking this kind of entertainment must necessarily have some effect in correcting the levity of the age; and let an audience be ever so thoughtless, they can scarcely come away, I should think, without being the better for an evening so spent." [1]

Samson was followed in due course by *The Messiah*, the first London performance of which took place on the 23rd of March 1743. It was then and for some years afterwards described merely as "a sacred oratorio," doubtless because Handel's enemies, who lost no chance of doing him a bad turn, would have raised hypocritical protests against the blasphemy of allowing the name of Messiah to appear on a playbill. No notice of *The Messiah* appeared in any London paper, but an anecdote relating to the first performance has survived in the correspondence of Dr. Beattie. "When Handel's *Messiah* was first performed," he says, "the audience was exceedingly struck and affected by the music in general, but when the chorus struck up 'For the Lord God Omnipotent' in the Alleluia, they were so transported that they all together, with the King (who happened to be present), started up and remained standing till the chorus ended. This anecdote I had from Lord Kinnoull." *The Messiah* does not at first seem to have pleased the taste of London musicians. "Partly," according to Lord Shaftesbury, "from the scruples some persons [2] had entertained against carrying on such a performance in a Play-House, and partly for not entering into the genius

---

[1] *Carter Correspondence*, 1808, vol. i. p. 29.

[2] Miss Catherine Talbot was one of these. Writing to her friend Mrs. Carter of a performance of *The Messiah*, she said: "To be sure the play-house is an unfit place for such a solemn performance."

12

of the composition, this capital composition was but indifferently relished." It was given only thrice during the season of 1743, while *Samson* was given eight times. Even Jennens, who ought to have known better, chose to find fault with it. " I shall shew you," he wrote to a friend, "a collection I gave Handel, call'd *Messiah*, which I value highly. He has made a fine entertainment of it, though not near so good as he might and ought to have done. I have with great difficulty made him correct some of the grossest faults in the composition, but he retained his overture obstinately, in which there are some passages far unworthy of Handel, but much more unworthy of *The Messiah*." Whatever the cause may have been, *The Messiah* was certainly slow in finding its way to popularity. During its first London season it was only given three times, as we have seen. In 1744 it was not performed at all, and only twice in 1745. After that it seems to have lain upon the shelf until 1749.

But England summoned Handel once more from his oratorios to celebrate her triumphs in the field. The war of " Jenkins's ear " had dragged on for some years without producing any incident that touched popular imagination. Englishmen hardly troubled to follow the devious mazes of foreign politics, and many honest citizens would have found it difficult to explain how it came about that after going to war with Spain to avenge Jenkins we found ourselves protecting Maria Theresa against the united forces of France and Prussia. But the victory of Dettingen in June 1743 gave the country something tangible to boast about. The idea of an English king leading his forces in person against our traditional enemies, and inflicting a sound beating upon them, was one that nobody could resist. George II's unpopularity was forgotten, and he became for the moment the national hero. With all his faults, he undoubtedly had personal courage, and the picture of him alighting from his unruly horse, and trusting to his own stout little legs, "which," as he said, "he knew would not run away with him," appealed irresistibly to English sentiment. So a national thanksgiving for the victory of Dettingen was decreed, and Handel, in his capacity of "Composer of Music to the Chapel Royal," wrote a *Te Deum* and an Anthem for it, which were duly performed at the Chapel Royal on the 27th of November. Both works met with general approbation. A newspaper of the period spoke of them as "so truly masterly and sublime, as well as new in their kind, that they prove this great genius not only inexhaustible, but likewise still rising to a higher degree of perfection."[1]

Mrs. Delany, after attending a rehearsal of the *Te Deum*, wrote enthusiastically to her brother: "It is excessively fine; I was all raptures and so was your friend D[octor] D[elany], as you may imagine. Everybody says it is the finest of Handel's compositions. I am not well enough acquainted with it to pronounce that of it, but it is heavenly."

For the Lenten season of 1744 Handel had a pleasant surprise for his subscribers in the shape of a secular oratorio, *Semele*, a return to the manner of his early triumph, *Acis and Galatea*. Handel certainly did all that he could to conciliate lovers of every sort of music, but the opposition against him and his music was still stubborn and powerful. Mrs. Delany,[2] writing after the first performance of *Semele*, observes significantly: "There

---

[1] Quoted by *Faulkner's Journal*, 26th November 1743.
[2] Delany, *Correspondence*, vol. ii.

was no disturbance at the play-house," as though a chorus of cat-calls might reasonably be expected at the production of a new oratorio.

She goes on: "The Goths were not so very absurd as to declare in a public manner their disapprobation of such a composer." But "the Goths," though they had the grace to refrain from open manifestations of hostility, were none the less determined to ruin Handel, whose concerts they looked upon as threatening danger to their favourite amusement of Italian opera. Ten days later Mrs. Delany returns to the subject:—

"*Semele* has a strong party against it, viz., the fine ladies, the *petits maîtres* and ignoramus's. All the opera people are enraged at Handel, but Lady Cobham, Lady Westmoreland, and Lady Chesterfield never fail it." Another who never failed to put in an appearance at Handel's concerts was King George II, who remained faithful to his favourite composer when his oratorios were deserted by court and society.

A famous *mot* of Lord Chesterfield's relates to this period of Handel's career. "What, my Lord," said some one to him, as he was coming out of Covent Garden one evening in the middle of the performance; "are you dismissed? Is there not an oratorio?" "Yes," replied he, "they are now performing, but I thought it best to retire, lest I should disturb the King in his privacies." The Prince of Wales was also a good friend to Handel at this time. He had, as we have seen, accepted the dedication of *Samson*, and he had long since forgotten the old squabbles about Bononcini and Senesino. It is true that Mrs. Delany refers to a quarrel between Handel and the Prince early in 1744, but from what she says Handel appears to have treated the affair as a joke. Handel used to hold many of the rehearsals for his oratorios at Carlton House, where the Prince had been established since 1732, and inside the walls of the music-room he behaved like a veritable dictator. Burney, who knew Handel well in his later years, says that if the Prince and Princess were not up to time in coming to a rehearsal, Handel was apt to become violent, whereupon the Prince, who must have been good-nature itself, used to confess himself in the wrong, and add that it was a shame to have kept these good people, meaning the performers, so long from their pupils and other concerns. Handel at rehearsal must have been a decidedly awe-inspiring person. If a maid of honour or any other female attendant talked while the music was going on, she rendered herself liable to a dose of Handel's most vigorous vernacular. Then the Princess of Wales, with her accustomed mildness and benignity, would smooth things over by saying: "Hush, hush! Handel is in a passion." At the performances in the theatre he was more terrific still. He had a way of shouting "Chorus!" at the close of an air, which Burney describes as extremely formidable. He used to wear an enormous white wig—the sort of wig that Edward Fitz-Gerald described as "a fugue in itself"—which his friends regarded as a kind of weather-glass indicative of the rise and fall of his stormy temperament. When things went well it had a certain nod or vibration which manifested his satisfaction, but without this outward and visible sign the initiated gathered that the composer was ill pleased with the performance, and looked out for squalls accordingly.

Semele was followed on the 2nd of March 1744 by *Joseph and his Brethren*, a work now entirely neglected, the libretto of which was written by the Reverend James

Miller, who dedicated it to the Duke of Montagu, a proof,
let us hope, that that effervescent nobleman had given up
his taste for practical joking as middle age approached,
and had begun to take life more seriously.

Joseph seems to have been born under an unlucky star.
At the final rehearsals, according to Mrs. Delany, " Handel
was mightily out of humour about it, for Sullivan, who is
to sing Joseph, is a *block* with a very fine voice, and Beard
has *no voice at all*.   The part which Francesina is to have
(Joseph's wife) will not admit of much variety, but I hope
it will be well received." *Joseph* did not, unfortunately,
fulfil expectations, and the season closed in disappointment.   Handel devoted the following summer to the
composition of *Belshazzar*, the libretto of which was
furnished to him by his friend Jennens.   Jennen's muse
was a lady of invincible prolixity, and Handel's utmost
efforts could do little to stem the torrent of her eloquence.
Several of Handel's letters to Jennens of this period are
extant, dealing principally with the new oratorio.   " Your
most excellent oratorio has given me great delight in
setting it to musick," he writes at one time, "and still
engages me warmly.   It is indeed a noble piece, very
grand and uncommon.   It has furnished me with expressions, and has given me opportunity to some very particular ideas, besides so many great choruses."

A little later the burden of Jennens's verbosity weighs
upon him more heavily: " I think it a very fine and
sublime oratorio, only it is really too long; if I should
extend the music, it would last four hours and more.   I
retrenched already a great deal of musick, that I might
preserve the poetry as much as I could, yet still it may be
shortened." Jennens was obstinate as well as wordy,
and, like Mr. Puff in *The Critic*, he determined to print

every word of it. When, therefore, the word-book of the oratorio was published, Jennens's rich fancies appeared in all their pristine and unshorn luxuriance, but a sinister black line in the margin indicated the passages, amounting in all to some two hundred lines, which the composer had not found it convenient to use. No wonder that Jennens was Handel's severest critic, and bewailed the base uses to which his "fine entertainment" had been condemned.

The collapse of the opera, which since Handel had retired from management in 1741 had been carried on by Lord Middlesex, seemed to leave the field open, and Handel now gave up Covent Garden and returned to his old quarters in the Haymarket, where he started a new series of subscription concerts in November 1744, on a more ambitious scale than ever. But if he imagined that it was going to be all plain sailing for him, now that the rivalry of the opera had ceased, he was grievously mistaken. The failure of their favourite entertainment only made his enemies more rabid than ever. It is difficult to comprehend the virulence of the feeling against Handel that raged at this time in aristocratic circles. The old quarrel about Senesino can have had very little to do with it, since many of Handel's persecutors were hardly more than children in those early days. Nor can the quarrel have turned on the nature and quality of Handel's own music; for very few of the opposition could tell a crotchet from a quaver. The matter was purely personal. Handel was an incarnation of the spirit of revolt against the old system of patronage that had ruled the world of music for so long. Here was a man who, while every other musician in the land remained at an angle of forty-five degrees in the presence of his princely patrons,

resolutely stood upright, went his own way, and snapped
his fingers in their ducal faces. What was to be done
with him? They had made him a bankrupt once—and
he had paid his debts to the uttermost farthing. They
had hounded him almost into his grave—and here he was
as strong and hearty as ever. But this time they vowed
one and all that there should be an end of him. It was
time that he should be taught his place. Was a mere
musician, a man who ought by rights to be a liveried
flunkey in the servants' hall—as Haydn a few years later
actually was—to defy the bluest blood in England?
Perish the thought! So the chosen leaders of the English
aristocracy laid their heads together, and devised a regular
campaign against the insufferable upstart. Women, ever
to the front when good works are afoot, led the crusade.
A certain Lady Brown,[1] not otherwise known to history,
is damned to everlasting fame by Burney as having
" distinguished herself as a persevering enemy of Handel."
She and her friends carefully chose the evenings of his
oratorios for their balls and card-parties, violating what

[1] Lady Brown belonged to the Cecil family. Her husband, Sir Robert,
had at one time been Resident at Venice, where his wife acquired a taste for
Italian music. On their return to London she posed as a patroness of foreign
singers, and was one of the first London hostesses to give regular musical
parties. Horace Walpole, writing to Mann in 1743, mentions the Sunday
evening concerts that she was in the habit of giving, according to Burney,
"at the risk of her windows," for the London mob in those days was nothing
if not Sabbatarian. Her match-making propensities, and later in life her
avarice, seem to have been a continual source of amusement to the *jeunesse
dorée* of London.

Lady Brown is also mentioned in Martinelli's correspondence as a leading
London hostess. " Every evening," he writes, "we go to Mylady Brown's
conversazioni, where beauteous ladies and charming cavaliers assemble in
large numbers, and music and play and men of letters combine with a good
supper to make up a delightful evening's entertainment." (Martinelli, *Lettere
familiari.*)

was then considered the sanctity of Lent in their endeavour to crush their enemy.[1]   If the fascinations of
these brilliant assemblies failed they eked them out with
mumming-shows, such as that supplied by a miserable
wretch named Russel, whom, after he had served their
wanton purpose, they allowed to be thrown into prison for
the debts contracted in their service.   There he lay rotting
until his munificent patronesses subscribed the sum of five
pounds, by means of which he was admitted to Bedlam,
where soon afterwards he died, a raving maniac.[2]

Victory crowned their generous efforts.   Handel's
season dragged wearily and hopelessly through the
winter.   His concerts were sometimes postponed, sometimes omitted altogether.   In vain did he produce
Hercules on the 5th of January, and *Belshazzar* on the
27th of March 1745—the one incomparably the greatest
of his secular oratorios, the other a masterpiece entitled
to high rank among his sacred works.   Nothing would
avail.   His own friends gave but lukewarm support, and
the strain of the ceaseless struggle seriously affected his
health.   We have a mournful glimpse of him in a letter
of his old friend Lady Shaftesbury written to her cousin
James Harris[3] in March 1745: "My constancy to poor

---

[1] Hawkins, *History*.

[2] Smollett refers to this unfortunate wretch in his satire *Advice* :—

> "Again shall Handel raise his laurelled brow,
> Again shall harmony with rapture glow !
> The spells dissolve, the combination breaks,
> And rival Punch no more in terror squeaks.
> Lo, Russel falls a sacrifice to whim
> And starts amazed in Newgate from his dream,
> With trembling hands implores their promised aid
> And sees their favour like a vision fade."

[3] James Harris was the eldest of three brothers, all of them devoted to
music, and intimate friends of Handel.   James, the eldest, was the father of

Handel got the better of my indolence, and I went last Friday to *Alexander's Feast*, but it was such a melancholy pleasure as drew tears of sorrow to see the great though unhappy Handel, dejected wan and dark, sitting by, not playing on the harpsichord, and to think how his light had been spent by being overplied in music's cause. I was sorry, too, to find the audience so insipid and tasteless (I may add unkind) not to give the poor man the comfort of applause; but affectation and conceit cannot discern or attend to merit."[1] Miss Catherine Talbot

the first Lord Malmesbury. He was nicknamed "Hermes" Harris after a philosophical work of that title which made some stir at the time. Dr. Johnson disliked him and called him "a prig, and a bad prig," but no one else had a word to say against him. He lived at Salisbury, where, according to a recent article by the present Lord Malmesbury (*The Ancestor*, vol. i.), Handel was a constant and welcome visitor to the family mansion of the Harrises, and often took part in amateur concerts. Harris was a practical musician, and did much for the cause of music in Salisbury and its neighbourhood. His son wrote of him: "The superior taste and skill which he possessed in music, and his extreme fondness for hearing it, led him to attend to its cultivation in his native place with uncommon pains and success; insomuch that, under his auspices, not only the Annual Musical Festival in Salisbury flourished beyond most institutions of the kind, but even the ordinary subscription concerts were carried on by his assistance and directions, with a spirit and effect seldom equalled out of the Metropolis." An extremely interesting set of the rare word-books of these concerts has recently been placed at my disposal by my friend Mr. Randall Davies. It is worth noting that in a letter recently published (*Hist. MSS. Comm.*, Report xv. Appx. pt. 2.) Handel's librettist Morell mentions a performance of *Jephtha* given at Salisbury under James Harris's direction as having been the best he ever heard, and the word-books testify that the concerts were carried out in the most complete and elaborate manner. Thomas Harris, the second brother, was a master in Chancery. He witnessed Handel's will and three of the codicils appended to it. Under a fourth and last codicil he received a bequest of £300. William, the third brother, was the parson of the family. He was chaplain to the Bishop of Durham, and rector of Egglescliffe in that see.

[1] *Malmesbury Papers*, vol. i. p. 2.

joined in deploring the decadence of fashionable taste. No one, she complained, seemed to care for anything but crowded assemblies. "Friendly visits and private parties are things gone out of the world; and Handel, once so crowded, plays to empty walls in that opera-house, where there used to be a constant *audience* as long as there were any dancers to be *seen.*" She did not profess to be a musician, but her criticism of *Belshazzar* is admirable. "Unfashionable that I am, I was, I own, highly delighted the other night at his last oratorio. 'Tis called *Belshazzar*, the story the taking of Babylon by Cyrus; and the music, in spite of all that very bad performers could do to spoil it, equal to anything I ever heard. There is a chorus of Babylonians deriding Cyrus from their walls, that has the best expression of scornful laughter imaginable. Another of the Jews, where the name Jehovah is introduced first with a moment's silence and then with a full swell of music, so solemn that I think it is the most striking lesson against common genteel swearing I ever met with."[1] Soon after this the end came. The season closed abruptly on the 23rd of April. Only sixteen of the promised twenty-four concerts had been given, but the performances did not cover their expenses, and Handel's own funds, the proceeds of his successful visit to Ireland, were exhausted. His health forbade further efforts, and once more he was declared a bankrupt.

Already in 1743, according to Hawkins, he had had a slight turn of that disorder which had driven him to Aix-la-Chapelle,[2] and the fact that he was unable to take his usual share in the performance of his oratorios proves

---

[1] *Correspondence of Mrs. E. Carter*, vol. i. p. 59.
[2] Hawkins, *History*, v. 358. Horace Walpole wrote in May 1743: "Handel has had a palsy, and can't compose."

plainly enough how ill he was. A few months' rest, however, and probably a visit to one of his favourite watering-places, Tunbridge Wells or Cheltenham, put him on his legs again. His indomitable spirit rose superior to every trial, and instead of giving up the struggle in despair he hired the Covent Garden theatre for the ensuing Lent.

In a letter from William Harris to his sister-in-law, dated 29th August 1745, we find the composer back in London: "I met Mr. Handel a few days since in the street, and stopped and put him in mind who I was, upon which it would have diverted you to have seen his antic motions. He seemed highly pleased and was full of inquiry after you and the Councillor [Thomas Harris]. I told him I was very confident that you expected a visit from him this summer. He talked much of his precarious state of health, yet he looks well enough. I believe you will have him with you ere long." [1] The health-giving breezes of Salisbury Downs and the motherly care of friendly Mrs. Harris doubtless combined to expedite Handel's return to health, and in October Lord Shaftesbury could report progress: "Poor Handel looks something better. I hope he will entirely recover in due time, though he has been a good deal disordered in the head." [2] Recover he did, and to such purpose that his apparent defeat at the hands of his malignant enemies was converted into a victory, the most brilliant and lasting of his career.

[1] *Malmesbury Papers*, vol. i. p. 3.   [2] *Ibid.* vol. i. p. 9.

CHAPTER XIII

THE TURN OF THE TIDE, 1745–1751

WHEN one fine August morning in the year 1745 the news reached London that Prince Charles Edward Stuart had landed in Scotland, everybody laughed incredulously. People had almost forgotten about the Jacobites. They seemed to belong to the dim past of childhood, and to be the stock-in-trade of the elderly bores who babbled about the 'fifteen and the times of good Queen Anne. But the days passed by, and the news was confirmed. The Pretender unfurled his standard at Glenfinnan, and the clans gathered round him. London's incredulity changed to annoyance. The Scottish rising was a ridiculous piece of impertinence—why did not some one go out and put a stop to it? Thereupon Sir John Cope did go, but it needed more than his blundering and bewildered efforts to check the rebellion. Prince Charlie easily eluded him among the fastnesses of the Grampians, and was at the gates of Perth while Cope was marching upon Inverness. However, London still preserved its superior attitude, and when the ministers proposed any preventive plans to the King, he merely replied, " Pho! don't talk to me of that stuff." Then came the Prince's triumphal entry into Edinburgh, and the crushing defeat of Cope at Prestonpans. London began to get nervous. Horace Walpole admitted in a letter to Horace Mann that the defeat had frightened everybody, though the King still pooh-poohed the whole business. When the rebels crossed the border, fear changed to consternation. Horace Walpole called it an ugly business, and prided himself upon not despairing. Then followed the siege and capture of Carlisle, and the march south to Derby. With the Highlanders almost at their doors the citizens of London made up their minds for the worst. Shops were shut, and all business was suspended. There was a run on the Bank, and the Guards were marched out to Finchley. " It is beyond the power of words," wrote William Harris to his sister-in-law, " to describe to you the hurry both court and city were in."[1] All over the country the terror was the same. At King's Lynn they talked seriously of cutting down their bridges to keep out the rebels, and beaching ships to prevent the French from entering the harbour.[2] But the alarm was needless. In a few days came the news of the rebels' retreat. London breathed a vast sigh of relief, and resumed the ordinary avocations of life. But while it lasted the alarm had been a real one, and the sense of having had a narrow escape was so strong in men's minds that it occurred to Handel to write an *Occasional Oratorio* celebrating the general delight at the country's escape from what seemed at the time a grave peril. The *Occasional Oratorio* was somewhat hastily put together, and Handel made free use in it of several of his earlier works, notably of *Israel in Egypt*, but it is hardly fair to call it a pasticcio, as many of Handel's biographers have done, since it contains no fewer than thirty-one

[1] *Malmesbury Papers*, vol. i. p. 21.
[2] Edmund Pyle, *Memoirs of a Royal Chaplain*, p. 113.

original numbers. It was performed for the first time on the 14th of February 1746, and was twice repeated, the performances being specially designed, according to Handel's advertisement, " to make good to the subscribers that favoured him last season the number of performances he was not then able to complete."

It has been suggested by some of Handel's biographers, notably by Schoelcher and Rockstro, that the word " Occasional " refers to this tardy fulfilment of Handel's obligations, and that the work has nothing to do with the rebellion. It is true that it was produced before the battle of Culloden finally shattered Charles Edward's hopes, but the following letter, written by William Harris to his sister-in-law on the 8th of February 1746, shows that the work was none the less regarded by Handel's contemporaries as expressive of the general rejoicing: "Yesterday morning I was at Handel's house to hear the rehearsal of his new *Occasional Oratorio*. It is extremely worthy of him, which you will allow to be saying all one can in praise of it.   He has but three voices for his songs—Francesina, Reinholt, and Beard ; his band of music is not very extraordinary.   Du Feche [1] is his first fiddle, and for the rest I really could not find out who they were, and I doubt his failure will be in this article. The words of his oratorio are scriptural, but taken from various parts, and are expressive of the rebels' flight and our pursuit of them.   Had not the Duke carried his point triumphantly, this oratorio could not have been brought on." [2]

But the rebellion of 1745 was destined to give birth to a more famous work than the *Occasional Oratorio*. The victory of Culloden on the 16th of April 1746 finally

[1] William Defesch.   [2] *Malmesbury Papers,* vol. i. p. 33.

crushed the Jacobite cause, and raised the Duke of Cumberland to the rank of a national saviour. The horrors of the red reign of terror that followed Culloden were ignored or condoned, and when " Billy the Butcher " —as even his own soldiers and partisans called him— returned to London in July he was the hero of the hour.

A medal was struck in his honour, and the thanks of Parliament, together with a grant of twenty-five thousand pounds a year, were poured at his feet. The principal cities of England vied in offering him civic honours, and the poet Collins sang his sweetest numbers in the young warrior's praise. Handel lent his voice to the general acclamation, and celebrated the Duke's triumph in the martial strains of *Judas Maccabæus*, which was written in July and August 1746 to a libretto by Thomas Morell, and produced at Covent Garden on the 1st of April 1747, after repeated postponements on account of the trial of Lord Lovat, which occupied public attention to the exclusion of everything else. Morell was an amiable man and a good scholar. He furnished Handel with the librettos of several of his most famous oratorios. In a letter written after Handel's death, Morell has given some interesting details of the manner in which he and the composer worked together : " And now as to Oratorios :— There was a time (says Mr. Addison), when it was laid down as a maxim, that nothing was capable of being well set to Musick, that was not nonsense. And this I think, though it might be wrote before Oratorios were in fashion, supplies an Oratorio-writer (if he may be called a writer) with some sort of apology ; especially if it be considered, what alterations he must submit to, if the composer be of an haughty disposition, and has but an imperfect

acquaintance with the English language.[1] As to myself,
great lover as I am of music, I should never have
thought of such an undertaking (in which, for the reasons
above, little or no credit is to be gained) had not Mr.
Handel applied to me when at Kew in 1746, and added
to his request the honour of a recommendation from
Prince Frederick. Upon this I thought I could do as
well as some who had gone before me, and within two or
three days carried him the first act of *Judas Maccabæus*,
which he approved of. 'Woll,' says he, 'and how are
you to go on?' 'Why, we are to suppose an engagement, and that the Israelites have conquered, and so
begin with a chorus as " Fallen is the foe," or something
like it.' 'No, I will have this,' and began working it,
as it is, upon the harpischord. 'Well, go on.' 'I will
bring you more to-morrow.' 'No, something now.'
'So fall thy foes, O Lord——' 'That will do,' and
immediately carried on the composition as we have it
in that most admirable chorus. That incomparable air,
'Wise men, flattering, may deceive us' (which was the
last he composed,[2] as ' Sion now his head shall raise ' was
his last chorus) was designed for *Belshazzar*, but that not
being performed, he happily flung it into *Judas Maccabæus*.
N.B.—The plan of *Judas Maccabæus* was designed as a
compliment to the Duke of Cumberland, upon his returning victorious from Scotland. I had introduced several
incidents more apropos, but it was thought they would
make it too long, and they were therefore omitted. The
Duke, however, made me a handsome present by the
hands of Mr. Poyntz. The success of the oratorio was

---

[1] Obviously a reference to Handel.

[2] This is a mistake. " Wise men, flattering " is an adaptation of the song
" Se vuoi pace," in *Agrippina*.

very great, and I have often wished that at first I had
asked in jest for the benefit of the 30th night instead of
a 3d.   I am sure he would have given it to me ; on which
night there was above £400 in the house.   He left me a
legacy, however, of £200."[1]   *Judas Maccabæus* marks a
very important point in the history of Handel's career.
Its production was the turn of the tide of his fortunes.
During the season of 1747 Handel abandoned the system
of subscription performances, and threw his theatre open
to all comers.   This change of policy brought its own
reward.   Finding that his aristocratic patrons had failed
him, Handel turned to the great middle class, who became
his ardent supporters and brought him new fame and
fortune.

Fielding's *Amelia* gives a typical description of a
visit to the oratorio about this time.   Amelia and her
friend start early so as to be in time to get a place in
the front row of the gallery.   Though they arrived "full
two hours before they saw the back of Mr. Handel," they
had plenty to amuse them.   A gentleman arrived on the
scene, who was at once smitten with Amelia's charms.
" He procured her a book and wax candle, and held the
candle for her himself during the whole entertainment."
Evidently there was not much luxury about oratorio-going
in those days, but it was the Amelias of the day and
their friends and relations who were the chief instruments
of Handel's ultimate triumph.[2]   Soon it became as much
the fashion to admire Handel as a few years before
it had been to decry him.   Lady Luxborough's steward,
who paid a visit to London in the spring of 1748, was
nothing if not up to date.   " He went," writes his mistress,

---

[1] *Historical MSS. Commission*, Report xv. Appendix, pt. 2.
[2] Fielding, *Amelia*, Bk. iv. ch. vii.

"to the oratorio of *Judas Maccabæus*, where he was highly entertained, and he speaks with such ecstasy of the music, as I confess I cannot conceive any one can feel who understands no more of music than myself, which I take to be his case. But I suppose he sets his judgment true to that of the multitude, for if his ear is not nice enough to distinguish the harmony, it serves to hear what the multitude say of it."[1]

Handel was not the only composer who tuned his lyre to celebrate the victor of Culloden. Gluck, who was then in London, wrote an opera called *La Caduta dei Giganti* in praise of the Duke of Cumberland. It was produced in 1747, but does not appear to have been much appreciated, indeed its failure is said to have had something to do with turning Gluck's thoughts in the direction of operatic reform. Handel thought very poorly of Gluck of whom he is said to have observed that he knew no more of counterpoint than his cook ; which very likely was hardly an exaggeration, since Waltz, the cook in question, had developed into an excellent bass singer after leaving Handel's service, whereas Gluck's operas were at that time very slight and trivial specimens of the fashionable manner of the day. To Gluck himself, however, Handel seems to have been more polite. Gluck called on him with the score of *La Caduta dei Giganti* under his arm, and took counsel with him as to the reasons of its failure. "You have taken far too much trouble over your opera," said Handel, whose operatic experiences seem not unnaturally to have left him rather cynical on the subject of aristocratic taste. "Here in England that is mere waste of time. What the English like is something that they can beat time to, something that hits them straight

[1] *Letters written by Lady Luxborough to William Shenstone*, 1775, p. 20.

on the drum of the ear."[1] Gluck had no opportunity of profiting by Handel's advice, as he left London soon afterwards never to return, but his gratitude to and admiration for the great man never failed. Forty years later, Michael Kelly, who sang in his *Iphigenia in Tauris* in Vienna, had a proof of this which he relates in his reminiscences: "One morning, after I had been singing with him, he said, 'Follow me upstairs, Sir, and I will introduce you to one whom all my life I have made my study and endeavoured to imitate.' I followed him into his bedroom, and opposite to the head of the bed saw a full-length picture of Handel in a rich frame. 'There, Sir,' said he, 'is the portrait of the inspired master of our art. When I open my eyes in the morning I look upon him with reverential awe and acknowledge him as such, and the highest praise is due to your country for having distinguished and cherished his gigantic genius.'"[2]

Apropos of *Judas*, Burney gives an amusing account of an encounter with Handel at the house of Signora Frasi, the famous singer: "At Frasi's, I remember, in the year 1748 he brought in his pocket the duet of *Judas Maccabæus*, 'From these dread scenes,' in which she had not sung when that oratorio was first performed in 1747. At the time he sat down at the harpsichord to give her and me the time of it, while he sung her part I hummed at sight the second over his shoulder, in which he encouraged me by desiring that I would sing out. But unfortunately something went wrong, and Handel with his usual impetuosity grew violent—a circumstance very terrific to a young musician. At length, however, recovering from my fright, I ventured to say that I fancied there was a

[1] Schmid, *C. W. von Gluck*, p. 29.
[2] Kelly, *Reminiscences*, vol. i. p. 255.

mistake in the writing, which upon examining Handel discovered to be the case; and then instantly, with the greatest good humour and humility said: 'I beg your pardon—I am a very odd dog. Master Schmidt is to blame.'"

Frasi was rather a favourite of Handel's. She had a beautiful voice, but was no musician, and incorrigibly lazy. One day she informed him that she was going to learn thorough-bass, in order to be able to accompany herself. "Oh," said Handel, "what may we not expect!"[1]

Judas Maccabæus gave some colour to the accusations which had been levelled against Handel in the days of *Saul* of loving noise for its own sake, at least if we may believe Miss Elizabeth Carter, who wrote to a friend soon after the production of the work: "In his last oratorio he has literally introduced guns, and they have a good effect."[2] Sheridan, it will be remembered, had a hit at the supposed noisiness of Handel's music in his burletta *Jupiter*, an early sketch for *The Critic*, in which the author whose play is being rehearsed directs that a pistol shall be fired behind the scenes, observing: "This hint I took from Handel."

Not a little of the success of *Judas Maccabæus* was due to the Jews of London, who hastened to patronise a work in which the glory of their national hero was extolled with so much spirit and eloquence. Their numbers were not very imposing, for there can hardly have been more than 7000 Jews in all England at that time,[3] but they were for the most part men of substance, and Handel, realising that he had tapped a new fount of profit, bade his trusty Morell draw the subject of his next

[1] Burney, *Commemoration*.   [2] *Carter Correspondence*, i. 134.
[3] Hertz, *British Imperialism in the Eighteenth Century*, p. 63.

oratorio from the same Hebrew source. Morell obeyed with alacrity: "The next year," his record continues, "he desired another, and I gave him *Alexander Balus*, which follows the history of the foregoing in the Maccabees. In the first part there is a very pleasing air, accompanied with the harp, 'Hark, hark, he strikes the golden lyre!' in the second two charming duets, 'O what pleasure past expressing,' and 'Hail, wedded love, mysterious law.' The third begins with an incomparable air in the affetuoso style, intermixed with the chorus recitative that follows it. And as to the last air I cannot help telling you that when Mr. Handel first read it he cried out, 'Damn your iambics!' 'Don't put yourself in a passion, they are easily trochees.' 'Trochees, what are trochees?' 'Why, the very reverse of iambics, by leaving out a syllable in every line, as instead of "Convey me to some peaceful shore," "Lead me to some peaceful shore."' 'That is what I want.' 'I will step into the parlour and alter them immediately.' I went down and returned with them altered in about three minutes, when he would have them as they were, and had set them most delightfully, accompanied with only a quaver and a rest of three quavers."

Alexander Balus was written in June and July 1747, and produced on the 9th of March 1748. In spite of its subject it was never one of the more popular of Handel's oratorios, and was eclipsed in general favour by its immediate successor, *Joshua*, which was written in July and August 1747, and produced on the 23rd of March 1748.

In *Joshua* occurs the famous "See the conquering hero comes," afterwards transferred to *Judas Maccabæus*, with regard to which Miss Hawkins tells a characteristic story.

Soon after it was completed, Handel played it to Sir John Hawkins, and asked him how he liked it. "Not so well as some things I have heard of yours," was the reply. "Nor I neither," rejoined Handel; "but, young man, you will live to see it a greater favourite with the people than my other fine things."[1]

There is another story about *Joshua* told by Shield: "Travelling from London to Taplow with the father of modern harmony (Haydn), and having, the preceding evening, observed his countenance expressing rapturous astonishment during the Concert of Antient Music, I embraced the favourable opportunity of inquiring how he estimated the chorus in *Joshua*, 'The nations tremble.' The reply was, he had long been acquainted with music, but never knew half its powers before he heard it, and he was perfectly certain that only one inspired author ever did or ever would pen so sublime a composition."[2]

Joshua was followed in due course by *Susanna*, which was produced on the 10th of February 1749, and by *Solomon*, produced on the 17th of March 1749. The author of *Susanna* is not known. The libretto of *Solomon* has been attributed to Morell, but there is no authority for the ascription, and as Morell says nothing about it in his letter on Handel and his oratorios which has already been quoted, the probability is that he had nothing to do with it. By this time the tide had definitely turned in favour of Handel. Lady Shaftesbury, who was present at the first performance of *Susanna*, wrote: "I think I never saw a fuller house. Rich told me that he believed he would receive near £400." She did not, however, care much about *Susanna* herself: "I believe it will not insinuate itself so much into my approbation as most of

[1] *Anecdotes*, 1822.   [2] Shield, *Introduction to Harmony*.

Handel's performances do, as it is in the light operatic style."[1] But others seem to have regarded it more favourably. It was performed four times during the season, *Solomon* thrice, *Samson* and *The Messiah* each four times, and *Hercules* twice. During the oratorio season of 1749 occurred the public rejoicings for the Peace of Aix-la-Chapelle, which had been signed in October 1748. The Peace was a patched-up sort of business, and whoever profited by it, England certainly did not. But every one was tired of the war, and the news of peace was received with real enthusiasm in this country at any rate. Consequently the celebrations were carried out on a grand scale. The great feature of the festivity was to be a display of fireworks, for which a "machine," as it was called, representing a Doric temple, 114 feet in height and 410 feet long, was designed by the Chevalier Servandoni,[2] and erected in the Green Park. Handel was commissioned to write music for the festivity, which was to precede and accompany the display of fireworks. The building in the Green Park, though begun in the previous November, was only finished on the day before the celebration. Meanwhile the general excitement was working itself up to fever-heat. Even so long beforehand as December 1748, Lady Jane Coke wrote that she was tired of hearing about the fireworks, which it was feared would damage the houses in St. James's Street and break the windows in the Queen's Library.[3] Fireworks were

---

[1] *Malmesbury Letters*, vol. i. p. 741.

[2] An architect and artist famous in his day, and much in demand at the various courts of Europe. He had a genius for stage management, and at the production of an opera at Stuttgart designed a triumphal procession in which more than four hundred horses are said to have taken part. His best known architectural work is the façade of St. Sulpice at Paris.

[3] *Letters of Lady Jane Coke to Mrs. Eyre*, p. 14.

a rarity in those days, and everybody who could possibly manage it was coming up to London to see the show. "For a week before," wrote Horace Walpole, "the town was like a country fair, the streets filled from morning to night, scaffolds building wherever you could or could not see, and coaches arriving from every corner of the kingdom. This hurry and lively scene, with the sight of the immense crowds in the Park and on every house, the guards, and the machine itself, which was very beautiful, was all that was worth seeing." Horace had little to say in praise of the fireworks themselves, and Handel's music he did not so much as mention. "The fireworks by no means answered the expense, the length of preparation, and the expectation that had been raised. The rockets and whatever was thrown up into the air succeeded mighty well; but the wheels and all that was to compose the principal part were pitiful and ill-conducted, with no changes of coloured fire and shapes. The illumination was mean, and lighted so slowly that scarce anybody had patience to wait the finishing; and then what contributed to the awkwardness of the whole, was the right pavilion catching fire and being burnt down in the middle of the show. The King, the Duke, and Princess Emily saw it from the Library,[1] with their courts; the Prince and Princess, with their children, from Lady Middlesex's, no place being provided for them, nor any invitation given to the Library."[2]

Handel's music, which consisted of an overture and five short movements, the latter intended to illustrate some of the "set pieces," was scored for fifty-six wind instruments, including a serpent, this being the only

[1] Built by Queen Caroline on ground now occupied by Stafford House.
[2] *Letter*, vol. ii.

occasion on which he ever wrote a part for that now forgotten instrument, though a note preserved among the Handel manuscripts in the Fitzwilliam Museum seems to imply that it was used in performances of *Samson* and *Solomon*. At that time the serpent was said to be a good deal used in French orchestras, though it was rarely to be met with in England and Germany. When Handel first heard it he is said to have asked, "What the devil be that?" He was told that it was an instrument called a serpent. "A serpent!" he replied; "Ay, but not the serpent that seduced Eve." Handel's music, which was ready long before Servandoni's pavilion, was publicly rehearsed at Vauxhall Gardens a week before the actual peace celebration. According to the *Gentleman's Magazine* the audience on that occasion reached the almost incredible total of twelve thousand persons. This being so it is not surprising to read in a description of the proceedings: "So great a resort occasioned such a stoppage on London Bridge, that no carriage could pass for three hours. The footmen were so numerous as to obstruct the passage, so that a scuffle ensued in which some gentlemen were wounded." At the fireworks themselves there were accidents as well. Horace Walpole says that two people were killed, and some excitement was caused by the arrest of Servandoni himself, who completely lost his head when his cherished pavilion caught fire, and drew his sword upon the Controller of the Ordnance. He was taken into custody, but was discharged the next day on asking pardon of the Duke of Cumberland.[1]

Handel's music survived the occasion for which it was composed. He gave a performance of it at the Foundling Hospital a month later, together with a selection from

[1] *Gentleman's Magazine.*

VAUXHALL GARDENS

Solomon and a new anthem, " Blessed are they that consider the poor," which was written for the occasion. The Prince and Princess of Wales were present, and the Hospital must have netted a handsome sum by the performance, for the tickets were half a guinea apiece, and the audience amounted to over a thousand. Handel was nothing if not charitable. Through the darkest days of his managership he never omitted his annual performance in aid of the fund established for the benefit of decayed musicians. It will be remembered, too, that *The Messiah* was first given for a charitable object. The Foundling Hospital benefited more than any other institution by Handel's generosity. He followed up his performance of the Fireworks Music in May 1749 by presenting the Hospital with a new organ, which he opened in person with a performance of *The Messiah* on the 1st of May 1750. From that time until his death Handel continued to give at least one performance annually of *The Messiah* in the Foundling Chapel, each one of which meant an addition of some £500 to the Hospital exchequer. In his will, too, he bequeathed a full score and a complete set of parts of his masterpiece to the Hospital, a gift which, according to the custom of the time, carried with it the right, though not the exclusive right, of performance. The Trustees of the Hospital seem in this case to have acted rather a grasping part. Knowing of the bequest which Handel had made in their favour, they determined to take time by the forelock, and to petition Parliament, during the lifetime of the composer, to accord to them the sole right of performing *The Messiah*. This was more than Handel could stand. " The Devil ! " he cried ; " For what shall the Foundlings put mine oratorio in the Parliament ? The Devil ! Mine Musick shall not go to the Parliament."

Meanwhile the oratorios went serenely on. Some were more successful than others, but on the whole Handel's affairs were in a more favourable condition than at any previous period of his career. The tide had turned at last, and he was on the high road to prosperity. His health was good, too, and in every way fortune seemed to smile upon him. Lord Shaftesbury, in a letter to a friend dated the 13th of February 1750, gives a pleasant glimpse of the composer: "I have seen Handel several times since I came hither, and think I never saw him so cool and well. He is quite easy in his behaviour, and has been pleasing himself in the purchase of several fine pictures, particularly a large Rembrandt, which is indeed excellent. We have scarce talked at all about musical subjects, though enough to find his performances will go off incomparably well."[1] Curiously enough, it was with nature rather than with man that Handel had now to contend. In the early part of the year 1750 London was visited by an epidemic of earthquakes. People were thoroughly frightened, and numbers went into the country. "They say they are not frightened," laughed Horace Walpole, "but that it is such fine weather, Lord, one can't help going into the country."[2] Mrs. Montagu noted the effect upon Handel's audiences: "I was not under any apprehensions about the earthquake, but went that night to the Oratorio, then quietly to bed, but the madness of the multitude was prodigious. Near fifty of the people I had sent to, to play at cards here the Saturday following, went out of town to avoid being swallowed, and I believe they made a third part of the number I asked, so that you may

---

[1] *Malmesbury Papers*, vol. i. p. 77.
[2] Walpole, *Letters*, vol. ii. p. 435.

imagine how universal the fright must be. The Wednesday night the Oratorio was very empty, though it was the most favourite performance of Handel's."[1]

Theodora, which had been composed in June and July 1749, was produced on the 16th of March 1750, at the height of the earthquake scare. It never recovered from its unlucky start, or won a tithe of the popularity accorded to *The Messiah*, *Samson*, or *Judas*. This was partly due, no doubt, to the libretto, which was far from being one of the amiable Morell's triumphs. "Handel himself," Morell wrote, "valued it more than any performance of the kind, and when I once asked him, whether he did not look upon the Grand Chorus in *The Messiah* as his Masterpiece? 'No,' says he, 'I think the chorus at the end of the second part in *Theodora* far beyond it, "He saw the lovely Youth." ' The second night of *Theodora* was very thin indeed, tho' the Princess Amelia was there. I guessed it a losing night, so did not go to Mr. Handel as usual; but seeing him smile, I ventured, when, 'Will you be there next Friday night,' says he, 'and I will play it to you?' I told him I had just seen Sir T. Hankey, and he desired me to tell you, that if you would have it again, he would engage for all the Boxes. 'He is a fool; the Jews will not come to it (as to *Judas*) because it is a Christian story; and the ladies will not come, because it is a virtuous one.'"[2]

Apropos of Handel's smile, which had so invigorating an effect upon Morell's nerves, Burney records a somewhat similar impression of the great man. "His general look," he says, "was somewhat heavy and sour, but when

---

[1] Climenson, *Elizabeth Montagu*, vol. i. p. 274.
[2] *Hist. MSS. Commission*, Report xv. Appendix, pt. 2.

he *did* smile, it was his sire the sun bursting out of a black cloud."[1] *Theodora*, however, was no smiling matter. The public would not have it at any price. Some of Handel's friends, according to Burney, would not even take tickets for it as a gift, though they begged the composer shortly afterwards to give them seats for *The Messiah*. This was too much for Handel. " Oh, your servant, meine Herren," he cried, "you are damnable dainty! You would not go to *Theodora*. There was room enough to dance there, when that was performed." At another time, however, he took a humorous view of the situation, and when some one observed that the house was half-empty, replied: " Never mind, the music will sound the better."[2]

On the 1st of May 1750 came the performance of *The Messiah* at the Foundling Hospital, to which reference has already been made. This was so successful that it had to be repeated on the 15th, many persons who had actually bought tickets for the first performance being unable to get into the chapel. In June and July 1750 Handel was engaged upon a "musical interlude" entitled *The Choice of Hercules*. In the composition of the work he utilised a good deal of the incidental music which he had written a few months previously for Smollett's play, *Alceste*. Rich had intended to mount *Alceste* at Covent Garden with an unusual degree of splendour. Servandoni had been commissioned to paint the scenery, and Handel seems to have offered to compose the music in liquidation of an outstanding debt. But for some reason or other *Alceste* never saw the light, and the play itself now seems to be irretrievably lost. Soon after finishing *The Choice of Hercules* on the

[1] Burney, Sketch in *Commemoration*.   [2] Burney, *Commemoration*.

5th of July, Handel went abroad for the last time. Whether he went for another "cure" to Aix-la-Chapelle, or paid a visit to his niece Johanna Friderica, now married and living at Halle, is not known; in fact the only record of the trip is the following paragraph, which appeared in the *General Advertiser* of the 21st of August 1750:—

"Mr. Handel, who went to Germany to visit his friends some time since, and between the Hague and Haarlem had the misfortune to be overturned, by which he was terribly hurt, is now out of danger."

Meanwhile an old friend of Handel's had been getting into serious trouble. Earlier in the year Francesca Cuzzoni, the heroine of the operatic squabbles of twenty years before, had appeared upon the scene of her former triumphs. She was middle-aged by this time, and had squandered all the money that she had made in her youth. Her voice too was a mere shadow of what it had once been. Since her last appearance in England her career had been singularly chequered. Her first achievement on returning to Italy had been to poison her husband Sandoni in Venice. She was tried for her life, but got off with a sentence of perpetual banishment from the Republic. For the next ten years she sang chiefly in Germany. We hear of her at Hamburg and again at Stuttgart, where her quarrels with Marianne Pirker, a rival soprano, recalled the days of the Faustina-Cuzzoni riots.[1] When she arrived in England Handel gave her an engagement for old acquaintance sake, and she sang in one of his performances of *The Messiah*. But her day was over, and she soon sank into difficulties. In August 1750 Horace Walpole wrote: "Another celebrated Polly has been arrested for £30, even the old

[1] Sittard, *Musik am Württembergischen Hofe*, Bd. ii.

Cuzzoni. The Prince of Wales bailed her—who will do as much for him?"[1] She left London for ever soon afterwards, and died a few years later in great poverty at Bologna.

Handel was back again in London by the end of the year, and in January 1751 began the composition of *Jephtha*. He worked at this until the 23rd of February, when ill-health compelled him to break off, and he did not resume his task until the month of June. This forced cessation of activity was doubtless caused by a return of the mental disorder which first drove him to the baths of Aix-la-Chapelle, aggravated in the present instance by symptoms of the blindness which was shortly to descend upon him. Indications of the approaching failure of his sight are plainly revealed by a glance at the autograph of *Jephtha*. His health, however, permitted him to take part in two performances of *The Messiah* given at the Foundling Hospital on the 18th of April and the 16th of May respectively, at the second of which, according to the *General Advertiser*, he played a voluntary on the organ, "which met with universal applause." Soon afterwards he paid a visit to Cheltenham and tried a course of the waters there, returning to London on the 13th of June, presumably restored to health. He resumed work on *Jephtha* a few days later, and finished it on the 30th of August. The oratorio was produced on the 26th of February 1752. With *Jephtha* Handel brought to a close the long series of his oratorios. During his remaining years his failing eyesight made composition a difficult business, and his energies were devoted chiefly to presiding at the performances of his oratorios.

[1] Walpole, *Letters*, vol. iii.

CHAPTER XIV

HANDEL'S BLINDNESS AND DEATH, 1751–1759

THE battle was won at last. The struggle had been long and severe, but Handel had come out a conqueror in the end. With everything against him he had won by sheer force of personality. What Pitt was doing in the world of politics, Handel had done in the world of art. Different as were the spheres in which they worked, "the Great Commoner" and the composer of *The Messiah* had much in common, and the cause for which they fought was practically the same. Both were poets in an age of prose, transcendentalists waging mortal conflict with the forces of materialism. The era of Walpole was the apotheosis of common sense. Under a veneer of courtliness and polish society was coarse, selfish and sceptical—sceptical of faith and enthusiasm, sceptical even of itself. "Every one laughs," said Montesquieu on his visit to England, "if one talks of religion." Morality was out of fashion, drunkenness and obscenity were thought no disgrace to the highest in the land. Every man, according to Walpole, had his price. The throne was occupied by a dynasty which it was impossible to respect, loyalty was a thing forgotten, patriotism an empty name. But the very commercialism of Walpole's rule was forming a race full of promise for the future.

14

Through the long years of peace and prosperity a middle class was being created which held the future in its hand. Inarticulate at first, it was only to learn its power by years of struggle and endeavour. Of this class Pitt was the spokesman. He had sprung from it, and he knew its value. "It is the people who have sent me here," he cried to the Cabinet that opposed his will. In the Parliament of that day he stood alone, the depth of his conviction, his fiery energy, his poetic imagination, his appeal to the higher instincts of mankind contrasting strangely with the mercenary opportunism of the world in which he moved. England rallied round the man whose hands were clean in an age of corruption, whose life was pure in the midst of debauchery, and who loved his country with a passionate reverence that struck a new note in an age of self-seeking and party faction.

Handel's appeal was based on similar grounds. The turning-point of his career was when in 1747 he threw aside his subscription and appealed to the public at large. The aristocracy had failed him and he turned to the middle class. There he found the audience that he had sought in vain in the pampered worldlings of the court. The splendid seriousness of Handel's music, its wide humanity, its exaltation of thought, its unfaltering dignity of utterance, had fallen on deaf ears so long as he appealed only to an aristocratic audience. It was in the heart and brain of the middle class that Handel found at last an echo to his clarion call. For fifty years he had piped in vain to princelings; he turned to the people and found at once the sympathy that he sought.

But neither Pitt nor Handel could have done what he did had not English thought and feeling been guided to higher levels by the genius of one of the greatest men produced by the eighteenth century—John Wesley. To him the vast if gradual change that came over society during the later years of Walpole's rule was mainly due. The religious struggles of the Civil War and the political struggles of the Revolution had left in the minds of the middle class one overpowering sentiment—a craving for peace. This craving, fostered by Walpole, who saw better than any one what England wanted, became the parent of our later commercial prosperity, but with regard to the higher claims of life it induced something very like lethargy. Of the attitude of society towards these higher claims during the first half of the century we have already spoken. Under the first two Georges the upper class was frankly materialistic, the middle class apathetic, and the lower class not far removed from sheer brutalisation.

Doubtless beneath this lethargic exterior England was still religious, but the old Puritan spirit seemed asleep. It was the voice of Wesley that woke it to new life. The religious revival that he inaugurated is unparalleled in the history of the English people. It penetrated every part of the kingdom and every stratum of society. Its strength and importance lay in the fact that its results were not merely religious. Pitt's appeal was not religious, Handel's appeal was not religious, though his oratorios dealt for the most part with subjects technically termed sacred as opposed to secular. Both men appealed to the higher instincts of the nation from a wider standpoint, but without the influence of Wesley ever preaching the seriousness of life and the responsibility of the individual, they would have been but the voices of men crying in the wilderness. The audience that guffawed over the *Beggar's Opera* and the audience that rose to its feet to honour the sublime strains of *The Messiah* were one and the same, but

Wesley had breathed new life into dead souls, had opened blind eyes and unstopped deaf ears, had lifted England from its slough of sensual depravity and made it capable of understanding the noblest outpourings of human genius.

Meanwhile the threatening blindness was becoming a serious menace to Handel's future. Towards the close of the year 1751 he consulted Mr. Samuel Sharp, the Surgeon at Guy's Hospital, who gave a most unfavourable report of his prospect of retaining his sight. His spirits, usually so elastic, sank, it is said, beneath this terrible blow. But he would not give up the contest without a struggle. The sight of one eye was already gone, but there was a hope of saving the other. His symptoms were those of incipient *gutta serena*, a disease which necessitated a most painful operation. Three times Handel submitted to this, but in vain. His friends watched the course of the malady with anxious sympathy. In November 1751 Mrs. Delany wrote to her sister: "Did you hear that poor Handel has lost the sight of one of his eyes?" and a year later: "I hear he has now been couched, and found some benefit from it." But all hopes were delusive. On the 30th of January 1753 the *London Evening Post* informed its readers that: "Mr. Handel has at length, unhappily, quite lost his sight. Upon his being couched some time since, he saw so well that his friends flattered themselves his sight was restored for a continuance, but a few days have entirely put an end to their hopes."

Like Milton, whose poetry he had set to such incomparable music, he was to end his days in darkness, but like Milton he made up his mind to—

> "Argue not
> Against Heaven's hand or will, nor bate a jot
> Of heart or hope; but still bear up, and steer
> Right onward."

His eyes were useless or very nearly so — "so thick a drop serene had quenched their orbs"—but his fingers were as nimble as ever. He hastily summoned to his aid the younger Smith, the son of his old friend Johann Christopher Schmidt. Smith was then travelling on the Continent, but he returned at once, and with his assistance Handel contrived to continue the series of his oratorio concerts. Handel's own share of the performance was confined to playing organ concertos between the parts of his oratorios. "During the oratorio season," says Burney, "I have been told that he practised incessantly; and indeed that must have been the case, or his memory uncommonly retentive, for, after his blindness, he played several of his old organ concertos, which must have been previously impressed upon his memory by practice. At last, however, he rather chose to trust to his inventive powers than those of reminiscence, for, giving the band only the skeleton or ritornels of each movement, he played all the solo parts extempore, while the other parts left him *ad libitum* waiting for the signal of a shake, before they played such fragments of symphony as they found in their books." [1]

Another reminiscence of Handel's blindness tells of the emotion of the audience during a performance of *Samson*, when Beard sang with great feeling the famous air :—

> "Total eclipse ! No sun, no moon !
> All dark amid the blaze of noon."

The spectacle of the blind composer seated by the organ listening to the strains in which he seemed by some prophetic touch to have bewailed his own affliction,

---

[1] Burney, *Commemoration*.

affected those present so forcibly that many of them were
moved to tears.[1]

Handel was not the only blind musician of that epoch.
The feats of John Stanley had already excited the wonder
and admiration of his contemporaries. Stanley had been
blind since the age of two, but his affliction interfered in
no way with the exercise of his profession. In the first
days of Handel's blindness, when he was unable to take
part in the performance of his oratorios, his surgeon, Mr.
Sharp recommended Stanley to him, as a man whose
memory never failed. Upon this, Handel, whose sense of
humour never deserted him, burst into a loud laugh and
cried: " Mr. Sharp, have you never read the Scriptures ?
Do you not remember, if the blind lead the blind, they
both fall into the ditch."[1] Afterwards, however, he found
Stanley's assistance very valuable, and after Handel's
death the performances of his oratorios were continued by
Smith and Stanley in concert.

The closing years of Handel's life, in spite of the
grievous affliction under which he laboured, were smoothed
by the universal recognition of his genius and by the
enormous popularity which his oratorios enjoyed. He
lived a very quiet life, absorbed by music and the companionship of a few old friends. Even in his younger
days he had gone but little into society, save to preside
at the concerts given by the Royal Family, the Duke of
Rutland, Lord Burlington, and other patrons and friends.
Now his circle was sadly narrowed. The Prince of Wales
died in 1751, but Handel was not permitted to immortalise
his memory as he had immortalised that of his mother,
Queen Caroline. Frederick, pursued by his father's hatred
even beyond the tomb, was buried in Henry VII's chapel

[1] Coxe, *Anecdotes of Handel.*

"without either anthem or organ,"[1] and Handel's music was heard no more in Carlton House. During the last few years of his life he rarely left his house in Brook Street save to make an expedition to the City for the purpose of investing the money that he made by his concerts. Considering that these only took place during Lent, it is indeed a remarkable fact that although a bankrupt in 1746 he died worth £20,000. Burney relates that a friend of his, "who was generally at the performance of each oratorio in the year 1759 and who used to visit Handel after it was over in the treasury of the theatre's office, said that the money he used to take to his carriage of a night, though in gold and silver, was as likely to weigh him down and throw him into a fever, as the copper money of the painter Correggio, if he had as far to carry it." James Smyth told Bernard Granville that during his last season Handel made £1950 by his oratorios. Handel's blindness prevented him from composing much during these closing years. His most important work was the remodelling of his early oratorio, *Il Trionfo del Tempo*, which it will be remembered had been performed in a revived and enlarged form in the year 1737. It was now translated into English by Morell, and enlarged by the addition of seventeen additional pieces, a few of which were entirely new and must have been dictated by Handel to Smith. The rest were adapted from earlier works. In its new form *The Triumph of Time and Truth* was produced on the 11th of March 1757. It was evidently much liked, since it was given no fewer than four times in 1757 and twice in 1758. Time had not robbed Handel's touch of its old mastery. Still in his ashes lived their wonted fires. The new numbers in *The Triumph of Time*

[1] George Bubb Dodington, *Diary*.

and Truth are in no sense inferior to the old, while the duet and chorus, "Sion now her head shall raise," which was added to *Judas Maccabæus* in 1758, is one of the finest numbers Handel ever wrote. Up to the last he was still busy. In March 1759 *Solomon* and *Susanna* were performed, in each case "with new additions and alterations." These alterations, however, may very possibly have been made some years previously, and Burney states positively that "Sion now her head shall raise" was actually the last piece composed by Handel. It is worth noting by those who are exercised in mind by Handel's use of themes taken from the works of other composers, that this number is founded upon a melody by Bononcini. Whatever may be thought of Handel's artistic morality, it had at any rate the virtue of consistency! Handel seems to have relinquished few of his ordinary pursuits in consequence of his blindness. We hear of him playing at a concert at Mrs. Donnellan's in 1755, and helping Bernard Granville to choose an organ in the following year.[1]

One of the latest recorded incidents of Handel's career relates to his old friend John Christopher Schmidt, or Smith as he now called himself, who had been his constant companion for forty years. About four years before his death, he paid a visit to his favourite watering-place, Tunbridge Wells, accompanied by Smith. They quarrelled, as old friends will, over some absurd trifle, and parted in anger, vowing never to see each other again. The younger Smith, however, remained with Handel, and one day shortly after the quarrel Handel took his faithful secretary by the hand, and told him that he had made up his mind to put his name in his will in

[1] *Correspondence of Mrs. Delany*, vol. iii.

place of his father's. Smith, however, declared that if Handel did so, he would instantly quit him and take no further share in his oratorio performances, " for," he added, what will the world think, if you set aside my father and leave his legacy to me? They will suppose that I tried and succeeded in undermining him for my own advantage." Handel yielded the point, and shortly afterwards he was reconciled to Smith the father through the intercession of the son.

The end came with startling suddenness. Some months before his death, his appetite—usually a large one, as is not unfrequent in men of powerful intellect—had failed. He took this as a presage of his approaching end, but did not on that account give up his usual occupations. He conducted a performance of *The Messiah* on the 6th of April with no lack of his accustomed energy, but at the end of it he was seized with a faintness which sent him at once to his bed. He never rose again, but died some time in the night between the 13th and 14th of April 1759. It is curious, in the case of so celebrated a man, that there should be any doubt as to the hour at which he expired, yet such is the case. Dr. Warren, who attended the composer in his last illness, told Burney that Handel died before midnight on the 13th. James Smyth, on the other hand, who was Handel's most intimate friend, in a letter to Bernard Granville, the brother of Mrs. Delany, and another of the composer's dearest friends, distinctly states that he died on the 14th at eight o'clock in the morning. Neither, however, seems to have been present at the actual moment of death. Handel's funeral took place on the 20th of April at about eight o'clock in the evening. He was buried in the so-called Poets' Corner, in the south transept of Westminster

Abbey, in the presence of "a vast concourse of persons of all ranks, not fewer than three thousand in number."[1]

The monument by Roubiliac, which adorns the sepulchre, was erected in 1762. It has the faults of its creator and its period, but it is a spirited piece of work, and was pronounced by contemporary critics to be the best portrait of Handel in existence.

With regard to Handel's external semblance we are, indeed, rich in documents. Many excellent portraits survive, and we possess descriptions of him by contemporary writers, from which it not difficult to gather an idea of the man in his habit as he lived. His large and portly person, his awkward gait, his features—somewhat severe in expression until illuminated by a sudden smile—all these are as familiar to us as they were to his contemporaries. The character of the man is more difficult to come by. Like most men of exceptional power and grandeur of mind, he was too far above his contemporaries for them to realise his true greatness. They saw only the superficial aspects of his personality, and the little foibles or eccentricities of his character. Judging him by their own standard, they found him wanting in many of the minor graces that smooth the trivial round of life. He had a hasty temper, and habitually swore like a trooper. His manner was often rough and peremptory, but he never bore malice. He cared little for the world of civil formality, and was happier at home with a few chosen friends about him, than in dancing attendance upon empty-headed aristocrats whom he could not but despise in his heart. This independent behaviour of his often stood in the way of his success, but he never yielded an inch where dignity and self-respect were concerned.

[1] *Gentleman's Magazine.*

He was said to be ignorant and dull outside the affairs of his own profession—a charge often brought against those whose tastes happen not to coincide with the fashionable follies of the hour. He was, on the contrary, a man of considerable cultivation. His education had been far more complete than was then usual in the case of musicians, and his admirable taste in art matters is mentioned by several contemporaries who were well qualified to judge. His amiable biographers have unanimously attempted to persuade themselves and their readers that Handel was what is called a pious man. Everything on the contrary goes to prove that his religion was eminently of the type which, as Disraeli observed, all sensible men profess, but no sensible man talks about. According to Hawkins he often spoke of his good fortune in having taken up his abode in a country where no one suffered any molestation or inconvenience on account of his religious opinions. This does not sound like the utterance of a very ardent Christian, and there is something suspicious, too, about the sacred rapture with which the venerable Hawkins recorded the fact that during the last two or three years of his life Handel attended divine service at St. George's, Hanover Square. Dr. Beattie,[1] writing in 1780, professes to believe that Handel, "in spite of all that has been said to the contrary, must have been a pious man," so it is plain that his contemporaries were by no means unanimous upon the point. Handel's description of his feelings while composing the "Hallelujah" chorus : "I did think I did see heaven opened and the great God Himself," have often been quoted as an illustration of the sincerity of his religion. It has, as a matter of fact, nothing to do with the question.

[1] Forbes, *Life and Writings of James Beattie*, 1807, p. 331.

It merely shows that he was a man of powerful imagination. Doubtless while he was writing the " Hallelujah " chorus his imagination conjured up a vision of the glory of heaven. Similarly, while writing his famous chorus of devil-dancers in *Jephtha*, he saw with the inward eye the high places of Canaan and " the dismal dance around the furnace blue." But he has never been claimed on that account as a worshipper of Moloch. But speculations of this sort are idle at best. It is wiser to turn to Handel's works, where the man and his character, his hopes and beliefs, his dreams and ambitions are writ large for all to read.

CHAPTER XV

THE OPERAS

HANDEL'S operas are singularly difficult to discuss in terms of ordinary criticism. They were extravagantly praised by the connoisseurs of his time, but their vogue was brief. Five - and - twenty years after Handel's death they had passed almost entirely from the current repertory, and save for the revival of *Almira* in 1874 on the occasion of the opening of the new Hamburg opera-house, it must be considerably more than a hundred years since any one of them was publicly performed. Compared with his oratorios, they now seem sadly remote from the circle of modern sympathy. Opera since Handel's day has developed with extraordinary rapidity, whereas oratorio has tended to advance but little upon specially characteristic lines. To the average historian, therefore, Handel's oratorios still represent the highest point hitherto reached in this particular department of music, while his operas are usually dismissed as a negligible quantity. It is true that the most revolutionary changes in public taste could hardly restore Handel's operas to the stage, at any rate under the conditions in which they were performed in his lifetime. The disappearance of that repulsive anomaly, the male soprano, has made it impossible for us to give a faithful reproduc-

tion of eighteenth century opera. Yet in an adapted form
Handel's operas might still find a public, fit though few.
There is no reason why those who still have ears for
Gluck should not appreciate the beauties of Handel. It
is plain that a work written for the stage cannot be
properly judged in the study, and until Handel's operas
have been performed on the boards they cannot be
dismissed as trifling or ineffective. His conventions
differ widely, it is true, from those affected by the
composers of our day, but even here he has been mis-
judged by many who have discussed his methods. It is
generally said, for instance, that his operas are nothing
but a string of solos and duets, with a solitary chorus to
bring down the curtain.

A cursory examination of the works in question
reveals that this is not the case. Handel used the chorus
in his operas more freely than is usually stated, and when
occasion demanded he wrote concerted numbers for solo
voices in a manner ordinarily looked upon as the
invention of a later age. In the opera of *Alcina*, for
example, the chorus is freely used in the scenes in which
the victims of the enchantress Alcina appear, and there is
a trio in which the conflicting passions of three characters
are painted with extraordinary power. *Agrippina* has
several short concerted movements, and in *Radamisto*
there is an elaborate and highly dramatic quartet. It is
noticeable, too, that as Handel advanced in years and
experience he employed the chorus more extensively. In
his latest operas, such as *Giustino*, *Imeneo*, and *Deidamia*,
the chorus plays a decidedly more important part than in
his earlier works. But at no time did Handel permit the
rules and conventions that governed opera in his day
to override his own judgment. What these rules and

conventions were may be read in Rockstro's *Handel*, but as that learned historian was obliged to admit that Handel paid little attention to them, and indeed contravened them in every opera that he wrote, it does not seem advisable to linger over them. Handel followed the fashion of his day in the construction of his librettos, in the introduction of the inevitable confidantes and the no less inevitable underplot, but within certain limits he permitted himself all the freedom that he desired. The conventions of one age always appear foolish to another, but we must not let them blind us to the value of the work with which they are associated. But apart from convention, Handel's view of opera differed widely from that of our day. He treated it lyrically rather than dramatically, and who shall say that he was wrong? In our time opera has tended more and more to approach the confines of drama. Disregarding the one immutable convention by which opera exists as an art-form—the substitution of song for speech—we aim at a bastard realism, striving to bring the song of opera as near as possible to the speech of drama. Nothing can make opera realistic; it is conventional in essence; the less lyrical and the more dramatic it is, the less has it a reason for separate existence. Handel set his dialogue as recitative, and when a lyrical moment called for an intenser method of utterance he rose into song. With what success he did so cannot be declared until one of his operas has been heard upon the stage, but no one who accepts Mozart as a master of opera can condemn Handel on the ground of form. Certain conventions apart, the two men worked upon similar lines, and I have a strong impression that a performance of one of Handel's operas would be a surprise to the critics and historians

who habitually speak of them as a bundle of dry
bones.

In *Almira* we see Hercules in his cradle. It is the
one opera of Handel's Hamburg period that fate has
preserved for us, and fortunately it appears from contemporary accounts that it was the best of all of them.
Immature as it unquestionably is, it is an astonishing
work for a boy of nineteen to have written. As to the
libretto, the less said about it the better. *Almira* is a
comedy of love and intrigue, in which three amorous
couples and a comic servant plot and counterplot with
bewildering assiduity. A trained audience might con-
ceivably follow the devious mazes of the imbroglio with
some success, but the thing defies verbal description.
Handel's music is astonishing in its life and vigour.
From the sonorous overture, so different in its passionate
impetuosity from Keiser's pretty little preludes, to the
final ensemble the spirit of youth seems to breathe in
every bar of it. Weaknesses of course there are. The
vocal writing is often awkward, and the recitatives are
sometimes clumsily handled. But whenever a situation
shows a spark of dramatic feeling, as in that of Fernando's
farewell, Handel rises immediately to the occasion.
Already, too, his power of characterisation had begun to
develop. The passionate Almira is boldly and brilliantly
sketched, and most of the characters have distinguishing
traits. In this point if in nothing else Handel was
markedly Keiser's superior. Particularly good in the
comic servant Tabarco, whose music has often more than
a suggestion of the immortal Papageno. In many points
the maturer Handel is interestingly foreshadowed in
Almira. The orchestration has some characteristic
touches, and the little nature-sketches are in the true

Handelian manner. The breezes whisper divinely through the linden branches in Edilia's first air " Schönste Rosen," and Fernando's " Liebliche Wälder " is a charming woodland idyll. Very interesting, too, to Handelian students is the Sarabande—a rough sketch for the famous air which appeared in *Il Trionfo del Tempo* three years later, and figured again as the famous " Lascia ch' io pianga " in *Rinaldo*. In *Almira* it is a ballet-tune used to accompany a dance of Asiatics in the last act.

Handel's Florentine opera, *Rodrigo*, has only come down to us in an imperfect form. The second act is complete, but the beginning of the first and the end of the third are wanting. Enough of it, however, remains to give us a good idea of its style. It is very different in atmosphere from the semi-farcical entertainments that were popular in Hamburg. Ferdinand dei Medici found Scarlatti's operas too serious, but he must have thought that with *Rodrigo* he had fallen from the frying-pan into the fire. *Rodrigo* is all battle, murder, and sudden death. Roderick, the King of the Visigoths, is surrounded by enemies and traitors. His wife Esilena tries to buy his safety by offering to yield her share of the throne to her hated rival Florinda. Esilena and Florinda are happily contrasted in the manner of Elsa and Ortrud, and the scene in which Esilena makes her offer is very spirited and vigorous, the recitative being treated with a much firmer hand than in *Almira*. The character of Esilena is finely sketched. Her music has a warmth and tenderness which already shows the hand of the master, and the air in which she vows that not death shall part her from Rodrigo, and pictures herself wandering with him by the gloomy shore of Acheron is extraordinarily fine. Florinda has some fine music, too, though she flickers out towards

15

the close of the work; but the gem of the opera is Rodrigo's delicious air "Dolce amor," a melody of celestial loveliness which reappears in *Agrippina* and *Il Pastor Fido*. Handel used his *Almira* music a good deal in *Rodrigo*, and it is interesting to note the improvements resulting from the experience of two years' hard work and the study, perhaps, of Italian models.

In *Agrippina* Handel found himself in a totally different world from that of *Rodrigo*. *Agrippina*, for all its high-sounding name and the exalted personages who move through it, is nothing but a comedy of love and intrigue. The classical tradition died hard in Italy. The old operas had dealt solely with Greek mythology, and though the librettos of the eighteenth century had sunk deep in triviality, the fashion of naming the heroes after the great men of old was kept up merely for the sake of appearance. Thus in the world of opera Xerxes and Julius Cæsar still disported themselves upon the boards, even though the plot of the opera that they figured in might be borrowed from some Spanish comedy. *Agrippina* has only the very slightest connection with Roman history. It is a close-knit tangle of trickery and scheming, centring in Agrippina's endeavour to secure the throne for her son Nero. It would serve no good purpose to unravel its intricate network of intrigue. The plot is tedious, but the characters are well contrasted and skilfully drawn. The scheming Agrippina is a good foil to the light-hearted, frivolous Poppea, and Claudius, the amorous Emperor, is happily contrasted with the loyal Otho and the effeminate Nero; while the picture is completed by the two courtiers Pallas and Narcissus, whose alliance Agrippina secures by feigning love for the pair of then. Handel's hand is firmer in *Agrippina* than in *Rodrigo*. He sketches his

characters with a livelier and more vigorous touch. The
music was probably written in a hurry, and Handel
borrowed largely from his previous works. *Rodrigo*,
Il Trionfo del Tempo, and even *La Resurrezione* are
laid under frequent contribution. When changes are
made, they are always improvements, and almost invariably in the direction of conciseness and compactness.
Note, for instance, the altered rhythm in "Ingannata un
sol volta," an adaptation of the lovely air "Dolce amor"
from *Rodrigo*, and the pruning of the superfluous and
meaningless ornaments of "Crede l'uom" from *Il Trionfo*,
which in *Agrippina* becomes "Vaghe fonti," and, most
striking of all, the development of the rather commonplace "Un leggiadro giovinetto" from *Il Trionfo* into the
famous "Bel piacer." Now and then a song seems
to have been pitchforked rather unadvisedly into the
opera, mainly perhaps on account of its intrinsic tuneful-
ness. The dainty little air from *La Resurrezione*, "Ho un
non so che nel cor," sounds oddly on the lips of the
masculine Agrippina, and the two courtiers seem to have
been fitted with songs in somewhat indiscriminate manner.
But the new music shows all Handel's genius for characterisation. Claudius's "Vieni, o cara" is one of the most
voluptuous love-songs Handel ever wrote, and "Io di
Roma il Giove sono" has just the right note of pompous
splendour. Poppea's songs are grace and delicacy personi-
fied. One of them, "Bel piacer," appeared again in
Rinaldo, and became enormously popular in England.
Agrippina's music is appropriately vigorous and determined. Her great air, "Pensieri, voi tormentate," is
almost worthy of one of the passionate heroines of
Handel's later dramas. Handel seems to have had a
peculiar affection for *Agrippina*, and he often used it in

his later works. Pallas's vigorous air, "La mia sorte fortunata" (itself an adaptation, much altered and improved, of an air in *Aci, Galatea e Polifemo*), cropped up again in *Jephtha* nearly fifty years later, and the charming gavotte-song subsequently became famous as "Heroes, when with glory burning," in *Joshua*. A special feature of *Agrippina* is the unusual numbers of songs *alla Siciliana* which it contains. This alone, apart from documents, should have convinced Chrysander that it was written after Handel's visit to Naples, where, according to that learned historian, he first learnt to appreciate the beauty of this particular rhythm; but as a matter of fact, it need only prove that Handel had made acquaintance with the music of Scarlatti, whose operas abound in so-called *Sicilianas*, though their composer being himself a Sicilian, and knowing perfectly well what the real characteristics of Sicilian music were, did not so term them.[1]

With *Agrippina* Handel's apprenticeship ended. He had now learnt all that Italy could teach him. His style, so far as opera was concerned, was formed. Mr. E. J. Dent, in his valuable work on Scarlatti, has summed up so admirably the question of the extent to which Handel was influenced by Italy and Italian composers, that I cannot do better than quote what he says upon the subject. "On Handel Scarlatti's influence was strong at the beginning, but not very lasting or profound. Certainly the change of style that took place in his music after his visit to Italy is very noticeable. *Rinaldo* is as definitely Italian as *Almira* is definitely German in its manner. But although he began by modelling his phrases on Scarlatti after his visit to Italy, he very

[1] E. J. Dent, *Alessandro Scarlatti*, p. 151.

seldom enters thoroughly into Scarlatti's style. There
are several reasons for this. His acquaintance with
Scarlatti lasted a very short time, and his age made
him more suited to the companionship of Domenico,
whose influence can also be traced in much of his work.
Moreover, Handel, though only twenty-one when he came
to Italy, was a fully fledged composer. He was not very
familiar with the Italian style, but his Italian *Dixit
Dominus* is in some ways stronger than anything of
Scarlatti's in that line. Handel had had a Protestant
organist's training, which taught him to build up his
music on a strong, harmonic framework. But in spite
of the advantage of that wonderful German faculty for
translating and assimilating the work of other countries,
which accounts for much of the greatness of Handel,
Bach, Gluck, and Mozart, Handel had also the drawbacks
of his nationality. He set Italian, as he set English, like
a foreigner, never approaching that delicate intimacy of
declamation which is as characteristic a quality of Scarlatti as it is of Purcell. And it must be remembered that
a literary appreciation of the kind may take effect not
only in impassioned recitative, but also in the most
melodious and florid of arias. Handel's *coloratura* is
fairly effective in many cases, but it is commonplace in
detail. . . . Handel seems to nail his *coloratura* to its
framework; Scarlatti's often gains a priceless charm by
its wayward independence. Handel often reminds us of
some prudish nymph of Rubens, clutching her drapery
tightly about her, anxious and ungraceful; Scarlatti
recalls Tintoretto's Venus, her loose transparent girdle
fluttering crisply to the breeze, serving its whole purpose
in the delicate contrast that it makes with the pure firm
line of her perfectly poised and rounded form. Besides

Scarlatti, two other Italian composers exercised an equally strong influence upon Handel: the eclectic Steffani, from whom Handel learned to write overtures and dances in what we may call an Italian version of the style of Lulli; and Bononcini, who, in spite of his bad reputation among Handel's admirers, seems to have been the real originator of what is commonly described as the "Handelian style"—the straightforward, square-cut march, which Sullivan parodied so inimitably in *Princess Ida*. Bononcini even influenced Scarlatti himself, and it is therefore not surprising that a man of Handel's temperament should have seized more readily on the salient mannerisms of Bononcini and Steffani than on the more intricate subtleties of Scarlatti's music."[1]

Rinaldo is usually pronounced the finest, as it certainly is the most famous, of Handel's operas. It is easy to understand why this should be so. It had the great advantage of coming first; it introduced Handel to London, and lifted him at once to the position of the most popular composer of the day. It struck a new note of splendour and romance. It rang with the clash and glitter of arms. It had everything that could captivate the ear and eye of the crowd—brilliant music, a comprehensible story, gorgeous scenery, novel stage effects and admirable singers. But as a matter of fact it is far from being the best of Handel's operas, or even among the best. It has the advantage of a fine subject, it is true. After the puerile absurdities of *Almira*, the conventional melodrama of *Rodrigo*, and the pettifogging intrigue of *Agrippina* it must have been a relief to Handel to breathe the chivalric atmosphere of the *Gerusalemme Liberata*; and he contrived to pierce through the poor bald diction

[1] E. J. Dent, *Scarlatti*, p. 199.

of the librettist to the wonderful world of romance that
moved behind—Crusaders and Paynim warriors in shining
array, Armida and her sorceries, camps and ringing battle-
fields, and all the pomp and circumstance of war. But
not even Handel's genius could make Rossi's libretto a
good one. To see with what sedulous assiduity the poet
contrived to miss every opportunity one need only compare it with that of Gluck's *Armida*. By the side of
Gluck's tremendous heroine Handel's Armida is a mere
shadow, and it is a significant proof of the poor part she
plays in the drama that when *Rinaldo* was performed at
Hamburg, the authorities for once renounced their almost
invariable custom of calling the opera after the name of
the heroine.

Rossi, for instance, makes nothing whatever of Armida's
struggles between love and revenge, nothing of the voluptuous magic with which the enchantress strove to win Rinaldo
from his loyalty. Rinaldo is more sympathetically treated,
but he might have been made much more interesting than
he is. His constancy to Almirena his betrothed extorts
our respect for his virtues as a private individual, but it
detracts seriously from his merits as an operatic hero.
A Rinaldo who is not for a moment blinded by the
charms of the magic gardens, and an Armida who is
prepared to sacrifice her position as the leading sorceress
of Damascus without a struggle, cannot insinuate themselves very far into our sympathies. Armida is hardly
more than a sketch for some of the passionate heroines
of Handel's later dramas, and we shall find a far more
interesting Rinaldo in the person of Ruggiero in *Alcina*.
In a word, the psychology of *Rinaldo* is childish, and
Handel could make but little of it. He fell back in
despair upon the picturesque elements of the story, and

with them it is true that he did wonders. All the martial part of the opera is extraordinarily spirited, and fully justifies the high opinion which most critics have expressed of the work as a whole. Nor do the beauties of *Rinaldo* end here. With such meagre materials as his librettist afforded him, Handel contrived to do a great deal. The famous " Cara sposa " is a wonderful piece of musical characterisation, hitting off very subtly the effeminate side of Rinaldo's character before disaster had roused him to action, and " Ah crudel " shows what Handel might have made of Armida if Rossi had given him a chance. *Rinaldo* suffers a good deal from the haste with which it was written. A good deal of the music was introduced into the score from earlier works in Handel's usual manner, sometimes with surprisingly brilliant, but at other times with disastrous results. A great deal of Almirena's music had been used before, but it fits very well into its place, and the renowned " Lascia ch' io pianga " might well have been written for the situation. Argante's opening air, on the other hand, which was originally sung by the Cyclops in *Aci, Galatea e Polifemo*, though it makes a vigorous entry for the Paynim chief, is oddly out of place. What can one say of a plenipotentiary who opens negotiations for a truce by observing *à propos de bottes*:—

> " Alecto's snakes methinks I hear
> And hungry Scylla barking near."

The curious thing is that his diplomacy is successful. A good deal of the *Rinaldo* music is taken from an Italian cantata on the subject, written during Handel's stay at Rome, and this naturally enough fits into its place exceedingly well. One of these passages is the entrancing Sirens' song, which sounds as if it were an adaptation of an Italian folk-song, and makes one regret that time and his librettist did not allow Handel to make more of Armida's enchantments, which indeed are passed over with hardly a word. But when all is said against it that can be said, and when it is remembered that it was written in a fortnight, *Rinaldo* remains an astonishing piece of improvisation. Its freshness and vigour are beyond praise, and it is not difficult to understand how it kept its place on the stage when finer and subtler works passed into oblivion.

Of the other operas composed by Handel during his first two visits to England, *Teseo* and *Amadigi* are the most important. Both of them oddly enough are strikingly similar in subject to *Rinaldo*. In all three operas an important feature of the plot is the rivalry between a powerful and malignant sorceress and an innocent and trustful maiden. We have already in *Rinaldo* made the acquaintance of Armida and Almirena. Their counterparts in *Teseo* are Medea and Agilea, and the plot practically resolves itself into a duel between the two women for the love of Theseus. The characters of both are more carefully and elaborately drawn than their prototypes in *Rinaldo*. Agilea is far more of a human being than Almirena. There is a definite note of personality running through her songs, to which Almirena's music, hastily raked together from earlier works as it was, can lay but little claim. Almirena is only a typical *ingénue*, but Agilea is a tender and loving woman drawn with the utmost skill and sympathy. For sheer voluptuous beauty one of her airs, " Vieni, torna, idolo mio," is scarcely to be surpassed in the whole range of Handel's operas, and she has several other songs scarcely inferior. Medea is the finished portrait for which Armida was a hasty sketch. She is positively Æschylean in her rugged

grandeur and passionate force. By a skilful touch she
appears for the first time in a melting mood, singing a
lovely air in which the weary wanderer craves for peace
and tranquillity, but jealousy soon lashes her to fury, and
the rest of her career through the opera is a wild tempest
of conflicting passions. The great scene of the opera is
Medea's incantation, but her soliloquy in the third act,
when she has resolved upon the death of Theseus, is
another marvellous page.

   Amadigi as a drama is inferior to both *Rinaldo* and
Teseo. The libretto is clumsily put together, and gives
comparatively little opportunity for the delineation of
character. Melissa, the sorceress, is cleverly differentiated
from her two predecessors. She is cast in a tenderer
mould, and is much more seriously in love than either
Medea or Armida. She is perhaps less imposing as a
protagonist, and indeed is rather a weak-kneed sorceress
at best. She takes her discomfiture like a suffering
woman, rather than like an injured princess. The difference in character between Handel's three enchantresses
is neatly exemplified by their respective ends. Armida
makes the best of her defeat and becomes a convert to
Christianity, Melissa commits suicide, but Medea, still
defiant and undefeated, flies off in her dragon chariot.
Regarded purely as music, *Amadigi* is one of Handel's
most attractive operas. Not one in the long series is
richer in beautiful and expressive songs. It is remarkably
interesting, too, to the student of Handel's development
on account of its tendency towards a less conventional
treatment of the dramatic moments of the piece. In this
respect *Teseo* is an advance on *Rinaldo*, but *Amadigi*
shows a still more pronounced freedom in structure.
Handel had written nothing previously that can be com-

pared to the scene in which the ghost of Dardanus rises from the dead and bids Melissa refrain from persecuting the devoted lovers. Very striking too are the passages illustrating the swoon of Amadigi and Melissa's death-scene, and Amadigi's air, "T'amai quanto il mio cor," with its rapid alternations of *adagio* and *presto*, is a good instance of the increase in flexibility which experience gave to Handel's method.

Il Pastor Fido and *Silla*, though both contain much beautiful music, are not important to the study of Handel's operatic development.

After *Amadigi* Handel wrote no operas for five years. The foundation of the Royal Academy of Music brought him back to the stage with *Radamisto,* the first of the series of fourteen operas written for that institution.

Radamisto is one of his finest and most carefully written works. He had plenty of time, and was not driven, as in most of his previous operas, to use music already composed for other works. *Radamisto* is, I think, entirely original save for one air adapted from *Rodrigo*, and, clever as Handel was in working up old material, this fact alone gives it a decided advantage over its predecessors. The libretto is one of the best Handel ever set. The plot is fresh and interesting, and the characters are well drawn. Tiridate, the King of Armenia, has married Polissena, the daughter of Farasmane the King of Thrace, but he has conceived a violent passion for Zenobia, the wife of Farasmane's son Radamisto, and in order to get possession of her he goes to war with his father-in-law. Farasmane is taken prisoner, but Tiridate grants his life to the prayers of Polissena. Radamisto and Zenobia still hold out against the tyrant, and the first act ends with an assault upon their city.

When the second act opens the city has fallen, but
Radamisto and Zenobia escape by an underground passage, and come out beyond the walls. Zenobia is fainting
with fatigue and can go no further. They are surrounded
on all sides by the enemy, and escape is hopeless. Rather
than fall into the hands of Tiridate, she implores Radamisto to kill her. He has not the strength of mind to do
so, and she leaps into the river Araxes. Before Radamisto
can plunge in after her, he is taken prisoner by a body of
the enemy's soldiers. Their captain Tigrane, however, is
a friend. He allows Radamisto to disguise himself as
a slave, and so brings him to Polissena in safety while
he takes his garments to Tiridate as a proof of his death.
Radamisto tries to induce Polissena to help him to kill
Tiridate, but in spite of her wrongs she remains true
to her faithless husband. Meanwhile Zenobia has been
rescued from the river and is in the power of Tiridate,
who vainly endeavours to shake her fidelity to the
memory of Radamisto. Radamisto now appears in the
presence of Tiridate in his disguise, and is recognised by
Zenobia, who leaps from the depths of despair to wild
raptures of joy. Radamisto attempts the life of Tiridate,
who is saved by Polissena, and Radamisto is loaded with
chains. Meanwhile Tiridate's army has been roused to
mutiny by Tigrane, his guards desert him, and he is
at the mercy of Radamisto and Zenobia. But in an
eighteenth century opera a happy ending was *de rigueur*.
Tiridate is forgiven; he takes refuge in the arms of the
faithful Polissena, and the curtain falls on general rejoicing.

The opera is full of life and movement, the emotions
of the characters are well contrasted, and many of the
situations are admirable. Handel's music is superb

throughout. The first act rings with the noise of battle, while the anguish of the deserted Polissena, the savage fury of Tiridate and the noble dignity of the captured Farasmane are treated with incomparable skill. The second act opens with a lovely air for the despairing Zenobia, followed by the famous " Ombra cara," in which Radamisto invokes the shade of his lost wife. Later the music rises to wonderful heights of dramatic power. Radamisto's passionate appeal to Polissena, her distracted struggle between love for her husband and affection for her brother, Zenobia's haughty rejection of Tiridate's insolent proposals, and her alternations of hope and fear, when Radamisto appears, carry the interest on without a break. The last act is less thrilling as a whole, but it has what is perhaps the greatest thing in the work, in the shape of a wonderfully developed quartet, which seems to have escaped the notice of the historians who habitually speak of Handel's operas as a string of solos. The orchestration is throughout unusually rich and full. Horns make what is probably their first appearance in opera, and are used with singularly fine effect. If ever there should be a question of reviving one of Handel's operas on the modern stage, the claims of *Radamisto* would deserve careful consideration.

After *Radamisto* came that curious experiment of tripartite authorship, *Muzio Scevola*. Handel's share of the work contains some splendid music, but in one solitary act he naturally found comparatively little scope for his genius. His next opera, *Floridante*, shows a complete change of style. Bononcini had appeared upon the scene, and the success of his *Astarto* gave Handel food for reflection. *Radamisto* was obviously far above the heads of the audiences of that day, and, besides, the singers whom he then had at his command, particularly Anastasia Robinson, were not equal to the arduous tasks he imposed upon them. The fashionable subscribers of the Academy were bewildered by Handel's contrapuntal ingenuity, and they complained that his rich harmonies and fertile orchestration prevented their following the melodies of the songs.

Bononcini's simple little tunes were much more to their taste. What Handel thought about them and their criticisms we can easily imagine, but he took the hint notwithstanding. Thus while Bononcini was straining his slight, small talent in vain emulation of the sonorous splendour of his great rival, Handel consciously took a leaf out of the other's book, and wrote *Floridante* to suit the uncultivated taste of his patrons. *Floridante* presents a strange contrast to *Radamisto*. It is designedly slight in style; several of the songs are mere ballads, and the orchestration is simplicity itself. Only here and there does the lion's claw peep out, as in the lovely night-scene in which the heroine, like Agathe in *Der Freischütz*, listens for the footfall of her absent lover. *Ottone* and *Flavio* followed the same lines as *Floridante*. Handel now had Cuzzoni and Senesino to write for, and in their songs he could allow himself an occasional return to the grand style of *Radamisto*, as in the very expressive " Amor, nel mio penar" in *Flavio*, or in *Ottone* the splendid *scena* " Tanti affanni,"the plaintive " Affanni del pensier," and the pathetic " Vieni, o figlio," in which the divine forgiveness of a mother's love is painted in such moving colours. But for the most part he curbed his ambition, and gave his subscribers plenty of the pretty little Bononcinesque tunes that they could hum as they swung home in their sedanchairs. In *Giulio Cesare* he recanted his heresies, and re-

turned to his own gods. Either he felt that he had nothing more to fear from Bononcini, who had got into disgrace with the directors of the Academy, or he was tired of dancing in fetters. At any rate *Giulio Cesare* is freer in style than anything he had yet written. The libretto of *Giulio Cesare* covers very much the same period as Mr. Bernard Shaw's *Cæsar and Cleopatra*, but there unfortunately all resemblance between the two ends.

Giulio Cesare is an almost inextricable muddle of plots and counterplots, which positively defies analysis. But if the words are weak the music is superb. Its great strength lies in the accompanied recitatives. "Alma del gran Pompeo," the monologue which Cæsar pronounces over the tomb of his dead rival, has always been famous, but there are other pages in the opera scarcely less impressive, such as Cæsar's great *scena*, "Dall' ondoso periglio," in which recitative and *arioso* alternate in a manner no other composer of the time had dared to attempt. Very striking too is the note of romance that is struck in certain scenes, particularly in that of the vision of Parnassus with which Cleopatra attempts to beguile the amorous Cæsar. The music here is scored for harps, viola da gamba and theorbo, besides the usual strings and wind, disposed in two antiphonal orchestras. In other scenes four horns are used with surprising effect, probably for the first time in the history of opera, and doubtless with the intention of suggesting the barbaric character of Ptolemy's Egyptian cohorts. But the opera is full of interesting details of orchestration, and deserves careful study.

Tamerlano, in which the tenor Borosini made his first London appearance, is scarcely inferior. The principal characters are finely drawn and sharply contrasted—Tamerlane the insolent conqueror; Bajazet the defeated emperor, old, weak, and loaded with chains, but with spirit still unsubdued; and Asteria, fit daughter of such a sire. The opera abounds in scenes of keenly wrought dramatic fibre. There is a masterly trio in which conflicting passions clash in wondrous harmony, and the death of Bajazet is a passage of astonishing power, worthy of Gluck in his loftiest moments. The old man has drunk poison rather than witness his conqueror's triumph and his daughter's disgrace. Asteria clings about his neck, praying him to let her die with him. In broken accents he bids her farewell, and with his last breath hurls curses at Tamerlane, and bids him tremble at the terrors of a ghostly vengeance. The scene is wrought to a climax of astonishing power. Handel, who in his heart of hearts hated *castrati*, seems to have revelled in having at last a first-rate tenor at his command, and he wrote music for Borosini which it would have been idle to have put in the mouth of the effeminate Senesino. *Tamerlano* affords an instance of Handel's employment of the clarinet, which had been invented by Denner of Nuremberg about thirty years before. In the autograph the pastoral air, "Par che mi nasca," is accompanied by two *cornetti*, but in one of Smith's copies the *cornetti* are replaced by "clar. et clarin. 1° et 2°." Possibly some German musicians may have brought over specimens of the new instrument, and Handel, always ready for new experiments in orchestration, gave them a trial. He also wrote, probably for the same performers, a concerto for two clarinets and *corno di caccia*, the concertino parts of which are in the Fitzwilliam Museum at Cambridge. This work has never been published.

Rodelinda is cast in a gentler mould. It deals largely

with the woes of the deserted Rodelinda, wife of Bertarido, King of the Lombards, who believes her husband to have been slain in battle, and is hard put to it to repel the attentions of his successor. The opera opens very strikingly with the return of Bertarido, who finds himself confronted by his own tomb. His soliloquy, "Pompe vane di morte," is one of Handel's noblest accompanied recitatives, and it leads into the still finer air, "Dove sei," [1] in which Bertarido invokes the wife whom he believes to be lost to him for ever. Later in the opera occurs a wonderful dungeon scene, which has more than a suggestion of *Fidelio*, while if the passion of the imprisoned Florestan may be compared to that of Bertarido, Pizarro's famous song may no less fairly be quoted as a counterpart to "Fatto inferno," the tremendous *scena* in which Grimoaldo pours forth his soul in tempest.

Scipio and *Alessandro* are distinctly on a lower level. *Scipio* lives principally in the renown of its famous march, which is said to have been written originally for the Grenadier Guards and afterwards to have been incorporated into the opera.

In *Alessandro* Faustina made her début, and the

[1] The pious folk of the generation that followed Handel amused themselves with turning his operatic airs into sacred songs. "Dove sei" was one that fell into their clutches and came out as "Holy, holy, Lord God Almighty," in which version it is now probably better known than in its original form. Sometimes this peculiar method of paying a posthumous compliment to a popular composer worked rather neatly. As FitzGerald pointed out, "Nasce al bosco" bore its conversion into "He layeth the beams of His chambers in the waters" rather well, the passage about the shepherd sailing along on fortune's favouring gale fitting in happily enough to the words "and walketh on the wings of the wind." But "Dove sei" loses all its point by being canonised. The tortured passion, wild with all regret, of the original is completely smothered under the black coat and white tie of its Pecksniffian caricature.

16

dramatic interest of the work is largely sacrificed to the necessity of keeping the balance even between her and Cuzzoni. In *Rodelinda* and *Scipio* there are important tenor parts, but English amateurs just then would listen to nobody but the two prima donnas and their favourite *castrati*, so Handel had to bow to public opinion. There is an unimportant tenor part in *Alessandro*, but the rest of his Academy operas are written only for sopranos and contraltos, save for the thundering Boschi, whose popularity seems to have defied the dictates of fashion.

With *Admeto* we are once more in the presence of a masterpiece. The libretto is founded upon the world-renowned legend of Alcestis, which is treated with some skill, though the inevitable underplot is rather tiresome. Handel rose magnificently to the occasion, and his music is fully worthy of the noble story. Alcestis is one of his finest creations, and the sublime passion of her self-sacrifice is well contrasted with the light-hearted frivolity of Antigona, a youthful shepherdess, with whom Admetus consoles himself directly Alcestis has disappeared from the scene. Hercules is a splendid figure, and the selfish amorist Admetus is very happily drawn. The supernatural part of the opera is exceedingly impressive. The overture to the second act, which describes the gloomy horrors of the infernal regions, is a wonderful piece of tone-painting; and the opening scene, in which the dying Admetus is tormented by the Furies who gather round his couch, is no less striking than the corresponding scene in Gluck's *Iphigenia in Tauris*.

No more unfounded charge was ever laid at Handel's door than that his operas are all alike. On the contrary, no one ever appreciated more fully the value of contrast. *Riccardo* is as different from *Admeto* as possible. It rings with the noise of battle ; it is all martial ardour and patriotism. Dramatically it is not specially interesting, but it is full of interesting points, particularly as regards the orchestration. The elaborate storm-scene with which it opens is a very remarkable piece of writing for the time, and throughout the work there are signs of curious research in the choice of instruments. Some of the warlike songs have very spirited and effective parts for horns and trumpets. In a lovely *arioso* in which a despairing lover prays for death there is an obbligato for the bass flute, a " bird-song " sung by Cuzzoni has an elaborate and graceful part for a piccolo, and the charming pastoral air, " Quando non vede la cara madre," is quaintly accompanied by two "chalumeaux," a primitive species of clarinet. *Siroe* is on the whole rather disappointing, and gives the impression of having been written in haste. The Persian background tempted Handel to no experiments in orchestral colour, such as he had recently attempted, but there are some splendid songs in the opera. "Gelido in ogni vena" is a thrilling picture of guilty terror, and the monologue of the imprisoned Siroe is at least as fine as the corresponding scene in *Rodelinda*.

Tolomeo, the last opera written by Handel for the Royal Academy, bears, no less plainly than *Siroe*, traces of the untoward circumstances in which it was composed. Yet it contains many charming songs, such as the lovely " Fonte amiche," through which the breezes sigh and the waters murmur in such adorable concert, and the famous Echo song, " Dite che fa," in which Cuzzoni and Senesino scored a notable success. The great dramatic moment of the piece is the scene in which Tolomeo drinks what he believes to be poison, and sinks gradually into a lethargic slumber. This scene is in Handel's finest

manner. It opens with a noble recitative, and the air
that follows, "Stille amare," is one of the most expressive
he ever wrote. The ebbing tide of life is pictured with
marvellous skill and beauty, and the use of a *tremolando*
effect in the violins gives a curious touch of realism to the
scene.

The collapse of the Royal Academy and Handel's
start in management upon his own account opened a new
period in the development of his operatic style. It is not
easy to say how far the fact that he had a different
company of singers to compose for gave a fresh bent to
his genius, or how far the company was chosen to suit
the new style which he now adopted, but at any rate the
difference in manner between the old Academy operas
and those that he now produced is strikingly marked.
Lotario, the first opera produced under the new régime, is
not specially significant, but in *Partenope* the change of
style is unmistakable.

Handel's recent tour in Italy had introduced him to
many of the rising stars in the world of opera, such as
Vinci and Hasse, and in *Partenope* their influence upon
him can easily be traced in many of the airs. In general
structure, too, *Partenope* is curiously different from its
predecessors. The big *airs de parade*, which are so
prominent a feature of Handel's earlier operas when he
was still mainly under the influence of Scarlatti, have to a
great extent disappeared. In their place we find briefer
and more dramatic movement of the *arioso* type, and
variety is given to the action by frequent concerted pieces.
Partenope boasts a trio and a quartet, and no fewer than
four choruses, and there are numerous symphonic movements which form a welcome relief to the purely vocal
numbers.

Neither *Lotario* nor *Partenope* is particularly interesting as a drama, but both are crisp and vigorous in movement, and contain some capital characterisation. *Lotario* is a warlike story with the usual allowance of haughty tyrants and imprisoned damsels. The martial music is all very spirited and vigorous, but the best characters in the work are the hopeless lover Idelberto, who has some charming sentimental ditties, including the famous "Per salvarti," and his very bloodthirsty mother Matilde, a lady of truly Spartan fortitude, who goes through life with a drawn sword in her hand, ready to kill anything and anybody on the smallest provocation.

Partenope is lighter in character. It has of course a certain amount of fighting—few Handelian operas are altogether peaceable—but it is chiefly concerned with the quarrels and intrigues of three suitors for the hand of Partenope, the young Queen of Naples, and the efforts of Rosmira, a princess whom Arsace has thrown over for the sake of Partenope, to regain the affections of her faithless lover. Rosmira is a very high-spirited young lady, and, not content with disguising herself in male attire, goes so far as to challenge Arsace to mortal combat. The jealous fury of Rosmira is well contrasted with the light-hearted gaiety of Partenope, one of whose songs is the well-known "Qual farfalletta"; but the best songs fall to the share of Arsace, who is a distinctly variable person, and ranges between transports of rage, as in "Furibondo spira il vento," and depths of woe, as in the lovely "Ch'io parta," and the still more beautiful slumber-song, "Ma quai note," accompanied by flutes, muted strings and theorbo.

Poro follows much the same lines as *Partenope*, though the reappearance of Senesino in the company tempted Handel to return to some extent to the richer and more grandiose manner of his Academy days, at any rate in the songs allotted to the great *castrato*. *Poro* is in one respect somewhat disappointing, as there is little attempt in the orchestra at suggesting the Oriental colour of the background, though Handel had already made interesting experiments of this kind in his earlier works. In other respects *Poro* is fully up to the average Handelian standard. Many of the airs are intrinsically delightful, such as the pretty pastoral, "Son confusa pastorella," and the great dramatic moments of the piece are treated superbly. The death-song of the Indian queen is wonderfully beautiful, and the fact that it is written upon a ground-bass makes one wonder if Handel can possibly have made the acquaintance of Purcell's *Dido and Æneas*. One of the most striking and original things in *Poro* is an ironical duet between two jealous lovers, who in bitterness of heart quote passages from the love-songs that each has sung to the other earlier in the opera.

Ezio presents no very special claim to the attention of modern students. The plot is one of those interminable palace intrigues, in which every one seems to be conspiring against every one else at the same time in the most bewildering fashion. The music is no better and no worse than that of many other Handelian operas, but it is worth noting that the three bass songs, "Se un bell' ardire" (better known in England as "Droop not, young lover"), "Nasce al bosco," and "Già risuonar d'intorno," are still favourites with our latter-day singers. They were written for Montagnana, who made his first appearance under Handel's banner in *Ezio*. Montagnana was a singer of uncommon accomplishment, who seems, to judge from the music that Handel wrote for him, to have had an unusual accuracy of intonation in hitting distant intervals.

Sosarme is another of Handel's less important operas. The libretto deals in the received eighteenth-century manner with a number of amiable and abnormally credulous people, who are set at loggerheads by the purposeless malignity of a particularly double-dyed scoundrel. There are no dramatic situations worthy of the name, but Handel, as usual, contrived to make the most of every scene that had a spark of human emotion in it. There is a very fine *aria parlante*, "Cuor di madre," for a mother distracted by the emotions caused by the conflict of her husband and her son ; and the villain of the piece has a wonderful song, "Fra l'ombre," which seems to be enveloped in a weird atmosphere of guilt and horror. Still familiar to modern ears is the tranquil loveliness of "Rendi il sereno al ciglio," in which a devoted daughter soothes a mother's anguish, even as Manrico calms the raving Azucena in *Il Trovatore.*

Orlando is in every respect a finer work than its immediate predecessors. After the arid intrigues of *Ezio* and *Sosarme*, Handel must have been enraptured to find himself once more in the wonder-world of romance painted by the Italian poets of the Renaissance. He rose to his subject in characteristic style. *Orlando* is not, perhaps, particularly strong as regards plot, but there is a romantic charm about the story which fully atones for occasional weaknesses of structure. The savage figure of Orlando, whose hopeless passion for Angelica has turned his brain, stands out in striking relief against the graceful background of the shepherd life into which he bursts like a whirlwind. Very imposing, too, is the figure of Zoroaster, the magician who eventually restores

Orlando to sanity. The opening scene, in which Zoroaster, posted on a lonely mountain summit, invokes the aid of the silent stars, strikes a note of wild grandeur that echoes throughout the work. But the great moment of the piece is Orlando's mad scene, a passage of such concentrated force of imagination and such extraordinary inventive skill that by its side all the operatic frenzies of our modern Elviras and Lucias seem the most pitiful buffoonery. The details of the scene are worth careful study. The use of $\frac{5}{8}$ time is probably unprecedented in the history of music, and the contrast between the solemn passage on a ground-bass and the wild ravings of the peroration is extraordinarily fine. Writing half a century later, Burney still viewed the audacious innovations of this scene with grave suspicion. What the audiences of Handel's time thought of it, and of the opera as a whole, may be gathered from the fact that the production of *Orlando* was the signal for the foundation of the rival enterprise at Lincoln's Inn Fields, and that Senesino, who had certainly never in his career had music of such power and originality put unto his mouth, at once severed his connection with Handel, and went over to the enemy.

But the mad scene by no means monopolises the interest of *Orlando*. The opera is full of fine things. The scene in which Orlando, exhausted by his frenzy, sinks to sleep to the accompaniment of two *violette marine* —probably a kind of *viola d'amore*—is another masterly page. Zoroaster's three airs, " Lascia amor," " Tra caligini profonde," and " Sorge infausta una procella," are all magnificent, and, to our credit be it said, are still occasionally to be heard in our concert-rooms. The much-tried Angelica, when not being chased by her mad lover, has

some exquisite songs. Handel never surpassed the woodland magic of "Verdi piante," through which the voice
of the forest murmurs in such divinely soothing harmony,
and he gave the shepherd lovers some of the most
delicious pastoral music he ever wrote.

Ariadne, though one of the most popular of Handel's
operas with contemporary audiences, is far from being
among his best works. It may be regarded as in some
sort an apology for *Orlando*. In those days the English
public was just as impervious to new impressions as it
is nowadays—it never could have been more so—and
there can be little doubt that the freshness and originality
of *Orlando* repelled the average opera-goer as surely as
any attempt to enlarge the boundaries of music repels
our apathetic public to-day. *Ariadne* was a concession to
the conservatives. Handel, too, was doubtless anxious
that his new *primo uomo*, Carestini, who made his début
in *Ariadne*, should win the suffrages of his patrons, and
he gave him an unusually large number of commonplace
showy songs, by the aid of which he found no difficulty
in singing himself into general favour. Nevertheless
Ariadne has its fine moments. The scene of Theseus's
dream is effectively handled, and his combat with the
Minotaur is very spirited.

The most famous thing in the work, however, is the
minuet which is played at the opening of the first act,
while Theseus is disembarking from his galley with the
bevy of Athenian youths and maidens destined for the
jaws of the Minotaur. This piece enjoyed enormous
popularity throughout the eighteenth century. Its fate
foreshadowed that of the *Cavalleria* intermezzo in our
own day. It was transcribed for the harpsichord, arranged
for the violin, and even metamorphosed into a song.

Long after Handel's death it retained its vogue. The cultivated reader will not need to be reminded that in *She Stoops to Conquer* the performing bear, which "danced only to the genteelest of tunes," manifested a special predilection for its ravishing strains, and that so late as 1781 the fair Tilburina in Sheridan's *Critic* trod the ramparts of Tilbury "inconsolable to the minuet in *Ariadne*."

Handel's move to Covent Garden marks the opening of what may be called his third operatic period. At this epoch in his career he was hard put to it by the competition of the "Opera of the Nobility" in the Haymarket, and he left no stone unturned in the struggle to defeat his rivals. The distinguishing feature of his Covent Garden operas—the earlier ones, at any rate—is the increased importance assigned to the chorus and the introduction of dancing, which had figured but rarely in his previous operas.

Ariodante, the first of the Covent Garden operas, is particularly rich in dance music, each act terminating with an elaborate ballet, of which Mlle. Sallé, the French dancer, was the bright, particular star. In *Ariodante* Handel turned once more to his favourite Tasso, and produced a work which in grace and romantic charm yields to few of his operas. The plot is closely akin to that of *Much Ado about Nothing*. Polinesso, the villainous Duke of Albany, has been refused by Ginevra, the daughter of the King of Scotland, who loves Ariodante. In revenge he persuades Ginevra's confidante Dalinda to disguise herself in Ginevra's garments and to open a private door in the palace to him one night when Ariodante is wandering in the garden beneath his mistress's window. The plot succeeds. Ariodante, who has been a witness of what he believes to be Ginevra's perfidy, will have nothing more to say to her. Polinesso, however, overreaches himself. To close Dalinda's mouth, he plots to have her murdered. Ariodante saves her life, and in remorse she confesses her share of the plot against his happiness. The music, though not in Handel's grandest and most dramatic vein, is full of charming little vignettes, such as the garden scene in the first act, in which Ariodante breathes his passion in strains of the most voluptuous tenderness, and the wonderful orchestral picture of the rising moon at the opening of the second act. The dances are delightfully gay and sparkling, and the little pastoral symphony is a gem of the first water.

Alcina is another and even more successful experiment in the same style. The libretto, which is taken from Ariosto, has a good deal in common with those of *Rinaldo* and *Amadigi*. Ruggiero, a Christian knight, has fallen into the amorous clutches of Alcina, a Circelike sorceress, who has so bewildered his mind with her spells that when Bradamante, his plighted bride, appears on the scene to rescue him he shows a pronounced disinclination to leave his voluptuous bondage. He is brought to his senses by means of a magic ring, and he and Bradamante make their escape after breaking the urn on which Alcina's power depends, and reducing her palace and enchanted gardens to a dreary wilderness. *Alcina* has not perhaps the dramatic force of some of Handel's earlier works, but for sheer musical beauty it is without a rival, and the character-drawing is often curiously subtle. The opening scene in Alcina's palace, with its alternation of chorus and dance, is one of captivating loveliness, often foreshadowing very interestingly the style of Gluck, who may well have known *Alcina* and borne it in mind when he wrote his *Armida*. Alcina is one of Handel's most carefully studied characters. When she discovers Ruggiero's faithlessness she has a wonderful song, " Ah, mio cor," similar in feeling to Armida's " Ah, crudel" in *Rinaldo*, and to Melissa's " Ah, spietato" in *Amadigi*, in which she struggles with the conflicting emotions of grief and anger. To this succeeds a very striking incantation scene, in which she summons her minion spirits to assist her. Later her mood changes, and a lovely air, " Mi restano le lagrime," paints the anguish of her wounded heart in the most moving colours. Ruggiero is finely drawn also. His air, " Verdi prati," is well known in concert rooms, but apart from its context it loses all its psychological force. It is the knight's farewell to the enchanted splendour of Alcina's garden, and Handel, with his unrivalled knowledge of the human heart, has contrived to suggest a touch of that regret, which, so long as men are what they are, can hardly fail to make itself felt at such a time. Those who measure the works of earlier days by the suggestion of modernity that they exhibit, should compare Handel's treatment of the scene with Goethe's poem *Rinaldo*, in which the same idea is elaborated with truly Goethesque subtlety.

Atalanta was a *pièce d'occasion*, written in honour of the marriage of the Prince of Wales. It is appropriately brilliant and festive in character, and makes no pretence to dramatic interest, but it is nevertheless one of Handel's most charming operas, with its choruses of nymphs and shepherds, and its indescribable atmosphere of light-hearted gaiety and out-of-door freshness. Handel's later operas are hardly upon the same level as their predecessors. Ill-health and money troubles weighed heavily upon his spirits, and left their mark upon his music. Yet, though weak places occur in his last half-dozen operas, there is not one of them that does not contain beauties of a high order. In *Giustino* there is the romantic apparition of Fortune and a delightful sailors' chorus, which may possibly have been the model for Mozart's "Placido è il mar" in *Idomeneo*. *Arminio* is a return to the old heroic manner, and many of the scenes are poignantly dramatic. Arminio's great recitative, "Fier teatro di morte," and the noble air, "Vado a morir," are as fine as anything in *Radamisto*, but for the most part Handel seems at this time to have preferred lighter subjects. *Berenice* and *Faramondo* cannot be ranked high among the operas, though the minuet in the former is one of Handel's immortal tunes, and the latter has a very curious and successful experiment in realism in the song, "Voglio che sia," in which the hero, halting between two opinions, breaks off suddenly in the midst of his meditations, while the orchestra expresses his uncertainty in a passage of striking originality, which Handel a few years later worked up into a fine air in *Hercules*, dealing with a somewhat similar psychological situation.

Serse is Handel's one excursion into comic opera. It is a bustling little work, possibly founded upon a Spanish comedy of intrigue, in which only the names of the characters have anything to do with the classical world. *Serse* is now known chiefly as containing the beautiful air, "Ombra mai fu," which in its modern orchestral arrangement as "the celebrated Largo" is perhaps more popular than anything Handel ever wrote, but some of the lighter music is capital of its kind. There is a charming little song sung by the inevitable comic servant disguised as a flower-seller, which seems to be founded upon the street cries of the period. It is worth remarking that Handel is known to have taken a great interest in street cries. Lady Luxborough wrote to Shenstone the poet: "The great Handel has told me that the hints of his very best songs have several of them been owing to the sounds in his ears of cries in the streets."[1] An autograph note of his hastily jotted down on a loose sheet of paper together with the addresses of friends and other memoranda has preserved to us the cry of an itinerant match-seller :—

Buoy a - ny match - es,   my match - es buoy.

At the top of the page is written: "John Shaw, near a brandy shop, St. Giles's in the Tyburn Road, sells matches about." This interesting fragment is now in the Fitzwilliam Museum at Cambridge.

In *Imeneo* there is little to detain us, but *Deidamia*, Handel's last opera, contains some beautiful music. It is peculiar in having two important bass parts, to which many of the finest songs are assigned. The beautiful "Nel riposo" is one of those airs, like "Tears, such as tender fathers shed," in *Deborah*, and "How willing my paternal love," in *Samson*, in which Handel paints a picture of ripe and tender old age that no changes of time and fashion can cause to fade. In a very different vein is the bright and spirited hunting chorus, but *Deidamia* is full of good things, and had it appeared at a more favourable time and with a

[1] *Luxborough Correspondence*, 1775, p. 58.

stronger cast, it would have been one of Handel's most successful works. As it was, the public was tired of opera for the time being, and Handel was compelled to submit to the inevitable. With what feelings he did so we cannot tell. FitzGerald, who did not like oratorios, believed him reluctant. "Handel," he wrote, "was a good old Pagan at heart, and (till he had to yield to the fashionable Piety of England) stuck to Opera and Cantatas, such as *Acis and Galatea*, Milton's *Penseroso*, *Alexander's Feast*, etc., where he could revel and plunge and frolic without being tied down to Orthodoxy. And these are (to my mind) his really great works: these and his Coronation Anthems, where Human Pomp is to be accompanied and illustrated." That Handel was a thoroughgoing pagan I readily agree, but even pagans cannot endure misunderstanding, opposition and contempt for ever, and I cannot but think that it was with a sigh of relief that Handel turned his back upon the stage and devoted himself to the composition of the oratorios that were destined to bring him a wider and more enduring fame than the fickle world of the theatre could give.

CHAPTER XVI

ORATORIOS AND OTHER CHORAL WORKS

IT has been said by those whose aim is to belittle Handel and his works, that he did nothing to advance the development of music, that he initiated no new forms, but was content to work upon the lines already laid down by his predecessors. It is true that there was little of the revolutionary about Handel, and that for the most part he was content to carry existing forms to the highest possible point of beauty and perfection without embarking upon uncharted oceans of discovery, yet the charge of his traducers falls to the ground if we consider, to take but one instance, the work that he did in the development of oratorio. This alone gives him a right to rank among the greatest of those to whom we owe the modern forms of music.

Handel's oratorio style was the product of many mingled elements. Germany, Italy, and England all had a hand in its formation. When Handel reached Florence in 1706 he had little to learn from Italian composers as regards church music pure and simple. Very few authentic works of his Halle and Hamburg days have survived to our time. The early oratorios written under Zachow's influence are not now accepted as Handel's, and of late grave doubt has been cast upon the

authenticity of the little *St. John Passion* music. Bu
the *Dixit Dominus* which Handel wrote at Rome in April
1707 is quite enough in itself to show how completely he
had assimilated the best traditions of German ecclesiastical music. Mr. E. J. Dent, the biographer of Scarlatti,
admits indeed that in some ways it is stronger than
anything of Scarlatti's in that line. The vocal writing
is sometimes clumsy and inelegant, but the rich harmonic
foundation upon which the whole thing is built is typically
German in its breadth and solidity. Finer still are the
Laudate pueri and *Nisi Dominus*, which date from the
same period. The latter contains a particularly imposing
Gloria, which was independently performed at the Handel
Festival of 1891 and astonished every one by the
vigorous maturity of its style. But Handel's studies in
church music availed him little in the oratorios which he
was called upon to write during his sojourn in Rome. In
order to realise the position of oratorio in the world of
music at that time it will be necessary to turn for a
moment to the earlier history of the form.

Born almost contemporaneously with opera at the very
beginning of the seventeenth century, oratorio was in its
earliest form almost indistinguishable, save in subject, from
its sister art-form. The rudimentary oratorios of Emilio
del Cavalieri differ but slightly from the operas of Peri
and his fellows. There is the same dull waste of recitative,
broken by no oasis of melody, the same slight thin little
choruses, the same tinkling accompaniment. Carissimi
first led oratorio upon paths peculiar to itself. He gave
breadth and dignity to the choruses, and character to the
recitatives and airs. More important still for the future
of the art, he abjured the more specifically dramatic
effects which oratorio had hitherto shared with opera, and

17

invested all his works with an atmosphere of epic grandeur and sublimity, which more than aught else differentiated them from works written avowedly for stage representation. The death of Carissimi in 1674 left oratorio apparently established upon a firm basis, but his influence was not strong enough to overrule the pronounced leaning of the Italian genius towards drama in preference to epic, and in the hands of his successors, notably those of Alessandro Scarlatti, oratorio soon began to lose its characteristic outline, and to approach more and more closely to the confines of opera. Rome in the seventeenth century was as definitely the home of oratorio, as Venice was that of opera. Carissimi wrote his oratorios for the Oratory of San Marcello, and it was at Rome that his influence should have been strongest, but the fates were against him, and the Popes themselves unconsciously threw their influence into the opposite scale.

In 1667 died Clement IX, a man of artistic tastes, beneath whose amiable rule music of all kinds flourished like a green bay-tree. Innocent XI, who succeeded him, was cast in a different mould. He was a stern disciplinarian, and had no sympathy for the arts. He seems to have been particularly hard upon theatres. First he forbade actresses to wear low-cut dresses, and actually sent his *sbirri* to confiscate their short-sleeved garments. Finally he banished women from the stage altogether. His successor, Innocent XII, who ascended the papal throne in 1691, went still farther. In 1697 he closed the Teatro di Tordinona, and thus practically suppressed opera altogether. Artistic Rome was in despair, Cardinals wrung their hands, and the Arcadian Academy filled the air with lamentation. But opera, expelled by the papal fork, came back in a new disguise. In the Oratory of

San Marcello, the home of oratorio, she found a resting-place for the sole of her foot. A change came over the spirit of the place. Already the music of the oratorios there performed had contrived to secularize itself amazingly since the days of the severe Carissimi. Now the words also were to know the touch of worldliness. It is true that the performances were still in Latin, but to the *literati*, exiled from their favourite theatre, who took refuge in the oratory, Latin was a mother-tongue. Their influence made itself felt, and ere long the oratorios were nothing but operas in disguise. The characters were sacred, but their emotions and the language in which they expressed them were as secular as even a seventeenth-century Cardinal could desire. *Protoparentum Crimen et Pœna*, an oratorio on the subject of the Fall, is practically one long love-duet for Adam and Eve, and the fact that Tamar, Dinah, Susanna, and Bathsheba were the heroines of a few other oratorios produced at this time gives a good idea of the kind of subject which was popular among the cultivated circles in Rome.

This was the state in which oratorio was languishing when Handel came to Rome in 1707. It is no wonder that a stripling of two-and-twenty fell in with the prevailing taste, and wrote what he knew would find favour with his wealthy patrons. Not that there is anything distasteful in the libretto of *La Resurrezione*, but in spite of its subject the thing is opera pure and simple. There are only two choruses, both very slight in structure. All the rest of the work is given to the soloists. *La Resurrezione* is divided into two portions. The first takes place during the night preceding Easter Day. Lucifer is discovered exulting over the death of Christ, but an angel warns him that his triumph is to be shortlived. Two of the holy

women then appear, lamenting their dead Lord, and
St. John cheers them with the hope of His Resurrection.
The scene of the second part is laid in the garden of
Arimathea, but the actual incidents of the Resurrection
are not described. Christ is not introduced in person,
and the story of His appearance is narrated by Mary
Magdalene. The most striking figure in *La Resurrezione*
is Lucifer, whose music has many characteristically
vigorous touches. There is a suggestion of grisly horror
in his invocation to the powers below, " O voi dell' Erebo "
—the one air in the oratorio that is known to modern
audiences—and the rushing divisions and giant intervals
for the voice give an impression of concentrated fury,
while the long *glissando* scale-passages for the violins have
an eerie effect which the composer was to win by the
same means a few years later in the incantation scene
in *Teseo*. A proof of the close neighbourhood in which
opera and oratorio dwelt in those days is furnished by
the fact that Handel transferred a good deal of the
Resurrezione music to *Agrippina* a year later. Lucifer's
air already mentioned appeared in *Agrippina* in a sort of
drawing-room edition as an amiable ditty about constancy
being charmed by the placid ray of hope. A graceful little
song expressing Mary Magdalene's joy in her Saviour's
resurrection was put into the mouth of the triumphant
Agrippina without any alteration whatever. Such strange
transpositions were not at all uncommon in the eighteenth
century, and indicated no unusual levity on the part of the
composer. Many of the most edifying numbers in Bach's
Christmas Oratorio were taken from his own secular
cantatas. The lovely cradle-song of the Blessed Virgin, for
instance, had an earlier existence as a song of seduction
sung by the siren Pleasure to the youthful Hercules.

Handel's second Italian oratorio, *Il Trionfo del Tempo e del Disinganno*, is not perhaps intrinsically more attractive than *La Resurrezione*, but it has a special interest for the student as being the germ of the composer's latest work, *The Triumph of Time and Truth*. Originally written in 1708, it was revised for performance in England in 1737, still in its Italian form, and in 1757 it was translated, revised and enlarged, and finally performed in its familiar English form. In the main lines of its musical structure it resembles *La Resurrezione*, though its frigid allegorical libretto gives even fewer opportunities for dramatic effect, and there are sundry differences in detail between the two works. *Il Trionfo* contains no choruses at all, only a few ensemble numbers for the solo voices. There is much less instrumental *obbligato* work in *Il Trionfo* than in *La Resurrezione*, but on the other hand the orchestra plays a more important part. Handel's Neapolitan serenata, *Aci, Galatea e Polifemo*, is far slighter in construction. It has some pretty orchestral effects, as, for example, in the *obbligati* to a bird-song, and a duet for two violoncelli, but its chief musical interest lies in the beautiful song of the dying Acis and in the suggestions of humour that adorn the part of Polyphemus.

When Handel came to England in 1710, he thus had at his command two perfectly distinct styles, which he had not till then had occasion to blend, the German style of his church music—softened to some extent and rendered less angular by contact with Scarlatti and other Italian musicians, but remaining practically the art that he learnt at the feet of Zachow in Halle—and his operatic style which was almost purely Italian, though traces of Keiser's influence and the fashions that moulded *Almira* could still be traced in it. In England a third influence was

soon brought to bear upon him. His visits during his
first stay in England to St. Paul's Cathedral, where
Maurice Greene officiated as his organ-blower, introduced
him to Purcell and the English school of church musicians.
English church music was something very different from
anything Handel had ever heard before, and it could not
but exercise a decided influence upon his plastic genius.
The *Ode for Queen Anne's Birthday* (1713), the first
choral work written by Handel upon English soil, shows
this influence in a marked and unmistakable manner.
It opens with a curiously Purcellian recitative, and
throughout the work, particularly in the duet upon a
ground-bass, there are continual reminders of Purcell's
style. In the Utrecht *Te Deum* and *Jubilate*, which
followed close upon the Birthday Ode, English influences
are also to be traced, but less markedly. Chrysander has
pointed out how closely Handel followed the general
design of Purcell's *Te Deum*, which he undoubtedly heard
at the Festivals of the Sons of the Clergy, especially as
regards the alternation of chorus and solos. That is
true, but there is comparatively little that is distinctively
Purcellian in the music itself. Handel's mighty strength
of wing had already left Purcell far behind. His broadly
developed choruses owe little, if anything, to Purcell's
short scrappy movements. In the solo numbers the
influence of Purcell is felt more strongly. The duet,
" Vouchsafe, O Lord," and the alto solo, " When Thou
tookest upon Thee," would certainly never have been
written in anything like their present form but for
Handel's visits to St. Paul's.

In the *Brockes Passion*, which Handel wrote in 1716,
there is a return to the German style of his youth. The
work follows in its general lines the accepted formula for

Passion music as already adopted by Keiser and other composers, the sacred narrative, here presented not in the words of the Bible but in doggerel verse, being interspersed with dramatic choruses, reflective solos and chorales very much as we find it in Bach's familiar settings of the Passion story. It ought to be much more interesting than it actually is to set Bach and Handel side by side and to compare their respective treatments of the same theme. As a matter of fact the comparison is fruitless simply because the two men were what they were. To Bach, with his profoundly moral view of life and the pietistic Lutheranism that ran in his blood, the curious medley that German taste had made of the story of the Passion appealed with irresistible force. But Handel's artistic sensibilities were outraged by the sentimental moralisings with which the subject was overlaid, and by the aggressive didacticism that often obscured the simple majesty of the Biblical story. The frigid extravagances of Brockes's poem chilled the current of his inspiration. The truth is that his long absence from Germany had thrown him out of touch with his countrymen's view of religion. Italian culture and English Laodiceanism had given him a fresh point of view, and he could not fall back into the groove of his childhood's belief. If his *Brockes Passion* is one of the least satisfactory of his works, it is from no failure in musicianship—for it contains many vigorous passages, and at least one scene, that of Christ's agony in the garden, of deep and moving beauty—but because it gives throughout the impression of a man working with uncongenial material. If Handel wished to prove that he could pit himself successfully against his old rival Keiser he won his case, for his *Passion* seems to have been popular in Germany, but he did not repeat the experiment, and the *Brockes Passion* was the last work in which he set his mother tongue to music.

Handel's excursion into the realms of German music did not retard the development of his English style. Soon after his return to England he entered the service of the Duke of Chandos, and during the next few years produced the famous series of anthems universally known by the name of his princely patron. Anthems in the ordinary sense of the word the Chandos anthems emphatically are not. With their imposing chain of choruses and solos, their elaborate overtures and full orchestral accompaniment, they have really more in common with the church cantatas which Bach was pouring forth in such profusion at the same time. But here, as in the case of the *Passion* music, the superficial resemblance in form only makes the essential difference in feeling between the two composers the more striking. No two men ever envisaged sacred things with a more profound diversity of view. The burning sincerity of Bach's genius and his deeply religious nature animate every note of his cantatas. The story of Haydn offering up a prayer before beginning to compose may be perfectly true of Haydn, but it would be much truer of Bach. The production of sacred music was to him an act of adoration, whereas to Handel it was merely an artistic exercise. Bach's cantatas breathe the inmost secrets of his pious heart. Handel's anthems are the brilliant improvisations of an accomplished artist. While Bach is on his knees in the Holy of Holies, Handel is leading a gaily robed procession through the echoing aisles of the church. To modern taste, and indeed to all taste that values the spirit rather than the body, the end rather than

the means, Bach's sacred music must rank far above
Handel's, but it is only fair when we are comparing the
two composers to look upon the other side of the picture,
and to remember that though Bach is without a rival in
his own organ-loft he never strayed from it, whereas
Handel's range of thought was boundless, and he was as
superior to Bach in secular music as Bach was to him
in sacred. Handel's church music was enthusiastically
admired and extravagantly praised during his lifetime,
but changes of fashion, which operate as drastically in
the religious world as in the secular, have estranged
public sympathy from this particular side of his activity.
The pomp and glitter of many of the anthems, their
ease of movement and their affluent inspiration, still
compel admiration, but they possess few of those qualities
for which we now value Handel. Every age reads its
own meaning in an artist and his work, and it is Handel's
soaring imagination and his sympathy with every phase
of human feeling that now enchain us. The eighteenth
century admired him for very different reasons, and the
works that they most appreciated leave us comparatively
cold. The conventional jubilations of the Psalms offered
Handel but little opportunity for the exercise of his
peculiar talents. His setting of such anthems as the
well-known " O praise the Lord with one consent," and
" O come, let us sing unto the Lord "—the only two of the
series that are ever publicly performed at the present time
—make no pretension to that imaginative power which
illuminates the oratorios. They are vigorous, straightforward and effective, but Handel's keenest admirer can
hardly say more for them than that. In some of the other
anthems, which it is almost impossible to perform
nowadays owing to Handel's employment of counter-

tenors in the choruses in place of contraltos and tenors, there are occasional passages which give a foretaste of what he was later to accomplish in his oratorios. In "The Lord is my light" there is a splendid sea-piece, "It is the Lord that ruleth the sea," which was afterwards elaborated into the great chorus in *Israel in Egypt* "But the waters overwhelmed them," and, finer still, a wonderful thunder and lightning chorus, a rough sketch for the great chorus in *Joshua*. Perhaps the noblest of the Chandos anthems is "Let God arise," with its impressive opening chorus, in which the scattered enemies flee in all directions in the most realistic manner, and its very poetical setting of the words, "Like as the smoke vanisheth." In a tenderer vein is the beautiful "As pants the hart," an anthem of which, as of many of the others, several versions exist, the alterations and revisions being due partly to changes in the Canons choir, and partly to the necessity of adapting them to the less elaborate choir of the Chapel Royal. Three *Te Deums*—the third a free adaptation of the second—also date approximately from Handel's Chandos period. They are grandiose and sonorous works in the "big bow-wow" manner that was so much admired by his contemporaries, but now seems a trifle too much bewigged and beruffled for modern taste. That in B flat is the most elaborate and is usually considered the finest, but all three are works of uncommon dignity and grandeur of style. They express the pomp and circumstance of religion rather than its holiest and most sacred raptures, but, like the anthems, they compel admiration by the consummate ease and fluency of their technique, and they furnish a triumphant proof of Handel's superb mastery of his material.

But even the bright array of Chandos anthems fades

into insignificance by the side of the two great works which Handel produced while an inmate of Canons, *Esther* and *Acis and Galatea*. *Esther*, the first oratorio ever written to English words, is all-important in the history of Handel's artistic development. Like many other art-forms, English oratorio owed its birth to what may be called a happy accident. We know nothing of the circumstances that led to the composition of *Esther*, but there can be little or no doubt that it was intended for stage performance. It was originally described as a masque, and was performed with scenery and action when revived in 1732 by the children of the Chapel Royal. Only the prohibition of Bishop Gibson prevented Handel from giving it as a drama on the stage of the King's Theatre. Thus *Esther*, though rightly called an oratorio in the modern sense of the word as being the harbinger of the mighty succession of masterpieces that Handel was subsequently to produce in this form, is in itself a hybrid work, tracing its descent to Greek tragedy through Racine's drama, of which it is a free adaptation. Racine avowedly followed Greek methods, seeking to establish a due balance between chorus and principals, and Pope, if the libretto of *Esther* was actually his handiwork, reduced the drama to a minimum and gave additional importance to the chorus, unconsciously accentuating the epic element which was eventually to distinguish oratorio from drama. *Esther* can hardly have been very effective as a drama owing to the preponderance of the choral element, and its real value probably only became apparent when it was performed as an oratorio. It is, naturally enough, somewhat tentative in style, and the fact that Handel used a good deal of his *Passion* music in its composition, sometimes in a rather indiscriminate manner, tends to blunt the sharpness of the characterisation. But though as a whole *Esther* is a work of more promise than actual performance, it is rich in the seeds of what was afterwards to develop into the grand manner of Handel's later days. The overture has always been a favourite, and it is valuable, apart from its sheer musical value, as a rejoinder to the often repeated accusation that Handel's overtures have nothing to do with the works that they precede. In this respect, indeed, Handel was far in advance of his age. The *Esther* overture has an obvious connection with the unfolding of the drama. The first movement, closely allied as it is in rhythm to Haman's first song, plainly portrays the arrogance of the tyrant ; the second movement is no less obviously a picture of the Jewish exiles' grief and despair, while the note of triumph sounds clearly in the final fugue. As to the oratorio itself, its strength most emphatically does not lie in its solos, though it is surprising how well some of them fit the situation, considering to what very different words they were originally written, and what very different emotions the music was intended to illustrate. Thus Ahasuerus's graceful love-song was originally a lament sung by a believer over his crucified Saviour, and the duet in which Esther is reassured by her lord is an adaptation of that sung in the *Passion* music by the Blessed Virgin and Jesus Christ in His last moments. Strangest of all, the moving strains in which Haman pleads for his life with Esther are taken from Christ's agony in the Garden of Gethsemane. But if the solos in *Esther* are not altogether satisfactory, many of the choruses are magnificent, and give rich promise of what Handel was subsequently to accomplish in handling vast masses of sound. The plaintive "Ye sons of Israel, mourn," is a highly successful

HANDEL

first essay in a manner of which the beautiful "For Sion lamentation make," in _Judas Maccabæus_, is perhaps the most familiar example. "He comes to end our woes" is a ringing song of victory in Handel's most brilliant vein, and in the splendid finale he put to triumphant use the experience that he had gained in his Chandos anthems.

Acis and Galatea was, like _Esther_, originally called a masque, and like _Esther_ was doubtless intended for stage performance, but there the resemblance between the two ends. _Esther_ was a pioneering excursion into an undiscovered country, but in _Acis_, Handel was on ground that he had already traversed during his Italian days. The English _Acis_ has nothing in common with the Neapolitan _Aci, Galatea e Polifemo_, save subject, but it is a nobler and richer development of the "pastoral" that had been popular all over Europe for many years. In its exquisite strains the masques of Jacobean times reached a brilliant climax. _Acis_ was the most perfect work Handel had yet written, some might say the most perfect work he ever wrote. Gay's pretty poem inspired him, and his music is wrought with a touch at once delicate and sure. "Do you know the music?" wrote Edward FitzGerald to Frederic Tennyson. "It is of Handel's best, and as classical as any man who wore a full-bottomed wig could write." Wig or no wig, it has the magic that only genius can evoke, and the romantic charm that is for all time. The sunny life of old Sicily sparkles in its pages, the very spirit of Theocritus breathes through its delicious melodies. We know it nowadays, alas! only as a cantata, but its proper place is in the theatre, as the few who can remember Macready's wonderful revival in 1842, of which FitzGerald was writing, can testify. It has often been performed on the stage since those days, and always with remarkable success. Even the grotesque exhibition given ten years ago by the now defunct Purcell Operatic Society did not wholly obscure its beauties.

After leaving the Duke of Chandos, Handel devoted his energies almost exclusively to opera for many years. The coronation of George II in 1727 drew him for a moment from the stage to the church. The four anthems that he wrote for the festal service rank among his most famous works, and in their own particular line have never been surpassed. Never before or since have the pomp and splendour of human things been set to music of more regal magnificence. The voice of a great nation speaks in Handel's majestic strains. The flash of jewels and the glitter of gold is in his music. The spiritual note is not touched—what place, indeed, could it have in the coronation of George II?—but so far as earthly things can compass the sublime it is compassed in Handel's Coronation music. The superb dignity of the anthems has extorted eulogy from men more famous in literature than in art. Edward FitzGerald, a devoted, though narrow Handelian, thought them his masterpiece. " Handel never gets out of his wig—that is, out of his age. His Hallelujah chorus is a chorus, not of angels, but of well-fed earthly choristers, ranged tier above tier in a Gothic cathedral, with princes for audience, and their military trumpets flourishing over the full volume of the organ. Handel's gods are like Homer's, and his sublime never reaches beyond the region of the clouds. Therefore I think that his great marches, triumphal pieces, and Coronation anthems are his finest works." One of De Quincey's opium-dreams refers to the magnificent opening of *Zadok the Priest*, the first of the four anthems : " Then suddenly would come a dream of far different character—a tumultuous dream, commencing with a music such as now I often heard in sleep, music of preparation and of awakening suspense. The undulations of fast-gathering tumults were like the opening of the Coronation anthem; and, like *that*, gave the feeling of multitudinous movement, of infinite cavalcades filing off, and the tread of innumerable armies."

The revivals of *Esther* and *Acis* in 1732 turned Handel's attention once more in the direction of oratorio, and in 1733 he produced *Deborah*, which was thus the first of his sacred oratorios conceived and executed as such. *Deborah* differs totally from *Esther* in structure. *Esther* was an oratorio only by accident, but *Deborah* was specially designed to bring into play those mighty forces which in *Esther* only made but a fitful appearance. There is nothing dramatic about *Deborah*. It has no action and very little characterisation. The scheme of the work is purely epical. It tells the story of a battle of nations. The protagonists are no mere individuals, but the rival powers of Israel and Amalek, the worshippers of Jehovah and of Baal, joined in bitter and deadly strife. The plot is unfolded almost entirely by means of narrative and chorus, the utterances of Deborah, Barak, and the other characters being for the most part merely comments on the situation. Thus the structure of the work differs entirely from that of drama, with its quick play of chequered feeling, and approximates far more closely to that of the epic, in which, though the characters appear and pronounce speeches, they seem to move in a world far removed from that of real life. The stately splendour of Handel's style harmonised incomparably with the form that he had practically invented. His solemn slow-moving airs fit as perfectly into their places in the general scheme as do the speeches in *Paradise Lost*. The varied passion and strenuous emotion that in his operas he painted with so fine a touch would here strike a jarring note. Dignity is the note of *Deborah*, though within the limits that he assigned himself Handel found room for powerful contrasts and felicitous descriptive effects. The overture, even more patently than that of *Esther*, is a disproof of the assertion that Handel's preludes have nothing to do with the works that they usher in. Two of the themes are actually taken from choruses in the work itself, one sung by the priests of Baal and the other by the Israelites, and the overture is obviously designed as a brief compendium of the struggle between the opposing nations. The solos are the least interesting part of the work. Many of them are taken from earlier works, from the *Passion* and from various anthems. They are often skilfully adapted to new uses, but there is little attempt at characterisation, and the characters are for the most part merely types. Abinoam, the father of Barak, is an exception. He is the first of the wonderful series of old men, whom Handel drew with so loving a hand. His song, " Tears, such as tender fathers shed," though an adaptation of an air in one of the Chandos anthems, is a perfect little picture of the tenderness of paternal love. But the great strength of *Deborah* lies in its choruses, which are something altogether different from anything the world had seen before. In grand procession they stride along, with necks with thunder clothed and long resounding pace. Several are taken from the Coronation anthems, but the new ones are more imposing still. "Immortal Lord of earth and skies," " See the proud chief," " Lord of Eternity " — each one seems more tremendous than the last, for Handel's coursers never tire.

In his later days Handel did far finer and subtler work than anything in *Deborah*, but he rarely surpassed the ringing choruses in which the might of Israel defies the pride of heathendom.

Deborah, as we have seen above (p. 119), was very far from being an unequivocal success. The raised prices of the seats got Handel into serious trouble, and it is easy to believe that the sonorous splendour of the music was a good deal above the heads of the audiences of Walpole's London. Handel had yet to educate his followers into appreciating his sublime epics. He seems to have felt this himself, and his next oratorio *Athaliah* was much slighter in design. The grave majesty of *Deborah* here gives place to a lighter and more lyrical manner, and the functions of the chorus are considerably curtailed. The libretto of *Athaliah* was doubtless partly responsible for this. It is an adaptation of Racine's *Athalie*, and has a good deal more of the drama about it than *Deborah*. The characters are more carefully treated, and the solos are on a distinctly higher level. Athaliah herself dominates the scene. There is an almost Æschylean grandeur in her guilty pride and insolence, and the superstitious terror inspired by her boding dream gives a curiously heathenish touch to her strange and imposing figure. In charming contrast is the group of pious Israelites, the inspired seer Joad, the gentle Josabeth, and the delightfully boyish Joash. As in *Deborah*, the Israelites and the worshippers of Baal are employed to balance the picture with striking effect, but the contrast is more subtly elaborated in *Athaliah*. The voluptuous beauty of heathendom is emphasized in a remarkable way. The chorus, " Cheer her, O Baal," in which Athaliah's disturbed spirits are soothed by her attendants, has a strange

18

languorous charm that breathes all the potent magic of the perfumed East, and no less insinuating is the caressing tenderness of the lovely air, "Gentle airs, melodious strains." The Israelites' music, too, if less overpowering than the stupendous choruses of *Deborah*, has a special charm and character of its own. Several of the choruses are fine specimens of Handel's grand manner, but it is the lighter numbers, such as the exquisite chorus of virgins in the opening scene, and the delicious duet, "Joys in gentle train appearing," that impart to *Athaliah* its special character, and give it a place of its own among Handel's oratorios.

The two works which Handel wrote in 1734 for the marriage of his patroness and pupil the Princess Royal, were almost entirely concocted from his earlier compositions. *Parnasso in Festa* was mainly drawn from *Athaliah*, though two of the best numbers in it, the choruses of hunters and of sylvans, are new, and the Wedding anthem was altogether an adaptation of old material. A grander note was struck in *Alexander's Feast* (1736), a work which during Handel's lifetime was as popular as anything that he produced. It is curious to note, as the years pass by, how each generation in turn seems to find something to suit its own special requirements in the works of the great masters. Handel, for instance, is treasured to-day by those who know anything of his music outside *The Messiah* chiefly for his imaginative qualities, but the eighteenth century preferred him in his more rhetorical vein. The critics of the day set little store by even such a tremendous masterpiece of imagination as *Israel in Egypt*. *The Messiah* itself, judged as a work of art pure and simple, fell flat. It was only when it was definitely taken over by the Church that it became popular. What people preferred in those days was the sonorous dignity of the Dettingen *Te Deum* and the glittering pageantry of *Alexander's Feast*, and, as we have seen, the same view of Handel prevailed even down to the days of FitzGerald. *Alexander's Feast* is indeed a masterpiece in its own way. Handel's music is an admirable equivalent for the ringing rhetoric of Dryden. If one looks in vain for profound feeling or soaring imagination, Handel gives you instead admirable workmanship, inexhaustible vigour, and unfaltering dignity of utterance. *Alexander's Feast* is a wonderful series of pictures, each one dashed off in broad splashes of colour by the hand of a master. When Handel is in this vein his simple directness of method is overpowering. He seems to hurl his effects straight in your face. It was of such music as this that Mozart was thinking when he said, " When he chooses, he strikes like a thunderbolt."

The anthem written in 1736 for the Prince of Wales's wedding was a much better piece of work than the hastily put together pasticcio of 1734. Handel turned to it often in after-life, and the greater part of the music is familiar to us in the slightly altered form in which it reappeared in *The Triumph of Time and Truth* and other oratorios.

The spring of 1737 saw the revival in a remodelled form of Handel's Italian oratorio, *Il Trionfo del Tempo*, to which we will return in discussing the final form in which the work was presented in 1757.

In the following autumn he composed the beautiful anthem for the funeral of Queen Caroline, a work which, for dignity of utterance and depth of feeling, yields to nothing that he ever wrote. But all his previous triumphs paled before the two great oratorios that he composed in 1738, *Saul* and *Israel in Egypt*. In *Saul* Handel found a subject worthy of his powers. The libretto is skilfully put together, and Handel wedded it to music which combines the force and majesty of *Deborah* with the freshness of *Athaliah*. The special note of *Saul* is picturesqueness. Each scene in turn is handled with a graphic touch that makes every detail start into life with singular vividness. Take the opening scene, in which the people of Israel welcome the youthful hero, David, after his victory over the Philistines. First we hear the sounds of rejoicing in the distance, little more than a joyful marchlike movement accompanied by the ringing of a peal of bells. Then the maidens of Israel appear, leading the long procession. The music swells into a wonderful swaying rhythm as they dance forward singing a chorus of enchanting freshness and simplicity. The scene darkens for a moment while Saul passes along muttering envious curses, only to brighten again as the whole body of the people burst into triumphant chorus with the blaring of trumpets and the crashing of drums. Later in the work comes the appropriate pendant to this brilliant scene of rejoicing — the wonderful lament over the bodies of the slain king and his son. Never, even in *Samson*, did Handel give voice to the strains of a nation's lamentation in tones of a sublimer pathos. The varied emotions of the scene are depicted in his music with all that concentrated power of imagination which is Handel's special property. First comes the solemn procession bearing the bodies of Saul and Jonathan to the immortal strain of the Dead March, while the people lift their voices in a chorus of mourning for the fallen warriors of Israel. David's eulogy of the heroes strikes a sterner note. There is a touch of the fierce joy of battle in the music as he sings of the sword of Saul, and how it "drank the blood of slaughtered foes." The people catch the spirit of his words, and echo them in a short chorus of almost barbaric rapture. Then the music changes again, as David sings of Jonathan and the love that passes the love of women, leading into a chorus in which the very soul of passionate grief is transmuted into sound. After the tension of this scene, the relief of the final chorus is unspeakable. It is a jubilant prophecy of the future triumphs of David, and brings the oratorio to a close with the thunder of victory. These are only two of the many noble passages in *Saul*. There are others no less striking, such as the famous Envy chorus and the weird incantation scene in the witch's cavern at Endor. The character-drawing in the oratorio is more graphic than anything Handel had yet attempted, though his touch was to become surer in his later years. Saul's jealous misanthropy is well contrasted with the boyish charm of David, and another happy touch is gained by the contrasted emotions of the gentle Michal and the haughty Merab. Very striking, too, is the music associated with the "monster atheist," Goliath, which those who are interested in tracing foreshadowings of modern effects in the music of older masters should compare with Wagner's giant music in *Das Rheingold*. The orchestration of *Saul* is particularly interesting. Handel here employed effects which he never subsequently attempted in oratorio, feeling probably that the epic character of the form demanded an austerer method of treatment than was legitimate in opera. The score of *Saul* is enriched by trombones, and has an independent organ part — the latter a rare feature in eighteenth-century music. The use of a carillon of bells gives a special colour to the Israelite rejoicings in the opening scene, and two bassoons are employed with eerie effect to support the utterances of Samuel's ghost. A curious instance of Handel's occasional use of archaic instruments is to be found in David's exorcism of the evil spirit, which is accompanied by a theorbo.

Immediately upon the completion of *Saul*, Handel plunged into the composition of *Israel in Egypt*. No two works could present a more complete contrast. Handel seems to have been making experiments in the matter of form, and at this point in his career he was evidently wavering between the dramatic and the epic varieties of oratorio. The rapid play of individual emotion in *Saul* gives place to a severely epic manner of narration. Save for the few bars allotted to Miriam, the solos in *Israel* are purely impersonal. The tale of the salvation of the chosen people is told almost entirely in a chain of gigantic choruses, illustrating the sufferings of Israel in the land of bondage, the plagues inflicted by Jehovah upon the Egyptians, the escape of the Israelites, the passage of the Red Sea, and the final song of victory. The subject is colossal, and its treatment no less so. The possibilities of choral music as a means of expression are practically exhausted in *Israel*. Nothing like it had been heard before its day, nor has been attempted since. *Israel* remains one of the most astonishing *tours de force* in the history of music. As a combination of massive grandeur of style and picturesque force, it stands alone. It is like a vast series of frescoes painted by a giant on the walls of some primeval temple. The colours may have faded, but the sublime conception and the grand strength of line survive to astonish later and more degenerate ages. The range of Handel's genius was never more triumphantly displayed than in *Israel*. The skill with which each separate effect is gained is no less striking than the unfailing power of picturesque suggestion. Each of the plague choruses is a masterpiece in its way. There is, as it were, a shudder of disgust in the diminished sevenths and the passages of descending semitones in "They loathed to drink of the waters," which is considerably more impressive than the somewhat *naïf* realism of the succeeding solo, "Their land brought forth frogs." But if the frogs cannot be taken very seriously, the tremendous exordium of "He spake the word" transports us to a very different world, and the swarming flies and trampling locusts are painted with no loss of epic grandeur. Finer still is the famous Hailstone chorus, one of those big primitive things which are typical of one side of Handel's genius. The means by which the gathering storm is suggested are almost ludicrously simple, but they never miss fire, and the climax bursts upon us with terrific majesty. Finest of all is "He sent a thick darkness," in which the voices of a bewildered people cry to each other through the murky air with so strangely desolate a pathos. But space forbids a minute analysis of so familiar a work, and I must be content to touch on some of the most prominent features of the oratorio. It is characteristic of Handel that often a word or a phrase was enough to stimulate his genius to astonishing flights of imagination. Thus the words, "He led them forth like sheep," are responsible for the deliciously pastoral flow of the chorus, "But as for his people." Similarly in a later chorus, "The people shall hear," the composer fastened upon the phrase, "till thy people shall pass over, O Lord," and made it the foundation of an amazing picture of the weary march of the Israelites through the desert—a picture heightened by harmonies which, even to us, seem audacious in their rugged dissonance, and to an eighteenth-century audience must have sounded much as the harmonic experiments of Strauss or Debussy sound to modern ears. This is immediately followed by another picture, suggested by the words "Thou shalt bring them in," in which the serene loveliness of the land flowing with milk and honey is painted with a tranquil charm that is intensified by the harsh discords of the preceding chorus. Handel appreciated the majesty and splendour of the sea as perhaps no other composer in the whole history of music has done. His works are full of noble sea-pictures, and *Israel* is particularly rich in them. The solemn march of the children of Israel through the wild waters is grandly suggested in "He led them through the deep," and even finer is "But the waters overwhelmed them," through which the tumultuous glory of the lashing waves surges with such marvellous freshness and vigour ; but the greatest moment of all is the tremendous close of "And with the blast of Thy nostrils," where the depths congealed in the heart of the sea are painted with that awful simplicity of which Handel alone held the secret. "Egypt was glad" is a happy instance of Handel's ingenious use of other men's work for his own purposes. It is borrowed almost note for note from an organ canzona by an obscure German composer named Kerl, but it fits admirably into its place. Handel's conception of the Egyptians was that of a dull, hide-bound race, whom even the miraculous series of plagues scarcely disturbed in the narrow groove of their complacent apathy. He here contrasts their frozen conservatism with the progressive genius of the Israelites by the use of archaic methods of expression. The idea is felicitous, and, like most of Handel's experiments, is carried out with complete success.[1] But everything else in *Israel* pales before the astounding finale, in which triumphant rapture is tuned to such strains as Handel himself never surpassed. The tremendous "I will sing unto the Lord" soars to fabulous heights of sonorous splendour, and fitly brings to a close an oratorio which has a place of its own among the world's masterpieces. Handel might justly have said of *Israel*, as Wagner said of *Tristan und Isolde*, that it was an extravagance, not to be repeated nor imitated, but of all his works it is the most completely out of the reach of every other composer who ever lived.

After *Israel* Handel may well have felt that even his tireless coursers needed some repose, and his next two works were on a much less ambitious scale. *The Ode for St. Cecilia's Day*, though brief in compass, ranks among Handel's finest and most characteristic works. Dryden's poem, written as it was for musical setting, offers every possible opportunity for varied treatment. The opening recitative, "When nature underneath a heap of jarring atoms lay," is a curious piece of descriptive writing, in which odd little snatches of *naïf* realism jostle passages of real grandeur. In some of the airs that follow, the obbligato passages now sound sadly antiquated and meaningless, but there is a splendidly martial ring in the very Purcellian "The trumpet's loud clangour," and the air *alla Hornpipe*, "Orpheus could lead the savage race," into which Handel, who apparently liked Scotchmen no

---

[1] The question of Handel's indebtedness to earlier composers, of which *Israel in Egypt* affords perhaps more striking instances than any of his other works, is discussed in Appendix C.

more than did Dr. Johnson, introduced an unmistakable allusion to the bagpipes, is deliciously fresh and quaint. But the two great movements of the work are the lovely organ-song, "But oh! what art can teach," with its wonderful atmosphere of tranquil ecstasy, and the tremendous finale, in which the awful terrors of the Judgment Day are painted with a sublime majesty worthy of the brush of Michael Angelo himself.

Very different in scope is Handel's setting of Milton's *L'Allegro* and *Il Penseroso*, arranged by Jennens, and adorned with a singularly tasteless *coda* of his own devising, *Il Moderato*. Here Handel laid aside his wig, and wrote a work which stands by itself for freshness of inspiration and delicacy of treatment. *L'Allegro* is a series of exquisite *genre* pictures sketched with the lightest touch and yet elaborated with the most intimate detail. Nothing that Handel has left us shows more convincingly his love of nature. *L'Allegro* is full of delicious studies in *plein-airisme*. The country breezes blow freshly and sweetly through it, and the perfume of the wild rose lingers in its tender melodies. The recitative, "Mountains, on whose barren breast," is a wonderful piece of landscape-painting, and who has ever surpassed the romantic moon-rise in the second part of "Sweet bird," so rarely sung by the sopranos who revel in the faded *coloratura* of the opening section? In a different vein is the enchanted mystery of the "summer eves by haunted stream," and the woodland magic of "Hide me from day's garish eye." It is worth noting that *L'Allegro* was written during the great frost of 1740, yet there is no touch of winter in its merry strains. Snow-bound as he was in London, Handel seems to have harked back in imagination to the fields and hedgerows of Edgware.

L'Allegro rings with the sounds of rustic mirth. "Let me wander" is a delicious little idyll of the meadows, leading into the innocent gaiety of "Or let the merry bells ring round," with youth and maiden dancing in the chequered shade. Another perfect little vignette is the hunting scene pictured in "Mirth admit me of thy crew," and the note of honest English merriment rings clear in the splendidly vigorous laughing-song, "Haste thee, nymph." But *L'Allegro* is not all out-of-door life by any means. There is a charming little song in which the bell-man in the street and the cricket on the hearth have a quaint kind of duet, and the fireside picture in "Oft on a plat of rising ground," with the curfew tolling in the distance, is as perfect as a Dutch interior by Teniers or Ostade.

I have lingered over *L'Allegro* not merely on account of its intrinsic beauty, but because it is one of the best proofs we have of Handel's extraordinary breadth of sympathy. Nothing in man or nature came amiss to him. It is impossible not to feel that the man who wrote *L'Allegro* knew all about the scenes he was describing. Not only had he sat dreaming in close covert by some brook, and wandered over russet lawns and fallows grey, but he had discussed the hay crop with the mower as he whetted his scythe, and as like as not danced to the rebeck's sound with the buxom wenches of Edgware.

CHAPTER XVII

THE MESSIAH

FAMILIARITY breeds contempt, the proverb tells us. I am by no means sure that that is true as a general rule, and when it does happen I am inclined to think that the contempt is well deserved, so that the familiarity merely uncloaked the weaknesses which were not perceptible at a first acquaintance. However, familiarity breeds a good many other things as well, chiefly misunderstanding. It is the most familiar things that are the most misunderstood. Look at the Bible, for instance, which all of us are supposed to know by heart. Is there a more misunderstood book in the world? How many of the pious people who daily absorb a portion of it ever realise, to take one point, the transcendent literary beauty of our Authorised Version? How many even realise its value as a record of fact? They allow themselves to be hypnotised by its supposed sanctity, and forget that it purports to be a record of the actions of human beings. As a rule those who read it oftenest know least about it.

Look again at *Gulliver's Travels*, which I suppose, next to the Bible, *The Pilgrim's Progress*, and *Robinson Crusoe*, is the book that the average Englishman knows best. How strange has been its fate. The marvellous and terrible book in which Swift poured forth the stored

passion of his savage soul and glutted his hatred of the
animal man, has sunk to the rank of a nursery primer
from which lisping infants learn to spell. The fate of
The Messiah has been in some ways harder still.
The stupendous masterpiece in which Handel released
Christianity from the bondage of fact, and wrote the
romance of human redemption in characters of immortal
fire, is now degraded to the level of a mild digestive
which helps the struggling Nonconformist conscience to
tide over the festivities of Christmas. The ceremony of
attending a performance of *The Messiah* is to the average
Englishman as immutable a Christmas institution as going
to church or eating a slice of turkey. If you tell him that
The Messiah is a work of art, you either amuse or shock
him. A work of art, indeed—he would as soon apply the
phrase to a plum-pudding.

As a matter of fact, *The Messiah* is not only a very
great work of art, but it is actually the first instance in
the history of music of an attempt to view the mighty
drama of human redemption from an artistic standpoint.
We have only got to compare *The Messiah* with such a
work as Bach's *Matthew Passion* to see how entirely its
point of view differs from that of a work written, so to
speak, under the wing of the Church. Bach's *Passion*
is only a work of art by accident. It was primarily
written for edification, and edification, however excellent
a thing in itself, has nothing to do with art, though art
is often compelled to be its handmaid. Bach's *Passion*
is a church service, Handel's *Messiah* is a poem.
Bach deals with facts, Handel with ideas. I am continually reading in popular little musical handbooks of
the day that Bach is extraordinarily modern in feeling,
and Handel altogether old-fashioned. Very likely that

may be so in some way that I do not understand, but it strikes me that as regards their view of religion precisely the opposite is the case. Bach's attitude to Christianity is just what one would expect from a man of his bringing up and surroundings. He is a very good example of the average pietistic eighteenth-century Lutheran, with his bloodthirsty delight in the realistic details of Christ's passion, very much in the style of our own pious poet who wanted to be washed from his sins in a bath of blood or something of the kind. We have moved on a little since those days, and even the extreme Evangelicals, if any of them still survive, would now find Bach's Christianity slightly out of date. Handel's view of Christianity, on the other hand, is so surprisingly modern that the only book in which I have found it paralleled with any exactness is Mr. George Santayana's *Interpretations of Poetry and Religion*, which was published only a few years ago. I will venture to borrow a few passages from that very remarkable work, because I find Handel's attitude to Christianity as I read it in *The Messiah* better expressed in Mr. Santayana's words than in any that I could myself devise. In *The Messiah*, then, as I have said, for the first time in the history of music we find the drama of human redemption treated as a poem, not as a record of events. While his predecessors and contemporaries had exercised their art in presenting the story of Christ in its most human and realistic colours, Handel realised that the facts of Christ's life were nothing until they became symbols, and that the Christian system was in fact a picture of human destiny, an epic containing, as it were, the moral autobiography of man. The crucifixion, for example, seemed to him a tragic incident without further significance if regarded merely as an historical fact, as unessential to the Christian religion as was the death of Socrates to the Socratic philosophy. In order to make it a religious mystery, an idea capable of converting the world, the moral imagination must transform it into something that happens for the sake of the soul, so that each believer may say to himself that Christ so suffered for the love of him. Then, by ceasing to be viewed as an historical fact, the death of Christ becomes an inspiration. The whole of Christian doctrine is thus religious and efficacious only when it becomes poetry, because only then is it the felt counterpart of personal experience and a genuine expression of human life. This is the *idée mère* of *The Messiah*. The aim of the work is purely artistic. It has no didactic purpose. It is not a sermon, but a song—a magnificent effort of the human imagination, exercised upon the greatest and most inspiring of conceivable subjects. Incidentally it is also extremely edifying, but its edificatory purpose has been read into it by modern hearers who have found in *The Messiah* what they wished to find, rather than what the composer meant them to find. But it is the special property of great works of art that they mean one thing to one generation and one to another. *The Messiah* has a message to high and low, rich and poor, wise and foolish alike. By the side of imaginative flights of such measureless sublimity that they soar far beyond the ken of ordinary mortality, it contains passages so simple and direct that the dullest mind can comprehend them. *The Messiah*, if not Handel's greatest work, is undoubtedly the most universal in its appeal.

Thomas Jennens, the compiler of the text, has never had justice done to him. His libretto is really a very able piece of work. Knowing as we do how often

Handel stayed beneath his roof, we may take for granted
that the two worked together at *The Messiah*, and it is
possible that Handel had a larger share in the preparation of the text than Jennens, whose letter on the subject
has already been quoted, cared to admit. However that
may be, the ingenuity with which the words are selected
is remarkable. Jennens took especial pains to steer clear,
so far as was possible, of a mere statement of the facts of
Christ's life, emphasizing rather the ideas that underlie
them, and using the prophetic language of the Old
Testament in preference to the narrative of the New.
This alone did much towards raising the work from the
earthly region of prose to the ethereal heights of poetry.
But the libretto alone is, of course, nothing but a string
of texts, however skilfully juxtaposed. It was Handel's
genius that welded them into a sublime work of art.
The Messiah, as has been said, tells the story of man's
redemption. It is divided into three sections, the first of
which sets forth the promise of the Redeemer, the birth
of Christ, and His mission of healing and comfort ; the
second is devoted to His passion, resurrection, and ascension, the preaching of the gospel, the discomfiture of the
heathen, and the establishment of the kingdom of God
upon earth ; the third part deals with the Christian
belief in the resurrection of the body, and ends with the
triumph of the redeemed and the glory of heaven.

Face to face with a subject of this character, Handel
felt that the picturesque orchestration which is so
prominent a feature of *Saul* would be out of place. The
drama of human redemption demanded an austerer and
more reticent mode of treatment. The score of *The
Messiah* is one of the simplest that Handel ever wrote.
Save in the choruses, where the voice parts are doubled

by wind instruments, and trumpets and drums are
sparingly used, the accompaniments are written almost
without exception for strings alone. Yet within the
narrow limits that he assigned to himself Handel's
command of varied colour is remarkable, and Sir
Frederick Bridge's highly successful experiment of
performing *The Messiah* at the Albert Hall with the
original orchestration has opened the eyes of many, who
knew the oratorio only as disguised in the elegant
embroidery of Mozart's additional accompaniments, to
the real beauty and majesty of Handel's score.

Nothing is so difficult to criticise as the familiar;
and to English musicians, who have known every note
of *The Messiah* from their childhood, it is especially
difficult to get, as it were, outside the work, to banish the
sentimental associations that have clustered round it,
and to regard it as a work of art pure and simple.
There are many well-meaning persons to whom such an
attitude of mind is distasteful. *The Messiah* is to them
a thing above all criticism, occupying a place apart from
Handel's other works, indeed apart from all other music
whatsoever. But it is no good taking *The Messiah* on
trust as a sort of divinely inspired revelation. The only
way to understand and appreciate it is to pick it to pieces,
just as if it were a new work by a composer of our own
day.

The overture, gloomy and austere in tone, presents a
picture of the world plunged in sin and despair, before
the promise of a Messiah had kindled the hope of everlasting life. On this scene of doubt and darkness the
voice of the Comforter strikes with magical effect. The
change from minor to major at the opening of the accompanied recitative, "Comfort ye my people," is one of those

19

effects, all the more thrilling from their very simplicity, of which Handel held the secret. The following air, " Every valley," is on a distinctly lower level. Like so many of Handel's songs—and of Bach's too, for that matter, to say nothing of most of the other eighteenth-century composers—it is defaced by the interminable divisions, which were accepted by Georgian audiences as conventionally expressive of joy and gladness, but seem to modern ears as frigid and tasteless as the stucco ornaments of a barocco church—so little does one era accept the conventions of another! Apart from its divisions and its vigorous and spirited flow, there is very little in " Every valley" worth lingering over, and the *naïveté* with which the " rough places" are made plain is apt to provoke a smile. Nor is the chorus, " And the glory of the Lord," in any sense one of Handel's greatest achievements. There is a certain straightforward vigour about it in which Handel's music is rarely deficient, but its rhythm sadly lacks dignity and its development is long-winded, and the great effect of the repeated note is much better managed in the " Hallelujah" chorus, for which indeed " And the glory" is hardly more than a rough sketch. Far more striking is the great *scena* that follows, which was originally written for a contralto but is now, according to a precedent established by Handel himself, usually assigned to a bass.[1] The opening recitative, " Thus saith the Lord," is extraordinarily impressive; even the quaintly realistic divisions on the

---

[1] Considerations of space forbid me to discuss the questions raised by a comparison of the various MSS. of *The Messiah*. Numerous versions of many of the airs exist, and a study of the changes introduced by Handel into the oratorio is exceedingly interesting. With regard to details, students will find Sir William Cusins's pamphlet on *The Messiah* (Augener & Co., 1874) extremely valuable.

word "shake" seem to fit into their place very happily. The following air, " But who may abide," is one of Handel's most startlingly original productions. The mere form of the air was probably unprecedented in his time, and the contrast between the terrible desolation of the opening *larghetto* and the rushing flickering flames of the refiner's fire in the succeeding *prestissimo* is astonishingly fine. This is one of the passages in *The Messiah* that has gained most by the recent return to Handel's original accompaniment. Mozart, if the additions usually attributed to him are actually his, seems, as in many other instances, to have totally misapprehended Handel's meaning. His graceful embroideries completely obscure the carefully designed contrast between guilty man standing defenceless upon the bare earth and the advent of the terrible Judge in flames and tempest. The interest of the chorus, "And He shall purify the sons of Levi," is purely musical. I confess that I have not the least idea what connection the words have with the "plot" of *The Messiah*, and I doubt if Handel had much more. He adapted the music from one of a set of Italian duets that he had written just before beginning *The Messiah*, a blameless ditty about nothing in particular, and it fits the sons of Levi just as well as the flowers and sunsets of the original poem.

The little recitative that follows, "Behold, a virgin shall conceive," short as it is, is one of the most wonderful things in *The Messiah*. It has the tender exaltation of one of Giovanni Bellini's Madonnas, with a touch of sacred awe that was out of Bellini's compass. The same note of solemnity sounds through the rapture of "O thou that tellest good tidings to Zion," and lifts it above mere jubilation. One of the most striking features of *The*

Messiah is the skill which, in spite of its purely epical structure, Handel arranged his contrasts. The bass recitative and air, "For behold, darkness shall cover the earth," would be extraordinarily impressive in any context, but placed as it is between two of the "high lights" of the work it is doubly effective. Simple as are the means employed, it is one of the most speaking musical pictures ever painted. "The people that walked in darkness" affords a particularly good instance of the advantage gained by performing *The Messiah* as Handel wrote it, and not as other people think he ought to have written it. Mozart's wind parts, so beautiful in themselves and so utterly inappropriate to the subject, do not, as Rockstro truly observed, suggest darkness at all, but rather an enchanted atmosphere of soft golden light; whereas Handel's unison passages for strings and bassoons give a picture of a people groping its way through the blackness of night, to which music affords no parallel for force and intensity. "For unto us a child is born" is another of the choruses that owes its birth to one of the Italian duets already mentioned, and the process of its development deserves the most careful study. Here again those who have only heard it caricatured in Mozart's version know nothing of Handel's real meaning. Mozart's added brass not only ruins the effect of Handel's skilfully contrived climax in this particular chorus, but defeats the design of the whole oratorio. "For unto us" is the climax of the prophetic section, but it is still prophecy, not fulfilment. Handel carefully reserved his trumpets until the following section, just as he reserved the soprano voice to lend brightness to the advent of the promised Messiah. It is curious that Mozart, of all people in the world, should

have missed this important point, since he did very much
the same thing in *Don Giovanni*, reserving his trombones
to add impressiveness to the supernatural terrors of the
closing scenes.

In the Pastoral Symphony and the following numbers
we come nearer to drama than in any other part of *The
Messiah*. The birth of Christ is not described, but we
are taken to the fields where the shepherds abode by
night, and we listen with them to the angelic communica-
tion. The climax is contrived with Handel's usual care
and skill. The lovely Pastoral Symphony paints the
tranquil scene in colours the most delicate and subtle.
It is worth noticing that Handel, true to his principle of
keeping to low tones in the orchestration of *The Messiah*,
chose not to employ the traditionally pastoral hautboys
in this movement. The entry of the soprano voice, so
long delayed, strikes on the ear with a clarion note of
exaltation, and through the chain of recitatives that
follow—which cost Handel a great deal of trouble before
he arrived at the final form—the excitement grows with
each bar until the angelic choir bursts in with its jubilant
cry of "Glory to God," accompanied by the trumpets
that now are heard for the first time. The glitter and
sparkle of this chorus is astonishing. Here in good
truth are the "voices that seem to shine" of which the
old Elizabethan poet wrote, while the thrilling notes of
the trumpets and the rushing passages for the violins
seem to throw open the skies and give wondrous glimpses
of celestial radiance beyond. Mozart's treatment of
Handel's orchestration in this chorus is so incredible as
to raise a serious doubt whether the accompaniments
traditionally ascribed to him can possibly be by his hand.
Not only did he completely spoil the effect of the entry

of the trumpets by adding trumpet parts to "For unto us," but in "Glory to God" he actually cut out Handel's trumpet parts and wrote others of his own, leaving the voices in the opening bars supported only by strings and wood and reserving the trumpets until the words, "and peace on earth." The close of the chorus, with its exquisite *diminuendo* as the angels gradually disappear, is another characteristically Handelian passage, which may possibly have suggested to Wagner the close of his *Lohengrin* prelude where the angels who have brought the Holy Grail to earth disappear in the trackless blue, and indeed the whole number is a shining instance of Handel's extraordinary command of picturesque effect. The flashing soprano air, "Rejoice greatly, O daughter of Zion," is a fine example of the legitimate use of *coloratura*, to which the serene loveliness of the passage, "He shall speak peace unto the heathen," forms a perfect contrast.

In a very different vein is the succeeding air, "He shall feed His flock," in which Christ's earthly mission of comfort and consolation is painted in music whose infinite tenderness expresses, as only the greatest of all musicians could express it, the wonderful secret of Christianity, the charm that won the world from the radiant gods of Greece and taught it to bow at the feet of the Good Shepherd gathering the lambs with His arms and carrying them in His bosom. Never till Jesus Christ was born had the conception of a God of Pity dawned upon the world, and never till Handel wrote *The Messiah* had music clothed with her conquering magic the figure of the Divine Comforter whose message is to them that labour and are heavy laden.[1] Not alto-

[1] It has often been stated that the practice of allotting the first section of "He shall feed His flock" to a contralto and the second to a soprano is of

gether worthy of what has gone before, for all its rich musical beauty, is the chorus, " His yoke is easy," which brings the first part to a close. It is yet another adaptation from the Italian duets, and carries the mark of its origin in the curious opening phrase, which, however appropriate to the flowers laughing in the sunlight, to which it was first applied, is singularly ill adapted to the yoke that Christ laid upon His people.

The second part of *The Messiah* brings us to the passion of Christ, but the librettist, true to the spirit of the work, has carefully avoided any reference to the physical side of the tragedy, insisting rather on its inner meaning. We are bidden to contemplate not the bodily sufferings of Jesus, but the mystery of the atonement. It is not the human Christ, scourged, stricken and crucified, that is put before us, but the Lamb of God that taketh away the sins of the world. The solemn opening chorus, breathing the tragedy of infinite loneliness in its austere beauty, leads into the famous " He was despised," in which the note of utter desolation is still further emphasised. It is curious to note how the well-

modern origin, and a defiance of Handel's original intention. This, however, is not so; in fact, if the MS. notes in the copy of the original libretto now in the British Museum are to be relied on, the air was sung in this way at the first performance of *The Messiah*. It is true that in the autograph the whole of the air is in the key of B flat, but the Dublin MS. contains both versions. The version now used is unquestionably an improvement upon that given in the autograph. The device of giving the earthly message of comfort to a contralto and its celestial application to a soprano a fourth higher is nothing less than a stroke of genius, while the change to the key of F is a great relief to the ear, which would otherwise resent the monotony of three long pieces in the key of B flat. Possibly, too, a severely practical reason may be at the bottom of the transposition, for if only one soprano soloist were available, it would be too much to expect her to pass without any interval from the brilliant *coloratura* of " Rejoice greatly" to the suave *cantabile* phrases of " He shall feed His flock."

meaning persons who chose to embroider Handel's score with additional accompaniments contrived to ignore his obvious intentions on every possible occasion. In the thirty-third bar of this air, Handel, who well knew the majesty of silence, left a pause of half a bar before the entry of the unaccompanied voice. This pause Mozart filled up with meaningless chords, while Franz, not to be outdone in tastelessness and stupidity, actually added a passage for the clarinet, anticipating the vocal phrase and completely robbing it of its marvellous dignity and pathos. The wonderful second part of " He was despised " (almost invariably omitted at performances in England) adds a touch of poignancy by a reference to the actual sufferings of Christ, and so leads us on to the almost intolerable anguish of "Surely He hath borne our griefs." After this climax of emotion some relief was necessary, and Handel, whose artistic instinct was Athenian in its subtlety, relieves the tension with a chorus of purely musical interest, " And with His stripes we are healed "— just as Euripides in his *Troades* soothed the overtaxed feelings of his audience, after the terrible scene in which Astyanax is torn from Andromache's arms, with the purely sensuous beauty of the famous Salamis chorus. I have myself no very great admiration for "And with His stripes," but I recognise its value in the picture.

"All we like sheep" is a picture painted in Handel's broadest manner. The colour is positively hurled at the canvas. But the result is colossal. The sheep wandering without a shepherd seem to have the whole world for their pasture, and the tremendous *coda*, in which the promise of atonement is thundered forth, seems to be written upon the skies for all the nations to read.

We now exchange the general for the particular, and

the libretto, leaving the purely epical treatment of the atonement, leads us as it were to the foot of the cross. Yet even here the physical side of Christ's passion is left out of sight; it is the contrast between His mental agony and the scoffs of the crowd of unbelievers that forms the subject of the picture. Similarly, the actual facts of the resurrection and ascension are barely hinted at, the triumph of the Saviour over death and the grave and His ascent to heaven amidst throngs of chorusing angels being suggested rather than described in the two beautiful airs, "But Thou didst not leave His soul in hell," and "Thou art gone up on high," and in the accompanying choruses, "Lift up your heads," and "Let all the angels of God worship Him."

The libretto then turns to the evangelisation of the world by the apostles and their followers. The opening number of this section, "The Lord gave the word, great was the company of the preachers," is far from being one of the most impressive choruses in *The Messiah*, but it is technically interesting to the Handelian student as an instance of Handel's ingenious manner of working up old material. The opening notes at once recall the thrilling opening of the chorus, "He spake the word," in *Israel in Egypt*, and the device for expressing the countless multitude of preachers is borrowed from the music illustrating "the busy hum of men," in *L'Allegro*. The following air, "How beautiful are the feet," gave Handel more trouble than anything else in the oratorio. Numerous versions of it exist in numerous forms, and it is characteristic of the composer that he finally decided upon the simplest of them all. But the well-known saying of Paesiello, *questo semplice com' è difficile*, is truer of Handel's music than of that to which it was originally applied. It is his simplest things that are most effectually beyond the reach of imitators.

The chorus, "Their sound is gone out into all lands," was an afterthought added to the work after the first performance, and is the only number in *The Messiah* that has independent parts for hautboys. Not only in this is it remarkable. To it as justly as to anything that Handel wrote can the epithet romantic be justly applied. The long sweeping phrases that paint the flight of the good tidings over land and sea have a soaring freedom of utterance that gives a character to this chorus distinct from anything else in *The Messiah*.

So far we have traced the spread of the gospel, but now comes a picture of the vain wrath of the heathen who flout its message, in the turbulent energy of the bass air, "Why do the nations so furiously rage together?" and the succeeding chorus, "Let us break their bonds asunder." But the divine vengeance follows closely. The impotent strivings of pagan insolence are crushed in the splendidly vigorous "Thou shalt break them in pieces," and the whole earth joins in a pæan of triumph over the final victory of Christianity in the world-famous "Hallelujah." Familiar as the "Hallelujah" chorus is, it is often profoundly misunderstood, particularly by those who have instituted comparisons between it and the "Sanctus" of Bach's Mass in B minor. The two compositions have nothing in common. In the "Sanctus" we hear the voices of the celestial choir, chanting the praise of the Omnipotent, and casting down their crowns upon the crystal sea. The "Hallelujah" chorus, on the other hand, is essentially of the earth earthy. Its place in *The Messiah* proves incontestably that it is a human song of rejoicing. "The kingdom of this world," it cries, "is become the kingdom of our Lord and of His Christ." We must wait until the close of the oratorio to hear the anthem of those which have come out of great tribulation and washed their robes and made them white in the blood of the Lamb.

The third part of the oratorio deals with the resurrection of the body and the life of the world to come. After the multitudinous thunders of the "Hallelujah" chorus a marvellous effect of contrast is gained by the austere simplicity of "I know that my Redeemer liveth," in which the chaste purity of the soprano voice, supported by a studiously unadorned accompaniment, suggests a cry of faith and hope rising from a world of doubt and darkness. The air is one of Handel's profoundest inspirations, but those who know it only when choked by additional accompaniments, can never have grasped its true meaning. To take but one instance, it is not until Mozart's intrusive viola part has been removed that the full force of the setting of "the first fruits of them that sleep" can be properly appreciated. Then and not till then is Handel's violoncello part properly heard, pulsating through the violins and organ with a strange throb of expectation, which tells in a language plainer than words of the sure and certain hope that lives even in death.

In the chain of brief choruses that follows, "Since by man came death, by man came also the resurrection of the dead," Handel contrasts the old and new dispensations with startling force, borrowing harmonies and cadences from the music of old time to emphasize the archaic dogmas of the Law, and leaving the unaccompanied voices of the chorus to tell of the old Adam and his death, while the sudden blaze of the orchestra illuminates the new Christ and His resurrection. But

before the promised life is won the mysteries of death
and judgment must be faced. The trumpet-call of doom
sounds in the stately recitative and air, "Behold I tell
you a mystery," and "The trumpet shall sound," and
in the succeeding duet, "O death, where is thy sting?"
leading into the chorus, "But thanks be to God," death
is swallowed up in victory. The last note of triumphant
faith sounds in the rarely heard air, "If God be for us,"
and in the final chorus, "Worthy is the Lamb," the
Christian is at last in the presence of his Maker. It is
only necessary to compare "Worthy is the Lamb" with
the "Hallelujah" chorus to realise the difference in
atmosphere between the two. The "Hallelujah" chorus
is an earthly song of praise, in which the thousand throats
of humanity unite to hymn the triumph of their Lord,
but in "Worthy is the Lamb" we hear the voices of the
redeemed. Even here the voice of the devil's advocate
is heard, pointing out how Handel lacks the spirituality
of Bach, how far, in short, "Worthy is the Lamb" is
beneath the great "Sanctus" in the B minor Mass as an
expression of rapturous exaltation. In a certain sense
this is true. Bach was unquestionably a more spiritually
minded, or, as we now say, a more religious man than
Handel. When he wrote the "Sanctus" he was rapt
away from earth, and stood in spirit among the harpers
harping with their harps beside the sea of glass, and
joined his voice to theirs. Handel's feet are always upon
solid earth. His imagination opened all portals, but he
passed none. When he wrote the "Hallelujah" chorus
he "did think he saw heaven opened and the great God
Himself," but he was not, like Bach, caught up in spirit
to the heaven that he beheld. Handel was an artist
rather than a seer. While Bach was in the midst of his

own imaginings, Handel contemplated the beatific vision from afar. The method of the one was subjective, of the other objective. Thus, in a word, must *The Messiah* as a whole be judged. It is a work of pure imagination, and to pretend that it is a record of Handel's private emotions is to misunderstand both the man and his genius. There was a good deal more of Titian than of Fra Angelico in Handel. For the rapture of spiritual ecstasy that animates the work of the pious Frate we ask of Handel in vain, but instead he gives us an all-embracing sympathy for every manifestation of human energy, that lifts his work far above sects and dogmas and makes it the common property of all mankind.

CHAPTER XVIII

THE LATER ORATORIOS

THE production of *The Messiah* was a turning-point in Handel's career as a composer of oratorios. It marks the close of what we may call his first or experimental period. Handel's first six oratorios all differ markedly in form. He seems to have been conducting a series of experiments, without being able to make up his mind as to which form of oratorio was best suited to his genius. *Esther* was originally a masque, frankly intended for theatrical performance, though its revision in 1734 naturally brought it more into the shape of oratorio. *Deborah* is an epic pure and simple. In *Athaliah* there is a return to the dramatic style, which is carried still further in *Saul*. *Israel* and *The Messiah*, on the other hand, are more definitely epical in treatment than *Deborah*. With *The Messiah* Handel's experiments ceased. After producing his two epical masterpieces he returned to the dramatic style of *Saul*, to which he adhered for the rest of his life. The reason for his decision is not far to seek. Handel was eminently practical, and his decision to abandon the purely epical style was probably due in great measure to the comparative failure of *Israel* and, in England if not in Ireland, of *The Messiah.* Within due limits, he was fully alive

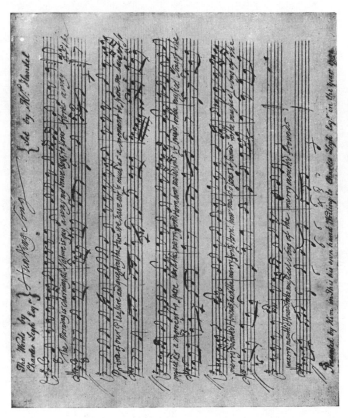

FACSIMILE OF HANDEL'S HUNTING SONG

to the wisdom of consulting popular taste, and doubtless
he recognised as clearly as his audiences that the emotions
of human beings, of like passions with ourselves, were a
good deal more interesting as a subject for artistic treatment than abstract discussions of the dogmas of theology.
At any rate, for the rest of his life he made no more
excursions into purely epical oratorio. The form that
he finally adopted has a good deal in common with
Greek tragedy. The attitude and functions of the chorus
are those of interested and sympathetic spectators who
rarely if ever take part in the action, but punctuate the
various scenes with choral odes of a meditative or gnomic
cast, often deducing a wholesome moral from the events
enacted before their eyes. The long set speeches which
are so important a feature of the Greek drama correspond
more or less accurately to the stately airs of Handelian
oratorio, while the more rapid dialogue or stichomythia
is represented by recitative. *Samson*, founded as it is
upon Milton's *Samson Agonistes*, which was written in
avowed imitation of an Athenian tragedy, is a particularly
fine instance of the oratorio-form that Handel finally
accepted. In dignity of style it yields to none of Handel's
works, while its dramatic power and the striking contrasts
of character in which it abounds give it a human interest
which is necessarily absent from the works conceived in
a more abstract vein. Newburgh Hamilton's libretto is
a more than tolerable piece of work. He knew his
Milton well, and besides making free use of *Samson
Agonistes*, he levied occasional contributions upon several
of Milton's other poems, including the Odes "On the
Nativity," " On the Passion," "On Time," and "At a solemn
Musick," the " Epitaph on the Marchioness of Winchester,"
and the translations of the Psalms. The result is a rather

surprising piece of patchwork, in which Hamilton's very prosaic muse cuts a poor figure in her august company, though the pedestrian numbers of the poetaster are to some extent atoned for by the skill with which the libretto is put together. A skilful piece of work it unquestionably is, and it is to be believed that Handel turned with no little satisfaction from the austere abstraction of *The Messiah* to the varied passions and pulsing life of *Samson*. What we may call the background of the work, the contrast between the idolatrous frivolities of heathendom and the august solemnity of the worship of the one true God, was often treated by Handel, but never with more consummate skill than in *Samson*. The Philistine revels are painted in the most glowing colours, and with a special touch of light-hearted and almost childlike gaiety that differentiates them from Handel's other excursions into the high places of paganism. In striking contrast are the nobly dignified choruses allotted to the Israelites, which are very far from being the merely conventional expressions of respectable piety to which in his later oratorios Handel sometimes condescended. On the contrary, many of them have a character peculiarly their own—a kind of rapturous exaltation which is very difficult to define in words. This quality I find particularly in the closing chorus, " Let their celestial concerts all unite," which, beginning rather dully, seems midway to be touched by some divine fire and to be uplifted into strange regions of spiritual ecstasy, and still more markedly in " Then round about the starry throne," a chorus on which, if I were condemned to the extremely difficult and unsatisfactory task of picking out one thing of Handel's as superior to all else, my choice, would, I think, alight. *Samson* is, I think, the most personal of Handel's oratorios, that of which the subject appealed most strongly to him, and into which he put most of himself. It is not so much that his own life was one long war against Philistines, or that he shared the hero's bodily affliction, though it is quite possible that at the time when he was writing *Samson* he may have had premonitory symptoms of his approaching blindness. The reason I believe, at the risk of being thought fanciful, to lie at the roots of Handel's character. We know but little of Handel's private life, but everything that has been handed down with regard to it points to his having been a man of singular personal purity. In his time obscenity of language and unchastity of life were regarded as the most venial of sins, but from the typical faults of the age Handel was entirely free, and the disgust with which he regarded the sensuality that he saw rampant around him is, I think, to be read in *Samson* by those that have eyes to see. I have already pointed out how fond Handel was of fixing on a word or a phrase and making it the text on which to ground a discourse. In " Then round about the starry throne " he seizes upon the words, " from all this earthly grossness quit," and turning as it were with loathing from the sordid and sensual amours of Samson and Delilah, he lifts his voice in a triumphant pæan in praise of chastity. It is difficult to describe the extraordinary ecstasy of this chorus. The music seems to glow with a white heat of rapture. There is nothing else like it in Handel, nor indeed in any one else. But the interest of *Samson* is far from ending here. The various characters of the drama are sketched with a masterly touch. Samson, the blind hero, is probably the most carefully studied figure in the whole range of Handel's oratorios. In him pathos and dignity are

20

mingled with an art that is beyond praise, and the flashes of the old fire that leap up from the ashes of despair give a wonderfully vivid touch to the character.

Micah, a figment of the librettist, is merely an excuse for the contralto solos, but the other personages are all happily drawn. Delilah, with her false beguiling, forms an admirable foil to the reverend figure of Manoah, whose music is a shining example of Handel's unequalled appreciation of the majesty and pathos of old age. The bitterness of unavailing sorrow was never set to more piteous accents than the close of the air, " Thy glorious deeds," nor has the tender sympathy of a father's love ever found truer or moving expression than in the beautiful " How willing my paternal love." In a very different vein is the masterly sketch of the Philistine giant Harapha, whose braggart cowardice is drawn with amazing boldness and vigour in the famous air, " Honour and arms."

Samson is more familiar to modern hearers than the majority of Handel's oratorios, but students should be warned that the abbreviated version now usually performed not only omits a great deal of fine music, but is arranged in a very happy-go-lucky manner, indeed the effect of several scenes is seriously marred by remorseless mutilation. Thus the omission of the solo, " To song and dance," deprives the ensuing chorus of much of its meaning, and the disappearance of the recitatives in the marvellous funeral scene at the close of the work, a masterpiece second only to the corresponding section of *Saul*, obscures Handel's carefully studied design, and, by omitting what we may call the stage-directions, robs the scene of much of its picturesqueness.

The victory of Dettingen in 1743 drew Handel for

the moment from his oratorios. The *Te Deum* and Anthem that he wrote to celebrate the triumphs of George II. are in the sonorous and splendid manner of his earlier Coronation anthems. The *Te Deum* in particular was extravagantly admired and praised during Handel's lifetime, and in public estimation it took the place till then held by the *Te Deum* that he had written in honour of the Peace of Utrecht thirty years before. Its pomp and glitter are now a little tarnished by time but it remains a fine specimen of ringing Handelian rhetoric.

Semele, Handel's next work, carried him to very different fields. Congreve's libretto had been published in 1720, described as an opera, but there seems no reason to suppose that Handel intended his work for stage performance. In *Semele* he put off to a great extent his "big bow-wow" manner, and produced a work which has a good deal more in common with *Acis and Galatea* than with any of the sacred or semi-sacred oratorios. There is the same lightness of touch, the same ease and gaiety of inspiration, and the same sunny background of the fresh, laughing, pagan life of old Greece. The choruses are as a rule slighter in construction than was Handel's wont, and many of them are founded upon sparkling dance measures. The ravishing love-chorus, "Now Love, that everlasting boy," is described as *alla Hornpipe*, and "Endless pleasure" is a lively gavotte. There is not much scope for characterisation in *Semele*. Juno is unquestionably the most striking figure in the work. Her jealous fury is painted in vivid colours, and her spiteful little air, "Above measure," gives a deliciously feminine touch to her grim personality. The other characters—the amorous Jupiter, the voluptuous Semele, and a host of minor figures—are less interesting on the whole, but the music of the drowsy god Somnus is very beautiful, and indeed *Semele* is full of charming songs, many of which, such as Semele's "O sleep, why dost thou leave me," and Jupiter's "Where'er you walk," are still famous. The score of *Semele* contains many of Handel's characteristically picturesque touches. The storm chorus, 'Avert these omens," is a brilliant piece of descriptive writing, and in another chorus later in the work the curiously realistic setting of the words, "All our boasted fire is lost in smoke," is very interesting. One of the *entr'actes* paints the sleep of Somnus effectively, and another gives a vivid picture of Juno's flight from Samos, while the passage for drums illustrating Jupiter's oath gives the lie to the often - repeated statement that Beethoven was the first to raise the drum to the rank of a solo instrument.

It is easy to believe that so whole-hearted a pagan as Handel enjoyed to the full the momentary escape that *Semele* gave him from sacred subjects, and that he returned to oratorio with no very great gusto. At any rate, *Joseph* is one of his least inspired efforts. To the present generation it is almost entirely unknown. It is the only one of Handel's oratorios that has never been published in vocal score, and though it is said to have been repeatedly performed in Berlin during the nineteenth century, there is no record of it having been given publicly in England since the death of the composer, though the fine chorus, "Blest be the man," has been heard more than once at the Handel Festival. The greater part of the music scarcely leaves the conventional track which Handel was now beginning to tread with somewhat mechanical steps, yet *Joseph* has its fine moments. There are several choruses of majestic dignity, and the wedding music is appropriately festive and jubilant.   Here and there, too, occur gems of melody in Handel's freshest manner, such as the exquisite pastoral, " The peasant tastes the sweets of life," and the graceful duet, "What's sweeter than a new-blown rose." But the finest music in *Joseph* is concerned with the erring brothers.   The guilty Simeon has a splendidly dramatic *scena*, and the recognition scene is handled with a masterly touch.   But as a whole *Joseph* is scarcely worthy of the hand that a few years before had written *Samson*.

The success of *Semele* tempted Handel to turn once more to Greek mythology, and his next work was *Hercules*, an adaptation by Thomas Broughton of Sophocles's noble tragedy, *The Women of Trachis*. *Hercules* stands in the front rank of Handel's works.   In dramatic power and masterly handling of character it is inferior to nothing that he wrote.   In style it leans to opera rather than to oratorio.   The choruses are comparatively few, and though striking in their kind depart widely as a rule from the accepted oratorio standard. The most remarkable of them are " Jealousy, infernal pest," a curious study in musical psychology, and the love-chorus, " Wanton God of amorous fire," which, though perhaps less engaging than the delicious " Now Love, that everlasting boy" in *Semele*, proves up to the hilt that Handel, old bachelor as he was, knew uncommonly well what he was writing about.[1]

[1] In Samuel Butler's notebooks there is a characteristic comment on the chorus, "Tyrants now no more shall dread," sung when the news of Hercules's death is announced, which I venture to quote : "The music to this chorus is written from the tyrants' point of view.   This is plain from the jubilant defiance with which the chorus opens, but becomes still plainer when the magnificent strain to which he has set the words, 'all fear of

But it is in the solo music that the real strength of *Hercules* lies. The character of Dejanira is elaborated with equal vigour and subtlety. Her changing moods are mirrored in music that gives its true value to every *nuance* of feeling. We see her first lamenting the absence of her lord in the pathetic air, " The world, when day's career is done," a melody of yearning beauty to which strange harmonies give an added poignancy. The news of Hercules's approach banishes her sorrow, and her new-found happiness breaks forth in the light-hearted strains of " Begone, my fears." The arrival of Hercules, accompanied by the captive princess Iole, sows the seeds of jealousy in Dejanira's bosom. Then follows an inter-

punishment is o'er,' bursts upon us. Here he flings aside all considerations save that of the gospel of doing whatever we please without having to pay for it. He remembers himself, however, shortly, and becomes almost puritanical over ' The world's avenger is no more.' Here he is quite proper. From a dramatic point of view Handel's treatment of these words must be condemned for reasons in respect of which Handel is rarely at fault. It puzzles the listener, who expects the words to be treated from the point of view of the vanquished slaves, not from that of the tyrants. There is no pretence that those particular tyrants are not so bad as ordinary tyrants, nor those particular vanquished slaves not so good as ordinary vanquished slaves, and unless this has been made clear in some way it is dramatically *de rigueur* that the tyrants should come to grief, or be about to come to grief. The hearer should know which way his sympathies are expected to go, and here we have the music dragging one way and the words the other.

" Nevertheless we pardon the departure from the strict rules of the game, partly because of the welcome nature of good tidings so exultantly announced to us about all fear of punishment being over, and partly because throughout the music is so much stronger than the words that we lose sight of them almost entirely. Handel probably wrote as he did from a profound, though perhaps unconscious, perception of the fact that even in his day there was a great deal of humanitarian nonsense talked, and that after all the tyrants were generally quite as good sort of people as the vanquished slaves. Having begun on this tack, it was easy to throw morality to the winds when he came to the words, ' all fear of punishment is o'er.' "

view with Iole, culminating in the bitter irony of " When beauty sorrow's livery wears." Later comes a long and carefully wrought scene with Hercules opening with a masterly song, " Resign thy club," the biting sarcasm of which is set to music of extraordinary force, and leading into the wonderful lament, " Cease, ruler of the day, to shine," which paints the anguish of a wounded heart in the most moving colours. But all else pales before the tremendous closing *scena*, " Where shall I fly?" in which the wretched woman, torn by terror and remorse, strives to hide her guilty head from the vengeful Furies that encompass her. The concentrated horror of this passage, wrought as it is to a climax of amazing power, can hardly be paralleled in the whole range of Handel's works. By the side of Dejanira the other characters of the drama sink into comparative insignificance. Hercules, a typical hero, bluff and beefy, is only interesting in his final agony, which is a page of poignant drama. The gentle Iole forms a graceful foil to the passion-tossed Dejanira. Though sketched with a light touch she is far from being a merely colourless *ingénue*. Her beautiful air, " My father," has power as well as pathos, while the scene in which she " chaffs" Hyllus is delightfully arch and vivacious. Exquisite, too, is the air, " My breast with tender pity swells," in which she endeavours to calm the frenzy of the stricken Dejanira. After the wild ravings of the guilty princess, the suave accents of Iole fall like balm upon the ear. The contrast is one of a kind in which Handel specially delighted, and he has here treated it with a magical touch; but *Hercules* is throughout full of Handel's finest workmanship, and it is curious that it should be so little known. Present-day critics, who are always

on the look out for "modern" effects in the works of
the classical masters, would find much in *Hercules* to
interest them. In particular, it is worth while to call
attention to the curious little symphony that precedes
the third act, a piece of primitive programme music
describing the agony of Hercules in the most realistic
fashion.

With *Belshazzar* Handel returned once more to the
Old Testament and his trusty Jennens. *Belshazzar* is in
his stateliest style, abounding in fully developed choruses,
and trusting but little to dramatic interest or play of
character. Of its kind it is a fine example. Handel
rarely surpassed the massive grandeur of such choruses
as "By slow degrees the wrath of God," "See from his
post Euphrates flies," and "Sing, O heavens," to name
but a few out of many. In a very different vein is the
mocking chorus of Babylonians, who from the height of
their impregnable walls deride the vain efforts of the
besiegers below—a passage brimming over with that
peculiarly ironic humour which was characteristic of
Handel. Admirable, too, is the whole scene of Belshazzar's
feast, the insolent arrogance of the king, the drunken
chorus of his lords—one of the most "unbuttoned"
things Handel ever wrote, and full of effects that nobody
would dream of looking for in eighteenth-century music
—and finally the apparition of the hand and the writing
on the wall. This incident is treated with remarkable
power, the terrified cries of the king, the broken utterances
of the chorus, and the curiously descriptive orchestration
all contributing to the general effect. There are many
other interesting points in *Belshazzar*. Some of the solos
are in Handel's finest manner, notably the solemn "Great
God, who yet but darkly known," which in some

mysterious way conveys an impression of the awe felt by
a heathen in the presence of an unknown God, and the
splendid accompanied recitative, "Thus saith the Lord,"
a particularly fine instance of Handel's employment of a
ground-bass, not, as was so often the case in Purcell's
time, merely as an excuse for a meaningless display of
musical ingenuity, but for the purpose of expressing
a definite poetical idea, in this case the sureness of
the Divine support.   I must not forget the overture,
a very fine piece of programme music, painting in
the most picturesque and forcible manner the contrast
between the wild turbulence of the heathen and the
steady faith of the worshippers of God; nor the
curious little instrumental movement, marked in the
autograph as "Allegro postillons," which describes Belshazzar's messengers riding off post-haste in search of
the wise men who were to interpret the writing on the
wall.

The *Occasional Oratorio*, hastily put together to
celebrate the repulse of the Young Pretender, can hardly
be classed as an oratorio in the ordinary sense of the
word.   It is rather an anthem on an unusually extended
scale, being nothing but a string of texts from the Psalms
interspersed with songs, and boasting only the most
shadowy apology for a design.   Handel used a good deal
of old music in it, and of the new numbers hardly one
reaches his best standard, except perhaps the famous
overture, which through its stirring march has become
familiar to many who have but the vaguest idea what the
occasion was that called it forth.   Handel is usually
supposed to have lived before the days of "local colour,"
but in one of the songs in the *Occasional Oratorio*, "When
warlike ensigns wave on high," there occurs what looks

suspiciously like an imitation of the bagpipes, illustrating
the words:—

> " The frighted peasant sees his field
> For corn an iron harvest yield ;
> No pasture now the plains afford,
> And scythes are straightened into swords,"

which very possibly may be intended as a sly reference
to Prince Charlie's southern march, and to the apparition
of the Highland clansmen in the fertile meadows of the
Midlands.

Judas Maccabæus was in every way a nobler tribute
to the victor of Culloden than the *Occasional Oratorio.*
Its martial ardour has endeared it to many generations
of Englishmen, and it is still one of the most popular of
Handel's oratorios. This, however, is by no means the
same as saying that it is one of the best. As a matter of
fact it is inferior to many far less famous works. It is
totally devoid of anything like characterisation, and its
subject ties it down to the expression of none but the
simplest emotions of joy and grief, so that with all its
directness and vigour it tends decidedly to monotony.
What is worse is, that in *Judas,* more than in any of his
other oratorios, Handel lies open to the charge of writing
clap-trap. There are magnificent things scattered over
the score of *Judas,* superb choruses like "We never will
bow down," "Fall'n is the foe," and "Sion now her head
shall raise," and a few solo numbers of rare beauty, such
as "Pious orgies" and "O lovely peace," but there is far
too much music of the type of "Sound an alarm," and
"The Lord worketh wonders," for which the best that
can be said is that their energy makes some amends for
lack of inspiration.

Handel himself seems to have been fully alive to the

inferiority of *Judas*. His observation upon "See the conquering hero comes" (though this was subsequently borrowed from *Joshua*) has already been quoted, and a further record has been preserved which amounts to a practical confession that he was guilty of writing down to the level of an uneducated taste: "A gentleman whom he had desired to look over *Judas Maccabæus* having declared his opinion of it, 'Well,' said Handel, 'to be sure you have picked out the best songs, but you take no notice of that which is to get me all the money,' meaning the worst in the whole oratorio." As a matter of fact, Handel was totally lacking in the false pride that hinders a man from admitting his failures and deficiencies. He was walking one day in Marylebone Gardens with a reverend friend of his, named Fountayne, when the band struck up a piece of music. "Come, Mr. Fountayne," said Handel, "let us sit down and listen to this piece; I want to know your opinion of it." Down they sat, and after some time the old parson, turning to his companion, said, "It is not worth listening to, it is very poor stuff." "You are right, Mr. Fountayne," said Handel, "it is very poor stuff. I thought so myself when I had finished it." The old gentleman, being taken by surprise, was beginning to apologise, but Handel assured him there was no necessity, for the music was really bad, having been composed hastily, his time for its production having been limited, and that the opinion given was as correct as it was honest.[1] Handel, on the other hand, was ready to fight tooth and nail against what he thought was unintelligent criticism. One day his librettist Morell complained that the music of one of Handel's airs did not suit his words, whereupon Handel flew into a passion and

[1] Smith, *History of the Parish of Marylebone*, 1833.

cried, "What, you teach me music! The music, sir, is good music. It is your words is bad. Hear the passage again. There! go you and make words to that music."

Alexander Balus, though lacking in the qualities that captivate the vulgar ear in *Judas*, is in many ways a more remarkable work. To the musician indeed and to the student it is one of Handel's most interesting compositions, for the Oriental background tempted him to curious experiments in orchestration which often yield surprising results in the way of local colour. The libretto, which deals with the love of Alexander Balus, the King of Syria, for Cleopatra, the daughter of Ptolemy Philometor, who is quite a different person from the "Serpent of old Nile," is not particularly promising, but Handel contrived to infuse a good deal of life into the rather spectral characters. The youthful Alexander has some charming music, notably the delightful "O Mithra," one of the freshest and most ardent love-songs ever written, with a curious pulsating figure in the accompaniment which seems to indicate the haste of the young lover in flying to his mistress's feet. Cleopatra's music is among the most original that Handel ever produced, and seems to belong to a totally different world from the very conventional and commonplace songs in *Judas Maccabæus*. From her opening song, " Hark, hark, he strikes the golden lyre," to which a curiously exotic colour is given by an accompaniment of flutes, harp, and mandoline, to her marvellous death-song, "Convey me to some peaceful shore"—so different in its stoical resignation, illumined by no gleam of faith in a hereafter, from the rapture of exaltation with which a Theodora meets her doom—every note allotted to Cleopatra is worth careful study. One of her loveliest passages is a scene in the woods, in which her *rêverie* among the whispering trees and murmuring brooks is interrupted by a band of brigands who carry her off into captivity, her wild cries for help dying slowly on the ear as she is borne away. Singularly beautiful, too, is her marriage duet with Alexander, " Hail, wedded love," which seems to breathe a strange intensity of nuptial fervour. The other characters are more slightly drawn. Jonathan is a typical Hebrew, whose music is solemn and dignified without possessing any specially definite features, but Ptolemy is cleverly sketched. There is all the smooth duplicity of an Oriental statesman in his opening song, though later he shows himself in his true colours, and storms and threatens in the accepted tyrannical manner. Few of the choruses are in Handel's stately big-wig style. He seems to have felt the relief of getting for once out of his pious groove, and in *Alexander Balus* his heathen are quite as fresh and vigorous as in *Samson*. There is a curiously barbaric ring about the opening chorus, " Flushed with conquest," and the wedding music is very gay and spirited. The finest chorus in the work, however, is " O calumny," which is dragged in by the hilt *à propos de bottes*, obviously because of the success of the Envy and Jealousy choruses in *Saul* and *Hercules* respectively, but oddly as it occurs is none the less a marvellous piece of writing, weirdly grim and gloomy in feeling, and altogether one of the " creepiest " things Handel ever wrote.

Joshua seems to have been an attempt to repeat the popular success of *Judas Maccabæus*, but like most sequels it fell far below its predecessor. *Judas*, with all its faults, was eminently spirited and energetic, but *Joshua* is depressingly flat and tame. Here and there occurs a touch of the true Handelian fire, as in the magnificent chorus, " Glory to God," in which the tottering towers and strong-cemented walls of Jericho tumble to dust and ruin, and the amazingly fresh and vigorous "See, the conquering hero comes," one of those brave immortal things upon which the touch of Time is powerless. There are delicious little bits of landscape-painting, too, in *Joshua*, such as Caleb's song, "Shall I in Mamre's fertile plain?" with its wonderful suggestion of the far-away patriarchal life of the Old Testament, or the pleasant murmur of the waters in "While Kedron's brook," and the cool refreshing showers in "As cheers the sun." But some of the best songs are transplanted from earlier works. "O had I Jubal's lyre" is an adaptation of a song in a setting of the psalm *Laudate pueri*, dating from the old days at Halle, and "Heroes when with glory burning" is taken from *Agrippina*. On the whole, *Joshua* is of all the oratorios that upon which the lover of Handel is least inclined to linger.

If the flame of Handel's inspiration sank rather low in *Joshua*, it burned up as brightly as ever in *Solomon* and *Susanna*. Each of these two great works is a masterpiece in its way, yet there is hardly a point of resemblance between them. One of the most remarkable examples of Handel's versatility is his power of clothing each of his great choral works in an atmosphere peculiar to itself, and it would not be easy to find better instances of this than are afforded by *Solomon* and *Susanna*. *Solomon* is a work of pomp and circumstance. There is comparatively little in the libretto that calls for emotional power or for minute character - drawing. It is a glittering picture of the gorgeous court of the Jewish monarch, set forth in a series of choruses of superb breadth and grandeur. The music breathes of splendour and magnificence. There are many touches in the oratorio to relieve what might otherwise become the oppressive gorgeousness of the general texture of the work. There is the delicious love-music, and one would have to ransack Handel's works to find a tenderer love-song than "With thee the unsheltered moor I'd tread," or a more voluptuous chorus than "May no rash intruder." Excellent, too, is the incident of the judgment of Solomon, in which the characters of the two women are contrasted with the utmost subtlety, and there are several little nature-pictures in Handel's daintiest manner, such as "Beneath the vine and fig-tree's shade," and "How green our fertile pastures look," fragrant with the charm of rippling waters and murmuring breezes. But the final impression of the work is one of rich, even barbaric, splendour. It is like a series of gorgeously coloured frescoes in some wondrous palace of the East.

Susanna, on the other hand, is a picture of village life. It is painted in a scheme of quietly modulated colours. Many of the songs, like the Purcellian "Ask if yon damask rose be sweet," or the tender little love-ditty, "Ye verdant hills," or, most beautiful of all, the deliciously tuneful "Would custom melt," have almost a feeling of folk-music. The action of the story takes place during the captivity of the Jews in Babylonia, but only the opening chorus, written on what is practically the same ground-bass as that used by Purcell in Dido's death-song, and by Bach in the "Crucifixus" of the Mass in B minor, suggests anything like regret for a lost fatherland. The music for the most part is designedly simple in structure. Much of it is light, and at times almost humorous, as in the pretty little chorus in which the village gossips discuss Susanna's trial among themselves in whispered chatter. The last chorus again, in which the moral of the story is set forth in strains of enchanting simplicity, might well have served as a model to Mozart when he wrote the "Vaudeville" at the end of his *Entführung aus dem Serail*. Yet *Susanna* has its grand moments as well. "Righteous Heaven" is one of Handel's most stupendous choruses, and the scene between Susanna and the elders is treated with much dramatic power. The elders themselves are cleverly differentiated, the one sly and sentimental and the other violent and passionate, and Susanna's character, rising as she does under stress of circumstances to something very like heroism, is drawn with consummate art.

Theodora is a work that has never won a tithe of the consideration that it deserves. Handel himself thought very highly of it, and it is plain that he took unusual pains with it, and was proportionately mortified at its want of success. The weak point of *Theodora* is its dull libretto, one of Morell's most pedestrian productions, which all Handel's genius hardly sufficed to vitalise. The characters are the merest pasteboard, and even Handel could not turn them into human beings. On Theodora herself he expended untold pains. Many of her airs are exceedingly beautiful. Some of them, such as the great prison-scene with its curious and highly original little symphonies, are so elaborate as to suggest to certain critics that Handel had been studying Bach before writing *Theodora*. Others, like "Angels ever bright and fair," and "The Pilgrim's home," are in his simplest and most melodious manner, but the result somehow leaves one cold. The other characters are no less carefully treated— the sympathetic Irene and the ardent Didimus, Valens the black-hearted tyrant, and Septimius, the "friendly, social" pagan, who cannot understand why people worry about religion instead of enjoying themselves. The music

they are called upon to sing is often intrinsically fine,
but one and all they are merely types; there is no growth
in them, and they are just the same at the close of the
drama as at the beginning. The more generalised
emotions of the chorus gave Handel a better chance.
Often as he was called upon to set heathen ceremonial
to music, he never repeated himself, and in *Theodora* he
reproduced the frozen elegance of Roman ritual with
signal success. The very Purcellian " Queen of Summer "
is a model of clear-cut symmetry, and " Venus laughing
from the skies " is no less perfect in its way as a picture
of purely soulless religion. Handel's heathen are
invariably so delightful that his Christians (or Jews) are
often rather cast into the shade, but in *Theodora* they
are very well treated. " He saw the lovely youth," which
the composer ranked above the Hallelujah chorus in *The
Messiah*, is one of Handel's masterpieces, designed with
graphic decision, and elaborated with loving skill. Very
remarkable, too, with its atmosphere of brooding mystery,
is " How strange their ends," while the closing chorus,
so different in spirit from the usual jubilant oratorio finale,
keeps up to the end the air of peculiar distinction which
is the special property of *Theodora*. In this there is a
wonderfully characteristic Handelian touch in the sudden
burst of exaltation at the words, " That we the glorious
spring may know," which seems like the sun breaking
forth at noonday to dispel the mists of melancholy that
gather round the sombre opening of the chorus.

The "musical interlude," *The Choice of Hercules*, was
written with the eminently practical object of filling up
the evening's programme, of which the remainder was
supplied by *Alexander's Feast*. In it Handel used up a
great deal of the incidental music that he had composed

21

a few months before for Smollett's *Alceste*. It is one of the least known of his choral works, and though the *Alceste* music has been performed in recent years by the Handel Society, *The Choice of Hercules* is still buried in undeserved oblivion. It contains several lovely songs and one really magnificent chorus, "Virtue shall place thee in that blest abode," which alone should recommend the work to musicians.

Jephtha worthily closed the long series of Handel's oratorios. It is, in a sense, the summing-up of his career, exhibiting as it does to a great extent in its own compass the diverse merits that characterise its various predecessors. Many of the airs in *Jephtha* have the freshness and sparkle of Handel's early youth, and some of its choruses emulate the stupendous majesty of *Israel in Egypt* and *Solomon*, while in psychological subtlety and fineness of character-drawing *Jephtha* is on a level with *Samson*. Long experience had by this time given Handel an extraordinary certainty of touch, and the big effects in *Jephtha* "come off" with a sort of Nasmyth-hammerlike inevitability. Perhaps it would be hypercritical to say that this very certainty of touch occasionally gives an impression of something that might be called mechanical, but on the other hand there are many traces in *Jephtha* of a romantic feeling which is rarely met with in the work of a composer nearly seventy years of age. The subject of *Jephtha* is one of the most striking that Handel ever undertook; it is only unfortunate that the librettist, in deference to the fashion of the time, thought it necessary to introduce a foolish and quite superfluous love-interest, which adds nothing to the pathos of the situation, and obscures the main outline of the tragedy. *Jephtha* is one of Handel's most equal and sustained works. There are very few of those lapses into fluent commonplace which disfigure some of its predecessors. The choruses are exceptionally strong. The Moloch chorus at the beginning, with its "dismal dance around the furnace blue," is a particularly vivid musical picture of heathendom, while for sheer picturesqueness Handel never surpassed his great seascape, "When His loud voice in thunder spoke," with its boisterous surges and lashing billows. "How dark, O Lord, are Thy decrees," is a masterpiece of solemn grandeur, and "Cherub and seraphim" soars to unaccustomed heights of pure romance. The solo music is even more interesting. Each one of the characters, save the intrusive Hamor, who has really nothing to do with the plot, is elaborated with the most loving care. Particularly striking is the manner in which the development of the character of Iphis, as the librettist chose to christen Jephtha's daughter, is indicated. We see her first as a light-hearted girl, whose youthful gaiety finds charming expression in the pretty Bourrée, "The smiling dawn." Misfortune brings out the true nobility of her character. Resignation to the will of Heaven is the note of her lovely air, "Happy they," and her farewell to earth, "Farewell, ye limpid springs," seems to rise into wondrous regions of rapturous ecstasy. Jephtha is a still profounder study. His rapid changes of mood are painted with marvellous skill. Unfortunately the modern trick of linking the recitative, "Deeper and deeper still," to the air, "Waft her, angels," plays complete havoc with Handel's carefully wrought psychology. The two numbers have really nothing to do with each other. The recitative paints the conflict of Jephtha's emotions when he realises that his vow is to cost his daughter her life. The air comes at a later stage, when anguish has given place to resignation. It forms the conclusion of a great *scena* of which the opening movement, "Hide thou thy hated beams, O sun," touches the depths of gloom and despair, while the succeeding air, "Waft her, angels," is illumined by a ray of curious exaltation. The much-tried hero seems to realise in a dim way the wonderful conception, which was familiar to Greek minds, that in uttermost misery there is an element of beauty. Heavy fathers, as theatrical people call them, are common enough in Handel's oratorios, but the heavy mother is a rare bird. Storge is a fine specimen of the species, and her music is highly individual and characteristic. "Scenes of horror" is a very striking and dramatic *scena*, and "First perish thou" is a wonderful burst of passionate indignation.

During the last years of Handel's life his blindness proved a serious hindrance to composition, and he wrote little but a few additional numbers to grace the revival of some of his oratorios. The merit of these proves conclusively that the failure of his sight involved no corresponding failure of imaginative or technical power, indeed "Sion now her head shall raise," which was composed for a revival of *Judas Maccabæus*, and is said by Burney to have been absolutely the last thing that Handel wrote, is in his stateliest and most exalted manner. One other task occupied his declining years, the revisal of his early oratorio, *Il Trionfo del Tempo e della Verità*. This work, it will be remembered, was written during his stay in Rome in 1708. It was revised and enlarged, and, still in its Italian dress, produced in 1737. In 1757 a translation of the 1737 version was made by Dr. Morell, for which Handel wrote several new numbers and adapted others from earlier works, principally from *Parnasso in Festa*, which contributed the delightfully fresh and open-air choruses of hunters and dryads. In its final version, therefore, *The Triumph of Time and Truth* is uniquely interesting, as covering practically the whole course of Handel's activity, and it thus forms as it were a summing-up of his career as a musician.

It is curious, considering over how wide an interval its composition extended, that the work should exhibit so little discrepancy of style, but the fact that it is totally devoid of dramatic interest, and deals for the most part only with the lighter side of life, naturally narrows its range to sharply defined limits. Nevertheless, though it cannot be accepted as a representative work, *The Triumph of Time and Truth* has qualities of rare distinction, and it is significant that several of the new numbers, such as the delicious minuet, "Come, live with pleasure," are at least as conspicuous for youthful freshness and charm as those that were written when the composer was scarcely out of his teens.

But those whom the gods love, if they do not always die young, at least seem never to grow old, and it is pleasant to think that Handel, though bowed down by affliction, retained his lightness of heart and serenity of temperament to the end, and, like Rembrandt in his latest portrait, bade farewell to the world with a smiling face.

CHAPTER XIX

INSTRUMENTAL WORKS

HANDEL'S instrumental works, in spite of their many beauties, appeal far less strongly to the present generation than anything else that he wrote. The growth of musical form, the development of the orchestra, and the invention of the pianoforte have combined so completely to revolutionise public taste since his day, that a far greater mental effort is necessary to grasp Handel's point of view as exemplified in his sonatas and concertos than is the case with regard to his oratorios or even to his operas. To modern ears the instrumental music of the early eighteenth century speaks in a language that is now obsolete, and a certain amount of preliminary study is necessary before its meaning can be thoroughly grasped. Instrumental music has made such rapid strides since the days of the Georges that, though less than two hundred years separate Handel from Richard Strauss, they seem to us as far apart as is Chaucer from Browning. A somewhat similar intellectual exercise is demanded in each case if the modern student desires to enter into the heritage bequeathed by the older master, and in Handel's case no less than in Chaucer's the labour of mastering the dialect in which he wrote brings its own reward.

The earliest instrumental work of Handel's that has

survived is the set of trios for two hautboys and harpsichord, which is said by Chrysander to have been written
in 1696 in the composer's eleventh year. If it was really
written at that age it is an amazing proof of Handel's pre-
cociousness, for though it discloses few traces of originality,
the workmanship is skilful and singularly free from the
weakness and irresolution of childhood.

The advance on these boyish works shown in the
harpsichord suites, the first set of which was published
in 1720, is naturally very great. The latter were enormously popular in Handel's lifetime, and many of them still
hold their place in public estimation by the side of Bach's
similar works. Handel's harpsichord music is admittedly
unequal. At its worst it is the kind of fluent commonplace that almost any composer of the time could reel off
by the yard, but at its best it has all the great and distinguished qualities that we admire in his choral works.
The first set of suites is perhaps the strongest. It is full
of good things, and there are hardly any weak places in
it. The air with variations, which is known as "The
Harmonious Blacksmith," is of course the most famous
thing that Handel, or indeed anybody else, wrote for the
harpsichord, but it is far inferior to much that surrounds it.
The fugue that opens the E minor suite, with its three
defiant hammer-blows, is superb, and another splendid
movement is the "Overture" to the suite in G minor.
Some of the Allemandes and Courantes are now getting
a little musty, but the gigues are almost always first-rate.
That in the suite in A is particularly jovial, and those in
E minor and F sharp minor are very nearly as good,
while the whole of the F major suite, with its pensive
introduction, lively allegro, and brilliant fugue, is as fresh
and delightful as on the day that it was written.

The second book opens magnificently with the wonderful prelude to the suite in B flat, one of the most romantic things Handel ever wrote. Samuel Butler chose it as an illustration of the moaning of the statues in *Erewhon*, and there is indeed something almost unearthly in its wild weird chords. The rest of the collection contains nothing that can be compared to this marvellous piece. Many of the dance movements are charmingly graceful, and the gigues are invariably vigorous, but the interminable variations are rather wearisome. The third book, which was not published during Handel's lifetime, is a very miscellaneous collection. Some of the pieces date from Handel's early youth, and others are obviously written for childish performers, probably for the young princesses or for other aristocratic performers. Far finer are the six fugues, which were published in 1735. They are shining examples of Handel's smoothly flowing counterpoint. Two of them he subsequently used in *Israel in Egypt*, the first as " He smote all the first-born in Egypt," and the fifth as " They loathed to drink of the waters." The fourth had already done duty in the overture to the *Brockes Passion*. The last of the set has a grave beauty which gives it a character all its own. Samuel Butler refers to it in his *Way of All Flesh*, quoting the subject as a suitable epitaph for " an old man who was very sorry for things." A better description of it could not be devised.

Handel's sonatas for violin and other instruments accompanied by the harpsichord, though not so well known to musicians as his harpsichord suites, are still by no means forgotten. A set of twelve was published in 1732, and others taken from various sources bring the total up to nineteen. At what date they were composed

is not certainly known.   Chrysander attributes the
beautiful sonata for viola da gamba to the year 1705, since
it is known that the gamba was a favourite instrument
in Hamburg at that time.   The hautboy sonatas may
possibly date from still earlier times, when Handel,
according to his own account, composed for that instrument "like a devil."   The violin sonatas were very likely
written for Dubourg, who played Handel's music at
concerts as early as 1719,[1] or perhaps for the Prince of
Wales, who took lessons from Dubourg about 1730.
Many of these sonatas are delightfully fresh and
melodious.   The first of the two sonatas in A is still
popular, and those in E and D are occasionally to be
heard in twentieth century concert-rooms.   The Allegro
of the latter is a kind of preliminary sketch for the chorus,
"Live for ever, pious David's son," in *Solomon*, and in
several other movements occur reminiscences of works
already written or foreshadowings of those that were to
come.

Two sets of trios, for various combinations of instruments, published respectively in 1733 and 1739, also
exist.   The first follows the general lines of the early
Halle set of trios, as far as form is concerned, though
naturally with a far greater degree of technical skill and
melodic invention.   Many of these trios are indeed of
singular beauty and expressive power.   The first of the
set, which is written for flute, violin, and harpsichord,
has a slow movement of wonderfully tranquil loveliness
followed by an allegro, founded upon the highly
expressive melody associated with the words, "Why so

---

[1] The *Daily Courant* of 16th February 1719 refers to a new concerto,
"compos'd by Mr. Hendel, and perform'd by Mr. Dubourg at Hickford's
great Room in James Street."

full of grief, O my soul," in one of the Chandos anthems, which is worked up to a climax of remarkable force. Another is a transcription of the overture to *Esther*, ingeniously modified to suit its altered circumstances, while every one of the set presents some points of interest. The 1739 trios are rather lighter in style, dance movements being employed with greater frequency. On the whole they resemble the concertos in form rather than the earlier set of trios, and there is a more pronouncedly orchestral feeling about them. This is particularly the case with No. 4, which is an adaptation of the overture to *Athaliah*, with the addition of a Passacaglia and other dances, and it is difficult to believe that certain other movements, such as the march in the second sonata, can really have been intended for solo instruments.

An interesting point about Handel's solo sonatas and trios, to which attention has not, I think, been sufficiently drawn, is their value as links in the chain of the development of what is called sonata-form. It is the fashion, nowadays, especially with critics who have never taken the trouble to study his works, to repeat the old parrot-cry that Handel did not further the advance of music in any respect. I have already pointed out how groundless is this accusation in respect of oratorio. With regard to chamber music it is no less false. Much of Handel's chamber music is, in point of form, strikingly in advance of his time, and it is curious that his leaning towards modern methods should have been so little remarked by historians in their investigation of the beginnings of sonata-form. In many of his sonatas there are movements which within a comparatively brief compass conform strictly to the general outlines of sonata-form. The second movements of two of his best known sonatas, those in A and D, are good instances, and the second movement of the sonata in C minor for flute and violin (Op. 7, No. 1) is another. But throughout Handel's chamber music the tendency towards sonata-form is often to be traced in the most unmistakable fashion.

Considerably more important than his chamber works are the concertos which Handel wrote for various combinations of instruments. The concerto of the early eighteenth century was, it need hardly be said, a very different thing from the concerto of modern times. Handel's use of the form differs considerably from Bach's. Save in the case of the organ he wrote very few concertos for a solo instrument. The main characteristic of his concertos lies in the contrast between a small group of solo instruments, technically called the *concertino*, and a string band, called the *ripieno*. In his first set of *Concerti Grossi*, which were published in the year 1734, the disposition of instruments varies very much. Now and then we get a movement in which one solo instrument predominates, but as a rule the *concertino* is a group of two or more instruments. Thus in the first of the six concertos, the *concertino* of the opening movement consists of two hautboys and a violin; in the second movement two flutes are added and one of the hautboys is silent; while the third movement returns to the original arrangement. These *Concerti Grossi* are popularly known as the "Hautboy" concertos, from the prominent part assigned to the hautboys. The title, however, is decidedly misleading to modern ears, as there is very little actual solo work for a single hautboy, save in a few isolated movements, such as the lovely Largo in the second concerto, and the Andante in the fourth. There is a more decided approximation to the modern manner of treating the solo instrument in a second set of *Concerti Grossi*, published by Walsh in 1741, together with works by Veracini and Tartini, under the title *Select Harmony*, and in a couple of concertos, dating from a much earlier time, which were published by Chrysander in vol. xxi. of his edition of Handel's works. The *Concerti Grossi* are among the most attractive of Handel's instrumental works. They are as a rule light and even gay in sentiment, the slow movements being usually short, and in some cases omitted altogether. The allegro movements are among Handel's most vigorous efforts, and the dance movements, of which there are not a few, are invariably charming. Several movements are familiar to those who know their Handel well, being adapted or transcribed from earlier works, according to a fashion common at the time, to which Handel was particularly addicted.

The twelve "Grand" concertos for strings, which were written in 1739 and published in 1740, are on a far more imposing scale. Six of the concertos have five movements and four have six, and they are all planned upon a scale of grandeur and dignity that differentiates them entirely from the "Hautboy" concertos. They are written for strings alone, of course accompanied by the harpsichord, as was the universal practice in Handel's day, and the *concertino* in each instance is composed of two violins and a violoncello, contrasted with the *ripieno* band of strings. With these modest materials Handel produced effects often of surprising grandeur, varied by the touches of exquisite lightness and grace. In fact, one of the most striking features of the "Grand" concertos is the varied colour and feeling which Handel, in spite of all limitations, contrived to infuse into them. Not only with regard to changes of key—a point in which he

proved himself far more advanced than Bach—but by
novel arrangements of the movements, he sought with
signal success to avoid the charge of monotony so often
levelled against works for strings alone. The ninth
concerto is a good average specimen of Handel's treatment of the form. It opens with a magnificently solemn
and dignified introduction, Largo, $\frac{3}{4}$, in F major, leading
into a vigorous Allegro, C, in the same key. To this
succeeds a graceful Siciliana, Larghetto, $\frac{6}{8}$, in D minor,
leading into a splendidly forcible fugue in F major,
Allegro, C. Then comes a dainty little minuet in F
minor, $\frac{3}{8}$, and the concerto ends with a brilliant gigue in F
major, $\frac{12}{8}$. It is curious, considering how much popularity
Bach's suites now enjoy, that these concertos of Handel
should be so seldom performed. But at no time have
they equalled in popularity the organ concertos, of which
Burney observed that " public players on keyed instruments, as well as private, totally subsisted on these
concertos for near thirty years." The first set of organ
concertos was published in 1738, and the second, which
was largely made up of arrangements of the " Grand "
concertos, in 1740. A third set, which consisted mainly of
original music, was published a year after Handel's death
under the title of Op. 7. Handel's organ music is disappointing to those who come to it fresh from Bach. It
must be remembered, however, that his organ concertos
in their printed form represent but the skeleton, as it
were, of the works as conceived and executed by the
composer. His talent for improvisation was admitted by
all who heard him to be extraordinary, and it was his
custom to grace his concertos with long extempore
passages, for which the printed notes served but as the
foundation. We must bear in mind, too, the difference

that existed in Handel's time between English and German organs. Until the end of the eighteenth century the organ in St. Paul's Cathedral, on which Handel delighted to play as a young man, was the only one in the country that boasted a pedal-board. In writing his organ concertos, therefore, Handel was compelled to restrict himself to the manuals, and was thus driven to compose in a style which, though flexible and brilliant, seems slight and thin by the side of the massive splendour of Bach. It must be further remembered that Handel's organ concertos, as well as those written for other instruments, were intended for concert use, whereas Bach's organ music was primarily dedicated to the service of the church. Handel's concertos formed part and parcel of his oratorios, which indeed first called them into being, and were responsible for their very existence. It is hardly fair, therefore, to treat them as independent works, or to demand from them what we find, let us say, in Haydn's symphonies, the earliest of which were composed about the time of Handel's death. Handel's main design in writing his concertos was to afford a pleasant relief to his hearers between the acts of an oratorio, to lull them with the sheer beauty of sound, much as Euripides used the perfect music of his choral odes to soothe the nerves of his audience, strained to bursting-point by the poignant emotions of a tragedy. Did we know for what context each concerto was designed we might trace in it an echo of the scenes that it neighboured. But with regard to most of the concertos no such tradition has survived. We know that the organ concerto in B flat (No. 3 of the third act) was so much associated in the popular mind with *Esther* that the minuet in it was commonly known as the minuet in *Esther*, but the rest is silence. It would be exceedingly interesting to know something about the *provenance* of the so-called "Cuckoo and Nightingale" concerto (No. 2 of the second set). It is an adaptation of one of the "Grand" concertos, but the passages imitating the notes of the cuckoo and nightingale were added in the later version. There are very few instances in Handel's instrumental music of directly imitative music of this kind. His oratorios aad operas are, of course, full of it, either in the shape of dramatic symphonies, like those illustrating the pangs of the dying Hercules and the mad haste of Belshazzar's postilions, or as reproductions of the sights and sounds of nature in the accompaniments to songs. This concerto, however, stands as much alone among the works of Handel as does the Pastoral Symphony among Beethoven's, and it is curious that the two great composers, who had so little else in common, should join hands over their common love for the outdoor world.

In one other point Handel may be said to have given a hint to Beethoven, namely, in concluding an instrumental work with a chorus. In the British Museum there exists an autograph of the fourth organ concerto, to which is appended an Alleluia chorus, founded upon a theme in the concerto. It was written in 1735, and was used as the conclusion to the oratorio, *Il Trionfo del Tempo e della Verità*, which was revived in an amended form in 1737.

The most famous instrumental work that Handel ever wrote is unquestionably the Water Music. It undoubtedly owes a good deal of its notoriety to the circumstances of its production,[1] but its intrinsic beauty is quite sufficient to account for its popularity. Handel's dance music is

[1] See p. 73.

always delightful, and the sparkling series of movements that he wrote for George I's water-party are in his freshest and gayest manner. Somewhat less interesting, though no less well adapted for open-air performance, is the Fireworks Music which he composed for the celebration of the Peace of Aix-la-Chapelle in 1749.[1] Both works indeed bear convincing testimony to Handel's cleverness in adapting his style to the exigencies of the occasion, and to the forces that he had at his disposition.

Handel's other instrumental works must be briefly dismissed. Reference has already been made in various places to the overtures and other instrumental movements that adorn his operas and oratorios, but a few general observations may find place here. Handel borrowed the form of overture that had been invented by Lulli and improved by Scarlatti, and used it with but little alteration until the close of his career. He soon left his models far behind. It is not too much to say that the overture to *Almira* is finer than anything that had been written up to that date, and as his touch grew firmer and his knowledge of musical effect profounder, Handel soon surpassed the boyish efforts of his Hamburg days. It has often been said by musical historians who are in too great a hurry to read the works that they criticise, that Handel's overtures are all alike, and that one would do just as well as another as an introduction to any of the operas or oratorios. A very small amount of research will bring an unprejudiced student to a precisely opposite conclusion. I will not say that in the case of some of the operas which deal with similar subjects the substitution of one overture for another would be attended with fatal results. Working as he did at headlong speed, Handel

[1] See p. 200.

HANDEL

had not always time or inclination for psychological
subtlety, but as a rule it will be found that his overtures
fit the works that they precede a good deal more closely
than our historians suspect.   Usually it is only the general
tone of the work that is reproduced, as in the case of *The
Messiah*, where the solemn reticence of the treatment is
duly foreshadowed in the overture, or of *Susanna*, in which
the overture gives a foretaste of the village life that forms
the background of the oratorio.   In other works the idea
of a unity of atmosphere is worked out more fully.   The
overture to *The Triumph of Time and Truth* gives a brief
compendium of the struggle between duty and pleasure
that forms the theme of the oratorio—pleasure, as is usual
with Handel, being painted in far more agreeable colours
than her grave antagonist.   The overture to the *Occasional
Oratorio* sails nearer to the boundaries of programme
music.   It must be a very dull listener who does not read
in that stirring piece the whole history of the war that
formed Handel's subject—the mustering of troops for
battle, the lament over the fallen, and the triumphant
return of the victors.

In the overture to the second act of *Admeto*, which
precedes the descent of Alcestis to the shades, we get a
striking tone-picture of the gloomy regions of death,
extraordinarily modern in feeling, though fugal in
structure.   The overture to *Deborah*, again, in which
melodies from the work itself are used, gives a complete
and graphic picture of the struggle between the Israelites
and their heathen foes in the manner that is usually supposed to have originated at a much later date.   Enough
has been perhaps said to show that Handel's overtures
are by no means so monotonously uniform in style as is
generally affirmed, and the symphonies and other instru-

22

mental movements which occur in his operas and oratorios are no less interesting. Many of them are wonderfully vivid pieces of musical painting, and show Handel's genius in a light that is unfamiliar to modern musicians. Such passages as the sleep of Somnus in *Semele*, and the moonrise in *Ariodante*, to name but two instances out of many, form an important link in the history of programme music.

Mention should be made for the sake of completeness of the set of dance tunes which Handel wrote, or rather adapted from *Rodrigo*, for the revival of Ben Jonson's *Alchymist* under John Rich at Covent Garden Theatre in 1732, and of the music of *Terpsichore*, a ballet that he composed in 1734 for Mlle. Sallé. Handel's dance music is almost invariably fresh and charming, and even when he is in his lightest mood his grand manner never deserts him. His instrumental music is now sadly out of fashion, and it would probably be impossible to expect the average twentieth century concert-goer to take much interest in it. But to those who have mastered the Handelian idiom its beauty appears eternally new, and its unfailing dignity and loftiness of style recall the words in which Edward FitzGerald summed up his opinion of Handel: " His is the music for a great active people."

APPENDIX A

Merlini's Letter to Ferdinand dei Medici

ROMA, 24 *Settembre* 1707

"SERENISSIMA ALTEZZA,—Essendo costume degnissimo di V.A.S., che ha il suo grand' animo ornato di tutte le virtù, di far scelta de' virtuosi più rinomati in tutte le occasioni che se le appresentano di porre in lodata e dilettevole prova il lor valore: molto è doveroso che sia noto alla medesima S.A.V. un germe novello quale è un giovinetto di anni tredici Romano, che in età si tenera tocca l' arciliuto con fondamento e franchezza tale che postegli innanzi compositioni anche non pria vedute gareggia non senza grande ammiratione e meritato applauso con professori e virtuosi più inveterati e più celebri. Questo interviene alle Musiche e primarie Accademie di Roma, come è a dire in quella dell' Em̃o Sig^{re·} Card^{le·} Ottoboni, nell' altra che per tutto l'anno quotidianamente continua nell' Ecc^{ma·} Casa Colonna e nel Collegio Clementino; e si in queste come in altre pubbliche Accademie suona a solo ed in concerto con qualsiasi virtuoso. E tuttociò ben potrebbe testificarsi dal Sassone famoso che lo ha ben inteso in Casa Ottoboni, ed in Casa Colonna ha sonato seco e vi sona di continuo. Il Sig^{re·} Duca della Mirandola nel tempo di sua dimora in Roma sempre l' ha tenuto appresso di se. Per tanto se V.A.S. in congiuntura di cotesta opera havesse curiosità di sperimentarlo ardisco dire che ciò avverrebbe con istupore di chi che sia. E per essere il fancuillo figlio del Decano della Sig^{ra·} Prencipessa Altieri credo che esso di lui padre ne havera una somma ambizione. Lo stesso figliolo è di gran spirito, di bella presenza e di ottima indole. Et in humilità alla S.A.V. le faccio profondiss^a riv^za,

"ANIBALE MERLINI"

Archivio Mediceo, Filza 5897

APPENDIX B

LETTERS ON *ISRAEL IN EGYPT*

I HAVE not succeeded in finding a copy of the *London Daily Post* in which the first of the following letters appeared. It was, however, reprinted in the issue of April 1, 1740, on the occasion of a revival of *Israel in Egypt.*

Wedaesday morning, April 18, 1739

"SIR,—I beg Leave, by your Paper, to congratulate, not Mr. Handel, but the Town, upon the appearance there was *last* Night at *Israel in Egypt.* The glory of one Man, on this Occasion, is but of small Importance, in Comparison with that of so numerous an Assembly. The having a disposition to encourage, and Faculties to be entertain'd by such a truly-spiritual Entertainment, being very little inferior to the unrivall'd Superiority of first selecting the noble thoughts contained in the Drama, and giving to each its proper Expression in that most noble and angelic Science of Musick. This, Sir, the inimitable Author has done in such a manner as far to excel himself, if compar'd with any other of his masterly Compositions: As, indeed, he must have infinitely sunk beneath himself, and done himself great Injustice, had he fallen short of doing so.—But what a glorious Spectacle! to see a crowded Audience of the first Quality of a Nation, headed by the Heir-apparent of their Sovereign's Crown and Virtues, with his lovely and beloved Royal Consort by his Side, sitting enchanted (each receiving a superior Delight from the visible Satisfaction it gave the other) at Sounds, that at the same time express'd in so sublime a manner the Praises of the Deity itself, and did such Honour to the Faculties of human Nature, in first *creating* those Sounds, if I may so speak; and in the next Place, being able to be so highly delighted with them. Nothing shows the Worth of a People more, than their Taste for Publick Diversions: And could it be suppos'd, as I hope in Charity it may, or if this and suchlike Entertainments are often repeated, it will, that numerous and splendid Assemblies shall enter into the true Spirit of such an Entertainment, praising their Creator for the Care He takes of 'the Righteous' (see Oratorio, p. 6) and for the Delight he gives them:— *Did such a Taste prevail universally in a People, that People might expect on a like Occasion, if such Occasion should ever happen to them, the same* Deliverance *as those praises celebrate; and Protestant, free, virtuous, united, Christian England need little fear, at any time hereafter, the whole Force of slavish, bigotted, united, unchristian Popery, risen up against her should such a conjuncture ever hereafter happen.*

"If the Town is ever to be bless'd with this Entertainment again, I would recommend to every one to take the Book of the Drama with them: For tho' the Harmony be so unspeakably great of itself, it is in an unmeasurable Proportion more so, when seen to what Words it is adapted; especially, if every one who could take with them the Book, would do their best to carry a Heart for the Sense, as well as an Ear for the Sound.

"The narrow Limits of your Paper forbids entering into Particulars: But they know not what they fall short of in the Perfection of the Entertainment, who, when they hear the Musick, are not acquainted with the Words it expresses; or, if they have the Book, have not the proper Spirit to relish them. The Whole of the *first* Part [*i.e.* the Funeral Anthem] is entirely Devotional; and tho' the *second* Part be but *Historical*, yet as it relates the great Acts of the Power of God, the Sense and the Musick have a reciprocal Influence upon each other.

"'He gave them Hailstones for Rain, Fire mingled with the Hail ran along the Ground': And above all, 'But the Waters overwhelm'd their Enemies, there was not one left.'—The Sublimity of the great Musical Poet's Imagination here will not admit of Expression to any one who considers the Sound and the Sense together.

"The same of 'He is my God, I will prepare Him an Habitation: my Father's God.' Page 13 in the *third* Part.

"Again, 'Thou didst blow with the Wind; the Sea cover'd them; they sunk as Lead in the mighty Waters,' —and, to name no more, 'The Lord shall reign for ever and ever'; and Miriam's Song at the Conclusion.

"'Tis a sort of separate Existence the Musick has in these places apart from the Words; 'tis Soul and Body join'd when heard and read together: and if People before they went to hear it would but retire a Moment, and read by themselves the Words of the Sacred Drama, it would tend very much to raise their Delight when at the Representation. The Theatre, on this Occasion, ought to be enter'd with more solemnity than a Church; inasmuch as the Entertainment you go to is really in itself the noblest Adoration and Homage paid to the Deity that ever was in one. So sublime an Act of Devotion as this *Representation* carries in it, to a Heart and Ear duly tuned for it, would consecrate even Hell itself—It is the Action that is done in it that hallows the Place, and not the Place the Action. And if any outward Circumstances foreign to me can adulterate a good Action, I do not see where I can perform one, but in the most abstract Solitude.—If this be going out of the way, on this Occasion, the stupid senseless *Exceptions* that have been taken to so truly religious Representations as *this*, in particular, and the other *Oratorios* are, from the *Place* they are *exhibited in*, and to the attending and assisting at them by Persons of real Piety must be my *Apology*.

"I have been told, the Words were selected out of the Sacred Writings by the Great Composer himself. If so, the Judiciousness of his Choice in this Respect, and his suiting so happily the Magnificence of the Sounds in so exalted a Manner to the Grandeur of the Subject, shew which Way his natural Genius, had he but Encouragement, would incline him; and expresses, in a very lively Manner, the Harmony of his Heart to be as superlatively excellent, as the inimitable Sounds do the Beauty and Force of his Imagination and Skill in the noble Science itself.

"I can't conclude, Sir, without great concern at the Disadvantage so great a Master labours under, with respect to many of his *Vocal Instruments*, which fall so vastly short in being able to do due Justice to what they are to perform; and which, if executed in a manner worthy of it, would receive so great advantage. This Consideration will make a humane Mind serious, where a lighter Mind would be otherwise affected. I shall conclude with this Maxim, 'That in Publick Entertainments Every one should come with a reasonable Desire of being entertain'd themselves, or with the polite Resolution no ways to interrupt the Entertainment of others. And that to have a truce with Dissipation and noisy Discourse, and to forbear that silly Affectation of beating Time aloud on such an Occasion is indeed in appearance a great Compliment paid to the Divine Author of so sacred an Entertainment, and to the rest of the Company near them; but at the same time in reality a much greater Respect paid to themselves.' I cannot but add this Word, since I am on the Subject, That I think a profound Silence a much more proper Expression of Approbation to Musick, and to deep Distress in Tragedy, than all the noisy Applause so much in Vogue, however great the Authority of Custom may be for it.—I am, Sir, etc, R. W."

London Daily Post, 13 May 1739

" SIR,—Upon my arrival in town three days ago, I was not a little surprised to find that Mr. Handel's last oratorio, *Israel in Egypt,* which had been perform'd but once, was advertised to be for the last time on Wednesday. I was almost tempted to think that his genius had failed him, but must own myself agreeably disappointed. I was not only pleased, but also affected by it; for I never yet met with any musical performance in which the words and sentiments were so thoroughly studied and so clearly understood; and as the words are taken from the Bible they are perhaps some of the most sublime parts of it. I was indeed concerned that so excellent a work of so great a genius was neglected, for though it was a polite and attentive audience, it was not large enough, I doubt, to encourage him in any future attempt. As I should be extremely sorry to be deprived of hearing this again, and found many of the auditors in the same disposition, yet being afraid Mr. Handel will not undertake it without some publick encouragement, because he may think himself precluded by his advertisement (that it was to be the last time) I must beg leave by your means to convey not only my own but the desires of several others that he will perform this again some time next week.—I am, Sir, your very humble servant, A. Z."

APPENDIX C

HANDEL'S INDEBTEDNESS TO OTHER COMPOSERS

OF late years the question of Handel's indebtedness to other composers has occupied an altogether disproportionate amount of attention, indeed writers on Handel have devoted themselves to this particular point almost to the exclusion of all other phases of the composer's activity. Mr. Sedley Taylor's *Indebtedness of Handel to other Composers* (Cambridge, 1907), and Mr. P. Robinson's *Handel and his Orbit* (London, 1908), discuss the question so fully that it is hardly necessary for me to do more than refer my readers to their pages for a summary of the latest conclusions on the subject. However, as a certain amount of misunderstanding still exists with regard to Handel's supposed delinquencies, it may be as well to recapitulate briefly all that is known about them.

There is no doubt that Handel did make liberal use of the works of other men. The practice was by no means uncommon in his day, as Mr. Robinson proves up to the hilt, but Handel seems to have gone a considerable step farther than any of his contemporaries. Often he borrowed only a phrase or two and worked them up into elaborate choruses, but at other times he would take over a whole movement practically unaltered, as in the case of " Egypt was glad," and " Ere to dust is changed thy beauty." We know now, thanks to the labours of Mr. Robinson, that several of the works from which he borrowed most, *e.g.* the so-called Urio *Te Deum* and the Erba *Magnificat*, were in all probability early works of his own, but his indebtedness to many well-known composers of his own day remains an established fact. It is certain, too, that his borrowing was conducted upon a regular system. He had notebooks in which he jotted down passages which he thought would be useful, laying up a store of other men's ideas against a rainy day. This practice of his has proved a grievous stumbling-block to many of his latter-day admirers, whose pious minds have been severely exercised by the suspicion that their hero, though the soul of honesty in the ordinary affairs of life, was as unscrupulous as a highwayman in artistic matters. The difficulty is purely imaginary; the mistake is to judge Handel according to modern notions of property. Copyright legislation has in our times entirely altered the popular view of a man's rights in the productions of his own brain. In Handel's day the idea that literary or artistic works were the actual property of their authors

did not exist.　What we now call piracy was a recognised
institution, and Handel suffered from it as much as
anybody.　It is true that composers did not as a rule
venture to make free with his music, though Mr. Robinson
has shown that Muffat did so on occasion, but the reason
for their abstention is obvious.　Handel borrowed subjects
from his contemporaries because he saw that he could do
more with them than the composers had done, but he
would have been a bold man who ventured to go one
better than "the celebrated Mr. Handel."　But in other
respects the pirates had their will of him, and apparently
without any protest on his part.　When Walsh made a
fortune out of *Rinaldo*, Handel treated the incident as a
joke, and merely observed that the next time Walsh
should write the opera and he would publish it.　When
Arne gave a performance of *Acis and Galatea* under
Handel's very nose in the Haymarket, Handel made no
protest, but merely replied with a performance of his own.
Everything goes to prove that in those days a musical
work, so soon as it materialised into paper and ink, was
common property, and any one who chose could do what
he liked with it.　To pass off another man's work as your
own, as Bononcini is supposed to have done in the case
of a madrigal by Lotti, was a perfectly different thing,
and was regarded as a piece of shameless dishonesty, but
no one thought the worse of a man for making judicious
use of what was evidently regarded as the common stock.
The distinction appears a slight one to us, whose minds
are trained by modern legislation, but in the eighteenth
century it was evidently observed with the utmost nicety.
After all, who shall say that we are right and our
ancestors wrong?　We talk glibly nowadays about a thing
being right or wrong, when all that we really mean is
that it is legal or illegal.　Consciences are quite as elastic
now as they ever were.　When a law is passed we contrive
to adjust our moral standard to it in a very short time.
Even now, be it observed, with all our copyright legislation, we have by no means come to regard the products
of our brains as property in the same sense as lands,

houses, and money.   A man is only allowed to enjoy the proceeds of a patented invention for fourteen years.   The books that we write and the music that we compose are ours only for a limited period, which varies in different countries.   Yet what can be more essentially a man's property than the works of his own imagination?   Surely they are his in a far more intimate sense than the goods and chattels that he inherits from his forefathers.   True, says the modern legislator, but it is for the good of the world at large that books, music, and inventions should eventually become public property.   Undoubtedly, but would it not also be for the good of the world that the wealth of our millionaires should eventually be absorbed by the State?   However, so long as our laws are made by those who are richer in money than in brains the millionaires will be safe and the authors, composers, and inventors will have to suffer.   Truly the phantom Property leads us into strange passes!

But to return to Handel, there is no doubt that in his own day no one thought any the worse of him for taking his own wherever he found it.   No man had more enemies than Handel, and they left no stone unturned in their endeavours to ruin him, yet not one of them ever made his habitual borrowing an excuse for blackening his character.   Even his old enemy Mattheson, who would have been only too pleased to injure his artistic reputation, writing so early as 1722 refers at some length in his *Critica Musica* to the fact that Handel used a tune borrowed from Mattheson's own *Porsenna* in his *Agrippina* and *Muzio Scevola*.   Yet there is no trace of bitterness in his observations, indeed he does not go beyond a little mild chaff about Handel's excellent memory.   Scheibe in *Der Critische Musikus* (1737) remarks: " Handel has often worked out not only his own thoughts but those of other people, especially of Reinhard Keiser," without imputing any suggestion of blame.   The Abbé Prévost, who lived in London for several years, knew all about Handel's borrowings.   In *Le Pour et le Contre* (1733) we read: "Quelques critiques l'accusent d'avoir emprunté le fond d'une infinité de belles choses de Lully et surtout des cantates françaises, qu'il a l'adresse, disent-ils, de déguiser à l'Italienne. Mais le crime serait léger, quand il serait certain." Mr. Robinson, in *Handel and his Orbit*, quotes many additional passages which prove that Handel's use of other men's music was no secret to his contemporaries. Moreover, he conclusively establishes the fact that Handel not only took no pains to shroud his proceedings in secrecy, but on the contrary seems to have gone out of his way to advertise them to all whom they might concern. But the best summing-up of the views of the eighteenth century upon what we now call literary larceny is to be found in Byrom's lines on the famous Milton-Lauder controversy :—

> " Crime in a Poet, sirs, to steal a Thought?
> No, that 'tis not, if it be good for aught.
> 'Tis lawful Theft; 'tis laudable to boot;
> 'Tis want of Genius if he does not do't.
> The Fool admires, the Man of Sense alone
> Lights on a happy Thought, and makes it all his own;
>
> Flies like a Bee along the Muses' Field,
> Peeps in and tastes what any Flow'r can yield—
> Free, from the various Blossoms that he meets
> To pick and cull and carry Home the Sweets;
> While, saunt'ring out, the heavy stingless Drone
> Amidst a thousand Sweets makes none of 'em his own."

INDEX

INDEX